To Companion Friends, *With Love*

An inspiring true story of courage and compassion!

May 2007 - Photo by Peter d'Entremont

By Michelle Jameus

xulon PRESS

To Companion Friends, With Love
An inspiring true story of courage and compassion!
by Michelle Jameus

Printed in the United States of America

ISBN 9781498433594

www.xulonpress.com

This book is dedicated to everyone

who took this journey with me.

I couldn't have done it without you!

Contents

Introduction

When one goes through the grieving process, one "lives in" and passes through many difficult emotional phases. Spending time and energy in anger is normal; suffering through devastating depression is also normal. We must pass through these emotions and move on.

Moving into the depths of guilt is another healthy, but painful stop in the grieving journey. We all regret the thoughtless things we did to a lost loved one; we bemoan the wasted moments when we didn't help or express our love.

When the death of the loved one is due to something other than natural causes, the "stop in anger" often leads to passion for change for preventing future tragedies. Coroner's inquests are designed to address this.

For people who lose an animal, guilt is one of the most prevalent and difficult emotions with which to cope. Many people eventually let it go–they have to; they have to go on with their lives. They dismiss it out of emotional necessity.

Many people see what has happened and what society does and recognize the innate "wrongness" of our cultural norms. "This isn't right." "Why do we do this?" "There must be a better way." They cannot dismiss it. They cannot live in today's world and close their eyes. Once opened, they can never be closed. What are we on this earth for, if not "to use the gift or our lives to make this world a better place" (Jane Goodall)?

So one begins searching. Does everyone do this? Why? In other cultures, do they do this? Why not? When one finds that there are other practices and beliefs, action is born.

For Michelle Jameus, the grief of losing her two beloved dogs was such a motivation to change how we treat animals in this country. She felt so deeply that she herself needed to reach everyone in this nation to open his or her own eyes and to encourage another way. Too many animals are routinely euthanized in Canada. It is *not* necessary. It should *not* happen. There is a better way.

So, she embarked on a journey. Not of publicity campaigns, provocative letters to the editor, or public protests, but a personal one of reaching as many people as possible and talking to them face-to-face. To punctuate her powerful passion and commitment, she would not take the normal paths, but a private one, a solitary one, an incredibly difficult one–she would run alone across our nation and speak to everyone she could along the way about a better way–*the no-kill way.*

She started on a windy snowy day in St. John's Newfoundland on April 15th, 2007. She finished on a rainy, mild day in West Vancouver, British Columbia on October 29th, 2007. The adventures she experienced in the months in between, the Canadians she met, the lives she changed–these are all amazing stories yet to be told fully by this Canadian heroine!

She had no support vehicle - just a little tent to sleep in by the side of the TransCanada highway. She got to know some long-distance truck drivers who met her several times - and she got to know people, including media, who scorned her mission. There was extraordinary assistance by many who understood her motive; there were also bears to avoid, poison ivy to deal with, feet that ached, food to be found. There were lonely nights of feeling futile or useless when she needed to draw on every milligram of inner strength and faith; there were exhilarating days when the message was welcomed.

She survived it all–not without the help of some angels, she believes. She now has a story to tell about survival, about Canadians, about how Canadians treat animals. It is a remarkable one that has already inspired thousands.

Dorit Girash, Founder of Let Live Canada

Foreword

When Michelle Jameus touched the cold waters of St. John's, she had a dream to help save domestic animals from needless death. This is her mission, driven from experiences of her past. She will run–not walk–across Canada from the eastern edge to the western edge on the TransCanada highway, alone with no support vehicle or companionship. Every step she took plunged her deeper into truths and strengths that no one could have prepared her for.

Michelle's life has always been to give more than you can get, to win and succeed with hard work, integrity, and pure determination. This journey will challenge every aspect of Michelle: her physical strength, spiritual and emotional strength, and her cause to save animals killed by a disposable society. She has seen the depths of people's kindness and the darkness of people's ignorance along the highway; she has been forced off the road with vehicles and severe weather conditions. She has faced hunger and cold, wild animals, and suffered tremendous physical pain, but also seen the faces of angels.

Along the highway, in different cities and towns, she would contact media and various animal groups to listen to her message, but it seemed to be more of a hit and miss success. Little did she know that after six months of running, when she touched the waters of the west coast, no one would be there for her and her cause, other than Dorit, the founder of Let Live Canada. There was no glory, or congratulations, or fanfare. In fact, it was more like, "*who did what? For what?*"

The media and animal activists had been contacted that this was the end of a run by a female who had run across Canada alone for the life of domestic animals, but no one showed up; not even the local animal shelters and rescuers. On the surface, you might think that she ran across Canada and failed to enlighten many people about euthanizing healthy animals. In reality, Michelle did find life and this is her story.

Christine Jameus

Chapter 1

Newfoundland

When I think about how far I've run and how long I've been away from my family and friends, I wonder what it will be like to be at home again. After everything I've been through, will I be able to go back to the way things were before I started this incredible journey?

Tomorrow, I'll fly home to Ottawa after running six and a half months along the TransCanada Highway. I never really knew for sure if I could go the distance–at the time, it seemed impossible. Here I am, emerging in Vancouver, British Columbia, about to run across the Lion's Gate Bridge. My final destination is Ambleside Park and I've been looking forward to this day for such a long time. Finally, it had arrived.

Dorit has flown to be with me once again. She is the only person to be with me for both my first and last mile and I wonder if she really pictured back then that we would be here today. Did she really believe in the beginning it would be possible for me to survive a solitary run across our great country?

It's hard to imagine that I've come all this way alone on foot, completing 171 marathons in 198 days, or to conceive that it is even possible. The thought of having 7,358 kilometers behind me, considering how I got here, is overwhelming and in a few short breaths I started gasping for air and wiped away the tears from my eyes. The flood of memories is too much for me to handle.

For now, I just had to run a few more miles and my Cross Canada Marathon will be finished. It's a Monday morning, close to 9:30am on October 29, 2007, and the weatherman is calling for light rain most of the day.

Surprisingly I'm not in any hurry to get to the other side of the bridge. Maybe subconsciously I didn't want this marathon to end. I felt at peace with myself for the first time wanting to enjoy the last part of my run and take in what my eyes could behold of my surroundings. I barely noticed the rain or that I was chilled by the dampness. I didn't pay much attention to the pain in my feet or the aches in both my legs from the prolonged running.

Instead, the sound of splashing water under my shoes and the rhythm of my feet were soothing to my ears. Taking deep breaths of fresh air were invigorating and the thought of finishing made being out here more pleasurable.

For a moment I had a smile on my face, until someone walking a dog caught my attention. It was a reminder of the horrible regret I sheltered in the depth of my soul. It caused me to hang my head in shame and stop briefly to gaze out over the water. My thoughts going back several years to a dreadful night of images I can never erase from my head. They were as fresh in my mind as if it had happened only yesterday.

However, today is a glorious day like no other and I'm able to smile above my tears and know what victory feels like. I'm awe-struck by the kindness of strangers, family, and friends that helped get me here, and that God allowed an ordinary person like me to do something extraordinary.

Six and a half months earlier. . .
April 11, 2007 – St. John's, Newfoundland

On the morning of my departure to St. John's Newfoundland, a longtime friend and roommate, Sharron, dropped me off at the Ottawa Airport on her way to work.

"What's the name of the organization you're involved with again?" asked Sharron.

"Let Live Canada," I replied.

"Do you have a place to stay when you get there?" she continued to question me.

"I've got a room wherever I go," I said confidently and a tent tucked away in my backpack.

"What about money? I hope they're paying you something."

"I volunteered myself. Besides, I won't need much where I'm going."

"Well, good luck," she encouraged me. "Call me if you need anything."

"Thanks. I will. Try to stay out of trouble while I'm gone," I laughed.

I closed the door and watched her drive away. She had no idea that I was about to attempt a solitary run across Canada because I hadn't shared that part of my plans with her. "Hopefully she won't be too upset with me when she reads her email," I thought to myself.

Before we left the house, I sent an email to family and friends with the link to my blog hoping it would help them catch some of my passion. They would be seeing it for the first time and it will probably come as a surprise to them once they learn the extent of my plans.

Sitting in the airport waiting to board reminded me that somewhere in previous years a page had turned in my life and here I was, standing on the edge of my great adventure. "Every journey starts with the first step," I told myself, "and today, I'll take another one when I get on that plane."

All kinds of thoughts ran through my head, "Me and my big ideas! Why couldn't I just be satisfied with the way things were? Why did I have to be one of those people who has to cross the street to see what's on the other side?" I must be insane. I chuckled and couldn't believe I just packed up my life in a backpack and had a one-way ticket to St. John's Newfoundland. "This is pretty extreme, even for you Michelle," I uttered under my breath.

I began questioning if I was ready for this, if I had prepared myself well enough.

Haunting me was that faint voice of hesitation. "There's still time to turn back," it whispered in my ear, but my heart wouldn't listen. I knew that if I waited until I was ready, I would never leave.

After a short plane ride to Toronto, security let me through the gates with my little flagpole.

"I need it to hold up my flag," I told the security guard.

"No problem, we need more patriotism in our country," he responded and ushered me through.

"Thank you," I obliged.

Observing the behavior of people from different walks of life fascinated me and it helped to pass the time. There was a school choir singing and people rushing by. "Everyone has a story to tell," I thought. Maybe I should have shared more of mine with my family and friends, but I couldn't risk being stopped once they knew how far I was willing to go. To do something like this, you have to not care if you live or die and I didn't want anyone to talk me out of doing something I felt compelled to do.

Announcement after announcement, I watched as people boarded until my flight was called. Once we were airborne, the cabin lights were dimmed. The trip to St. John's was like the calm before a storm and the waves were yet to come. It had that feeling of being three in the morning and no one else awake.

There was a young couple sitting in front of me traveling with their dog under the seat. They had flown half way across the country, at great expense, to purchase their new puppy from a breeder in Ontario. Their love and effort for this animal was commendable, but it saddened me to know they could have rescued an abandoned animal in their own neighborhood.

We landed late that night and I needed to let the idea of my feet being in St. John's, Newfoundland sink in a little. In my place of new beginnings, I wandered around not really knowing what to do next. I had consciously under-planned my sleeping arrangements and thought I would just settle on what I would do when I got here. "Leave the consequences in the hands of someone else," I said. Good thing for me I was comfortable in unfamiliar surroundings.

When I finally stepped outside, there was a winter chill in the air and its wind blew right through me. It was a lot colder than I thought it would be. Kicking the snow on the ground caused me to wonder if what I had in my survival pack would be adequate for this time of year. Had I started at the wrong end of the country?

It was close to midnight and any ideas of camping were out of the question. Mostly because there were not any nearby campgrounds. I went back inside to reexamine my options and staring at me from the information desk was a brochure for the Downtown Hostel. It caught my eye and I embraced it as an invitation.

However, there was no answer when I called. I reasoned with myself that I would have plenty of time to enjoy my sleeping bag once I hit the highway, so I walked over to the airport hotel and spent a quiet first night in a warm bed.

The next morning, I felt a surge of excitement with the thought that this part of my journey was about to begin. You would have thought I had the cure for cancer the way I jumped out of bed and packed up my stuff.

I was responding to the emergency of my heart to make an impassioned plea for cats and dogs. Escalating was the anticipation of visiting local shelters and being with friends I hadn't met yet. First, I had to secure my stay at the Downtown Hostel for the next couple of days.

A man named Bill answered the phone and I was enchanted by his heavy Newfoundland accent. The price was right and he gave me directions how to find him. Riding the bus through the streets was enjoyable and gave me a glimpse of the city I might not have seen otherwise.

Meeting Bill made an impression on me. He was a true Newfoundlander with a wonderful sense of humor. His face was a picture of happiness and he took great pleasure in using Newfoundland lingo with his visitors. It didn't take long for me to feel comfortable around him. The people in St. John`s were so hospitable and gregarious.

After some orientation, he showed me to my room. The hostel was economical lodging and I would share quarters with an older woman from Vancouver who frequents St. John's. "They always come back," Bill smiled. Jeannie loved animals and we hit it off right away.

"What a wonderful thing to do for our four-legged friends," she marveled. "I wish I could do something like that. You must be in great shape."

"I feel pretty good," I replied.

"Yes, but to do something like this you must have trained for it."

"I did. Nothing professional though. Mostly, I self-trained for the past eighteen months. I run all the time, but I think it helped that I competed in a lot of different sports and have some athletic ability."

"Well, you're a brave woman to be doing something like this alone," she feared for me.

Trying something like this didn't feel like that big a deal to me the way some people made it out to be, but this definitely wasn't a task for the faint hearted. It had to be the very reason I got up in the morning and so worthwhile that I was willing to build my entire life around it. Once I made the decision to make it my priority, there was no turning back and I matched my desire with the will to complete it.

In the hallway, I met some of the other guests. There was a nice young man from the U.K. who came to visit but never left. "I started playing ice hockey and loved it so much that I didn't want to leave, so I found myself a job," he said happily.

There were no casual day-trippers here and I glanced at all the others whose memories lived on in Bill's guest book. Romancing with the history surrounding me on the walls, I signed my name as if to join a club of long lost voyagers.

Once I settled into my room, there were four animal shelters in the area I wanted to seek out over the next couple of days. My pursuit was to find out why our country uses the convenience of euthanizing to control the population of cats and dogs and to raise awareness about a problem our society appeared to ignore.

Heavenly Creatures was my first encounter. I tracked it down like an explorer looking for treasures yet to be discovered–treasures that are found by people who dig for them. As I approached the shelter, I snickered because I was nervous and began rehearsing how I should present myself. Finally I decided, "Silly, just be yourself."

My jitters subsided once I entered the building and made my climb to the top of the stairs. I entered a small room where there was a full-grown cat curled up in the back of a carrier on the table and a large dog lying on the floor, unbothered by my presence.

While I waited for the young girl to finish her phone conversation, I looked around the room and wondered where all the rescued animals were. When she got off the phone, I introduced my intentions and myself.

"Hello, my name is Michelle and I'm running solitary across Canada to raise awareness about the overpopulation problem with cats and dogs in our country. I'm following the TransCanada Highway and stopping at as many shelters as I can to speak with individuals, like yourself, to gain a better understanding of the problem."

"That's a great cause," she said with a surprised look on her face. "We're a no-kill shelter and we don't euthanize any of our animals; we keep them until a home can be found. I'm Jessica, the organization's co-founder."

"It's nice to meet you," I replied. "You don't have many animals."

"This is just an office and I have volunteers to foster animals until they can be adopted. How many people are with you?" she asked.

"Not many; just me."

"What about your support vehicle?"

"I don't have one - just a survival pack."

"You're running across Canada alone without a support vehicle!"

"As crazy as it sounds, I'll run a marathon a day, starting Sunday until I reach Vancouver."

"What about food and water?"

"I'll carry what I can, including a tent. For now I'm staying at the hostel until I leave."

Jessica's phone rang steadily and I admired the way she handled so many demands all at once. In between phone calls, we continued our conversation. "How did Heavenly Creatures get started?" I asked her.

"Well, we felt the need for an alternate rescue group in our community. This office is temporary until we can build a shelter. You probably need to rest your legs, but we're about to go on a dog walk. Would you like to join us?"

"I would love to, thank you. My legs could use the stretching."

As we walked to their favorite park, it allowed me to ask her some important questions. I listened to her insight into the problem and recognized that she spoke beyond her years.

"Why is there an overpopulation problem?" I asked her.

"For one thing, there are more animals than there are homes and animals keep breeding. Plus, irresponsible pet owners don't think through getting a pet and they either return them or don't spay or neuter them. Not everyone can afford it," she responded.

"What do you think is the cause of the problem?"

"Part of it is people's attitudes toward animals. They treat them like disposable items and there are not enough laws to protect them. We also need a low cost 'spay and neuter program' in the province. There is a local organization called Ruff Spots that tries to assist shelters with funding for spay and neuter costs for animals in their care. You might want to get in touch with them."

"Thank you, I will. Is the problem getting better or worse?"

"It's definitely getting worse, especially with cats. They can multiply quickly. From one cat there can be hundreds in a short time. There are so many strays wandering the streets breeding and looking for food. Lots of people can't bring themselves to take animals to the SPCA knowing there's a chance they might be euthanized."

"Do you think the problem could ever be solved?"

"I don't know. People's attitudes would have to change. Something would have to be done about breeding. It will take a miracle."

"Do you think our country would ever embrace the idea of a no-kill country?"

"Not if things stay the way they are. The government would have to step in. Shelters would have to work together. There are still people who think euthanasia is the only way to deal with the problem. The city has recently poured a lot of money into an expensive new facility, the Animal Care and Adoption Centre. People still think these larger organizations are taking care of the problem when the reality is healthy animals are still being euthanized if homes can't be found for them."

Jessica's frustration was heightened with the lack of funding available for the smaller shelters.

"Have you ever heard of Let Live Canada or Jazzpurr Society for Animal Protection?" I asked her.

"I think so. Didn't they have a conference not that long ago with Jane Goodall?"

"That's right; and the founder, Dorit Girash, is flying here tomorrow from Windsor Ontario to help kickoff this event."

It was comforting for me to know Dorit would be here and I was looking forward to meeting her for the first time. "I support their vision of a no-kill country and that spay and neutering is the next logical step for animal control. We have to stop killing so many healthy cats and dogs in our country. It's just not right. If the public knew that the overpopulation problem has been answered with prevention, wouldn't they want that?"

"You would think so, but lots of people don't like change, or want change," responded Jessica. "I think people want to do the right thing; they just need to know what that is. I'm hoping by raising awareness, people will respond favorably."

"Raising awareness should help. I'll send an email about your event to others in the area who I think would want to come out to the harbor on Sunday to support you."

"That's wonderful. I appreciate the help."

We parted and agreed to meet again the next morning. Jessica's support was a spark of encouragement and gave me the feeling I was on the right track. She was a local and would know the right people to contact. With a little help from her circle of influence getting the message out, I was hoping the ripple effect would be far-reaching. My fellow Canadians needed to hear about this.

Before returning to the hostel, I decided to take a stroll along Harbour Drive. Walking along the narrow streets, I observed the houses and historic buildings. While I walked, some friendly natives asked me, "What brings you here?" The reality of my answer begged the question: was I really going to go through with this? My mind tried to convince me there was still time to bail out, but for me, that was never going to be an option. I was hopelessly devoted to my heart's desire and the journey it was taking me on.

Later that night, I called my three sisters. First, I spoke with my oldest sister Chris who lives in Thunder Bay Ontario. She couldn't quite wrap her mind around what I was telling her.

"You're doing what. Why isn't anyone going with you?" Chris said in shock.

"Well, I asked a couple of people but I couldn't find anyone who could make the same kind of commitment as me. But don't worry. I'll be fine and I'll call every time I get to a public pay phone," I assured her.

"What about remote areas? How will you protect yourself? What if something happens and you can't get help? How will you make it through Sault Ste. Marie and Wawa? There's nothing there for one hundred kilometers except bears and wild animals. Are you nuts?"

"They won't bother me if I don't bother them. Besides, I won't be cooking or have any food in my tent and I'll be careful."

"Well, where will you get food and water? Don't you have to have a support vehicle to run a marathon, and you want to do this every day? Is that even possible? You're not twenty years old anymore, you know."

"Don't worry. I'm in the best shape of my life and I'll carry what I can with me," I said confidently.

"Can't somebody else do it?" Chris pleaded, wanting me to reconsider what I was doing and come home. Instead, I tried to reassure her that all was well.

Then, I spoke with my other two sisters–Marie, who also lives in Northern Ontario, and then Angel, who lives near Montreal. They all had similar concerns.

"That's a lot of time to be alone," they said.

"Won't you get lonely?" they asked.

"What happens if something goes wrong?"

Everyone was a lot more concerned than I was expecting. When I got off the phone, for the first time it felt like I might be on a suicide mission. I thought long and hard about what they had to say and asked myself several times if I could be making a mistake. I searched my heart and believed I was doing the right thing.

Before I went to bed, I phoned VOCM Openline, the local radio talk show, to appeal to the listeners. You never know whose ears your words will fall on. If I could just tell people what I knew, it might be enough to get everyone talking. I was grateful for the airtime, but didn't get to hear any of the feedback afterward. Good or bad, I thought it was better than nothing.

According to plan, Jessica and I met the next day back at her office. There, I met one of her volunteers, Ashley, who was quiet and didn't say much. I also met Jessica's boyfriend, Ivan, who shared with me his experience meeting Terry Fox in 1980.

"We didn't think a 'one legged guy' would get very far," Ivan confessed, "but at least he had somebody with him."

"Are you volunteering?" I laughed.

"Sorry, but you're on your own," he chuckled.

It was stimulating to talk with like-minded people and it helped to refocus my thoughts. However, they were concerned for my safety and a little skeptical too.

"Are you scared at all about being alone on the highway, especially at night?" asked Ivan.

"Well, I'm about to find out. I don't think I'll be afraid, but I've never done anything like this before, so we'll see what happens," I answered while keeping a brave face. I was more concerned with staying warm in this kind of weather. There would be no hot shower waiting for me at the end of my runs to take the chills away.

"We'll be at the harbor on Sunday to cheer you on," Ivan said.

"There will be other supporters coming as well," Jessica added and I was encouraged by their participation.

After I left Heavenly Creatures, I found my way to the Animal Care and Adoption Centre. Judging by the expression on Jessica's face, I sensed her confusion about me going there. My goal included dropping in on both traditional and no-kill shelters.

At the same time, I wanted to be cautious. It was not my intention to protest or come between people and organizations. Wherever I went, I conducted myself the same, respectful of everyone's position and mindful that local shelters know their communities best and can better identify with the issues.

However, shelters already know about the problems and animal lovers don't need convincing. Our country as a whole needed a wakeup call about our treatment of animals. Nevertheless, reaching the public is no easy task without the help of the media. Getting their attention, without celebrity status, was going to be a challenge.

When I arrived at the adoption centre, Abby the shelter cat and Tammy, who took me for a tour of the new building, greeted me cheerfully. It was an impressive facility and they unveiled what they had to offer with pride and excitement in hopes of satisfying the needs of many more animals.

"I don't work for a shelter," I told Tammy. "I'm just a concerned citizen speaking on behalf of cats and dogs."

"Your raising awareness is a good thing and should help," said Tammy.

"I hope so," I replied.

"I don't know that the overpopulation problem can ever be solved though. It's such a huge problem. There are just too many homeless animals that are puppies and kittens, victims of people who irresponsibly let their pets breed. Then, there are the many people who don't think through the responsibilities of pet ownership before they get an animal. They end up on the streets and we pick up as many cats and dogs that are more than a year old as we do litters. People just don't understand the consequences of their actions," Tammy said sadly.

"I think that's something I'm going to hear a lot of," I responded. "Well, thank you for taking the time to speak with me and I'm sure if animals could talk they would thank you for all that you do for them."

"Good luck on your journey," she said and waved good-bye.

From there, I hopped on a bus out of town to the SPCA. It was a much smaller and older building. Allison and Annie took a minute to tell me they too doubted it would be possible to solve the problem.

"What do you do with them all?" Allison stated emphatically. "You can't just let them roam the streets or lock them in a cage for the rest of their life. No-kill shelters turn away animals when they don't have room for them and guess where they end up? Here with us."

They did not respond well to questions. The subject of no-kill is charged with emotion and the idea disturbs the tranquility of traditional shelters, particularly when questions get uncomfortably personal. There was no tour of the building today.

It was a busy adoption day and I was heartbroken by the many abandoned animals waiting to be rescued. Before I left, I watched as a couple adopted an adorable kitten. Whenever a home is found for a pet, it was cause for a celebration, but it saddened my heart to see so many adult animals passed over. No one likes to talk about what happens to animals that don't get adopted. It's a difficult subject, but needs to be brought to the surface.

I hurried with excitement to the airport for Dorit's arrival. While I waited, it astounded me that she was flying all the way from Windsor Ontario to be here and that she had so much faith in someone she has never met. She trusted that I would do what I said I would do and I didn't want to disappoint her. However, I was also a little nervous about meeting her in person.

I recognized her right away from photos. "I'm so happy to finally meet you," I smiled as we exchanged a hug.

"Me too. You're a brave woman for trying something like this," Dorit said with amazement.

It was strange for me to hear someone say that. If I was being brave, it wasn't without fear. It's just that my conviction was bigger than my fear. Sometimes, your goals can be so compelling and inspiring that you think you can do anything. However, reality has a way of hitting you in the back of the head. Saying I could do this was one thing, but actually doing it was something else.

"Well, I'm really glad you're here, but I can't believe you flew all this way," I said.

"It's the least I could do considering what you are doing," responded Dorit.

"Thank you for your support and vote of confidence. I'm going to give this my best. I hope we have a good turnout on Sunday so you haven't come all this way for nothing."

After Dorit picked up her luggage, she rented a car and we drove to her hotel, the Marriott near the harbor. She offered to have me stay with her, but I had already settled in at the hostel.

Dorit was a vegetarian and once she was checked-in to her room, we went to the vegetarian restaurant nearby for something to eat. She spoke with a British accent and years of education as we spent some time learning more about each other. Even though she was retired now, her passion and commitment to improve life for animals was unmistakable and her background was impeccable. Everything she said was with conviction.

Our conversation then shifted to the journey I was about to embark on. "Julia will send out media releases for us and help out any way she can," Dorit said. Julia works at Jazzpurr Society for Animal Protection in Ontario (also known as Jazzpurr) and volunteers for Let Live Canada. "That's fantastic. I hope I get the opportunity to meet her too," I replied excitedly.

The media release for Sunday stated that the event would begin at Harbourside Park and continue along Harbour Drive to the Mile One Building. From there, I would start running.

"It's unfortunate that you won't be running through Windsor; we would have a lot of supporters there," Dorit said disappointedly.

"That would have been great, but it's too far from the TransCanada Highway and I'm concerned about making it to Vancouver before winter. Besides, I don't think I'm allowed to run on the main highways to get there," I responded.

"I understand. Not everyone is going to welcome you or accept the idea of no-kill, but don't be discouraged. Most people simply don't understand what 'no-kill' means," she cautioned me.

I hung onto every word Dorit said, listening intently to her experience and knowledge into animal welfare and what we were up against. All the while, I was wondering how our country could have let this problem get so big.

It had been a long travel day for Dorit and after some tea she retired to her room. We would get together again in the morning to continue our discussion over breakfast.

On my way back to the hostel, I thought about how glad I was that Dorit was here. Her presence gave me some confidence that there was value in what I was doing. I didn't think it was just coincidence that had brought us together and I recalled how our relationship began.

After I took the Veterinarian Assistant Program, I thought I wanted to open up my own rescue shelter. Then, I realized you couldn't build a shelter big enough to put all the homeless pets in. It didn't take me long to figure out that building another shelter wasn't going to solve the problem.

When I stumbled across no-kill information on the Internet, I knew instantly that this was where I wanted to help make a difference: to be a part of the solution and not the problem. If we continue to euthanize year after year, we have to recognize that there is something drastically wrong with the system and go in another direction. Half the population of Canada owns a pet and if they knew there is a better way to handle the problem, then surely everyone would want that.

In September 2005, I sent an inquiring email to Let Live Canada asking the question: Why is there not a no-kill law in Canada? Dorit replied:

> *Oh Wow. Wouldn't that be wonderful? There are various organizations attempting to make it happen – to no avail. Too many people make too much money from the lives of animals. Where are you Michelle? Would you like to join our organization?*

In April 2006, I approached her with my idea for this event. It was at that point that my decision to take this journey was irreversible. She was thrilled and I was excited to have her support, especially after the disappointment of being dismissed by both the Ottawa Humane Society (OHS) and the Canadian Federation of Humane Societies (CFHS) in 2004. The OHS couldn't support anything other than a local event so they directed me to CFHS. My meeting and correspondence attempts with CFHS had failed and I received this final reply:

> *Hi Michelle,*
>
> *I did receive your message, but really haven't had much time to give this attention. I'm still not convinced that you have a highly structured plan or that our member societies will give this their support. If I had to provide a firm answer today, it would be that I'm not prepared to give this more attention. However, if you're interested in shaping and refining your plans to finer detail, I will give it another look.*
>
> *As I've mentioned, there are a few key issues: these events have a spotty record of success (I'd*

be interested to see some evidence that you've communicated with others who have tried this kind of cross-country event); I am not in a position to say this is in the best interests of a shelter animal (i.e. the dog you would adopt); I'm not clear on the specific motivation behind the run (i.e. how is this run about animal welfare); liability issues need to be addressed. . .who is responsible for the undertaking, what risks would CFHS and member societies be accepting by involvement.

Do think about these issues and present a more developed case when you are able.

Thanks again,
Eric
Development Director
CFHS

My desire had fallen awkwardly on their ears, but their reluctance didn't discourage me. With a determined spirit, I made the decision to move forward with the support of Let Live Canada. In advance of leaving, I sent an announcement addressed to all known shelters across Canada, including the humane societies, as an invitation for their support and involvement. I received few responses.

Back at the hostel, Bill and Jeannie were outside on the back porch. I could smell the cigarette smoke as I walked in. Bill loved to head down to the local pub at the end of the day and had just returned. He was persistent that I should experience some Newfoundland traditions, or at least hear about them. I passed on drinking screech and kissing a fish, but I thanked him all the same. In true Newfie form, he loved to "live and laugh." I enjoyed some fun with them and I think Jeannie enjoyed Bill's company too. Maybe the hostel was something of a retreat for her.

As I lay in bed that night, I thought about people's reaction whenever I told them I was going to run across the country. They always looked at me as if I was out of my mind.

"Sure you are," they'd say.

"Without a support vehicle, that's impossible?"

"You'll never make it."

"Isn't it a little dangerous to be a girl alone on the highway with so many psychos running around?"

"Doing something like that to save cats and dogs might be considered a little fool-hearted."

I didn't look at it that way and my willingness was beyond them. They couldn't see what was hidden in my heart and that the true nature of my battle enabled me to turn a deaf ear to those who thought it was foolish. Anyone else's enthusiasm might have worn off by now, but not mine. I had the heart for it and a hope that was bigger than the eye could see.

> *"I am not moved by what I see or hear, I am moved by what I believe."*
>
> *-Smith Wigglesworth*

In the morning, Dorit took me out for breakfast and we continued our conversation. "Why is it so difficult for our country to solve this problem?" I asked Dorit, somewhat baffled.

"There are a number of reasons. Sadly, and to the detriment of animals, our country lacks national unity on the issues and about the only thing shelters can agree on is that there is a problem. It would take some time, but prevention would solve the problem once and for all."

"How does something like this happen when we have people and institutions put in place to protect animals?" I asked.

"Power and money. In shelter circles, there are basically two popular ways of thinking toward controlling the population: catch and kill, or 'Trap-Neuter-Return' (TNR). The failure of euthanasia is that killing the surplus of animals doesn't do anything to solve the problem. Animals keep breeding and repopulating. It's senseless, but there are some who think killing is the only way and that attitude doesn't go away easily. The no-kill movement answers the problem with a moral solution. TNR and prevention saves lives."

"It makes no sense to me that there is a proven solution and our country isn't jumping all over it. If the non-traditional shelters can be no-kill, what is stopping our country from being no-kill?"

"There will always be some who willingly refuse to act on doing what's right because money and power have a way of corrupting good intentions. Shelter's hide behind their budgets and blame the public for so many deaths. It's a cruel injustice and the problem won't go away as long as politicians ignore it. The sad truth is, some people don't think that saving the lives of cats and dogs is important," said Dorit.

You don't have to start from religious or philosophical conviction to arrive at the conclusion that an animal's life has value; even a brief examination of the consequences should be enough on which to base that decision. When we remove or diminish the value on an animal's life in any way, unthinkable things can happen. The consequences within our society are far-reaching and lethal for our companion friends. What needs to change is the public attitude that an animal is a disposable item. If we don't change that, what kind of message are we sending?

"Are we doing everything we can?" I asked.

"Lots of people are trying and it's only a matter of time before things change. What you are doing will help inspire others."

I had to pause for a moment and think about that. I was a nobody really, but, here I was, thinking I had just found out the biggest secret in the world and all I had to do was share it and the problem would be fixed. "Surely I'm not the only one who feels this way," I questioned. This is what was going on in my head. After listening to Dorit and others, it was becoming clear to me that this was going to be a lot harder than I thought. It was a thought I would have many times in the days to come.

Inspiring others would be great, but my marathon was about more than just running and raising awareness. It was equally about giving something back and expecting nothing in return. That was the kind of people I wanted to meet.

After we finished eating, we drove from the Mile One Building out to the TransCanada Highway to get a closer look at the route

I would run. It was a tremendous help to know what to expect ahead of time.

While we drove, I learned that Dorit's long resume of studies included the field of aviation and a teaching background. She had her flying license and to her credit organized several fly-a-thons for cancer and muscular dystrophy in the past. I was delighted when she shared some helpful tips with me about reading the skies.

"You can tell a lot by looking at the clouds," Dorit said. "Low stratus clouds will cause it to drizzle while the larger dark gray clouds produce the heaviest rain falls. The lighter gray clouds usually mean the water drops are not large enough to fall and it probably won't rain." Something told me I was going to get up close and personal with the skies before the end of my journey.

Once we left the city limits, any mystery about the landscaping quickly disappeared. Reality started sinking in. In this mysterious land there wasn't much out here except a vast unknown of isolation, a highway, and not a lot of payphones. To survive, I would have to lean on a lot of hope and virtue, and give it everything I had for a near-impossible task. The drive back was quiet and I fought to keep some nervous butterflies down.

We returned to town and dropped in on Beagle Paws, an organization dedicated to rescuing beagles and promoting them as pets and not just hunting dogs. We met Kelly and I admired how the dogs responded to her. Animals have a way of sensing good character in people, and people that are not a threat. "We don't euthanize animals here," Kelly said proudly. "We find homes for all our dogs."

There was something satisfying about hearing that. It was also a revelation. You can't legislate morality, or love, and there aren't any laws to make people good. All the laws in the world won't change human nature. The most vulnerable victims in our world today are children, the elderly, the sick, and animals. We have to and must defend the weak. Why not animals that are victims of multiplication?

Dorit had never been to St. John's before so we decided to take in some breathtaking views of the city and bay from Cape Spear and Signal Hill–attractions that were a reminder of their place in history.

We were captivated by the panoramic view of the harbor and the Atlantic Ocean, with dramatic shores and waves crashing against rocky cliffs. It was too soon to see any icebergs bobbing in the waters and we didn't see any whales feeding off the coast, but its natural beauty was unforgettable. The spectacular landscapes did not disappoint us, despite the chilling winds.

Daylight slowly faded. We headed back to Dorit's hotel where we talked for a while about tomorrow and the days to come. "You'll experience highs and lows, but don't let it get you down," she encouraged me. "I tried to think of something small and light that you could take with you. A good luck charm. This was the smallest thing I had. It was my Grandmother's," she said kindly and handed me a special amulet.

Moved by her thoughtful gesture, I gave her a hug. "Thank you Dorit," I said. "I'll return it to you when I'm done." Turning it around and putting the responsibility on myself to return the amulet safely, as if to guard it with my life, gave me another reason to act bravely.

"Get a good night's sleep," she said as I left.

Back at the hostel, I packed and repacked my survival pack several times to get it just right. It contained only ultra-light bare necessities: a one person tent, sleeping bag, three-quarter length body pad, one extra pair of shorts/shirt/socks/shoes, a one and a half liter hydration pack, vitamins, energy bars, two bagels, toothbrush, pair of wool socks, one fleece sweater, one t-shirt, one long dry wick tights, large Canada flags for people to sign, a rope and my TripTik from CAA. Anything else I would have to pick up along the way as needed.

On me, I would wear my rain suit, gloves, a ball cap, safety whistle, and a Garmin Forerunner GPS on my wrist. No other electronic device. Not even music. Mostly to keep the weight down, but also because I had no way of keeping them charged.

It was my last night at the hostel and I watched a bit of television with Jeannie. We switched to the weather station and there was snow in the forecast with temperatures well below zero. "You're not really going to run in this, are you?" she asked with concern on her face. "It's not ideal for sure, but I've run in worse conditions to train myself. I bought a fairly good tent and sleeping bag so I should be okay," I assured her.

Before I went to bed I called my youngest sister, Angel, and told her I probably won't get to a pay phone for a few days and not to worry. She agreed to be my single point of contact for this side of the country and if she didn't hear from me after three days, to send out a search party.

Her response was comforting. "Be careful and call the first chance you get. We're all thinking about you and wish we were there. Don't forget we love you." I think my being a little naive about what I was getting myself into was a good thing. By not knowing any different, I couldn't talk myself out of going ahead as planned.

Before I fell asleep, my thoughts drifted to an earlier phone conversation I had with Florence of Ruff Spots. I was disappointed to hear she wasn't able to come tomorrow because of the time change and her work commitment. I was glad I had the opportunity to speak with her, even if briefly.

"Ruff Spots is an animal welfare foundation and not a shelter," Florence informed me. "We provide some spay and neuter funding to charitable organizations in the province. It's always nice to hear about someone trying to help animals."

"One of Let Live Canada's goals is to have a national spay and neuter program across the country," I said excitedly.

"That would be wonderful. Good luck tomorrow," she said and hung up the phone.

When I got up in the morning, I quietly put my things together and then went downstairs for some coffee and toast. Jeannie sat in the kitchen with me and I was glad to hear that she was coming to the harbor, along with Miriam who was also staying at the hostel. "Keep in touch and let me know how you are doing," Jeannie said as she handed me a self-addressed post card. "I will and maybe I'll see you on the west coast when I get there," I replied.

I said good-bye to Bill. I don't think he likes good-byes. As I left, I thought how wonderful and unique the experience staying at the hostel had been for me. Here, I had found a place where there were no strangers, just lots of culture and friendly faces. One day, I hope to return under different circumstances.

Walking to Dorit's hotel gave me a chance to make any last minute adjustments to my backpack. I came with two bags full of provisions, but left with one. Carrying almost thirty pounds of extra weight on my back, and very little of that food, was more than I had trained with. It was as light as I could make it.

When I arrived at the hotel, Dorit was wearing the jersey I gave her. "It looks good on you. You look fit to run. Do you want to join me?" I smiled.

"I don't think so," she responded and asked me, "How are you feeling?"

"I feel great."

"Are you ready for this?"

"I'm as ready as I'll ever be," I responded.

The front desk clerk took our picture together before we left. Then, we drove to Harbour Drive but to our disappointment, there was no one there. Then, Ivan swung by in his car to let us know they were waiting for us near the Newfoundland Dog statues and we followed him.

We were delighted at the sight of a dozen or so supporters standing there with their dogs. Everyone had braved the weather and gathered to greet us. I was happy to see Jeannie amongst them.

Putting myself at the center of attention wasn't something I was comfortable with. I had to intentionally put my reservations aside if I was going to see this through. It was both exciting and nerve-wracking all at once. However, the friendly atmosphere helped to calm my nerves. Everyone seemed to enjoy the moment. Pictures were taken and conversations exchanged. A couple of people tried lifting my backpack and couldn't believe I would be running with it.

Words they wrote on my flag inspired me: "*We hope you succeed.*" "*Your journey inspires us.*" "*It only takes one. Our prayers are with you.*" Their faith in me was flattering, but deep down inside I wasn't sure I could live up to their expectations.

It was a windy and cold walk along Harbour Drive and I was uplifted by the support from everyone around me. Once we reached the Mile One building, Dorit addressed the crowd with some final thoughts. She had complete confidence that prevention would solve the problem and that it was a much more ethical solution.

"Other nations, including the States, have had great success with it and we can too. New York City is one example. In February 2007, they did not euthanize one healthy animal as a result of preventative methods. Statistics have proven that prevention does not cost communities any more money to spay and neuter than it does to euthanize. The facts are there, but they are ignored. We all need to speak out for those who cannot speak for themselves," said Dorit.

Humbled by her introduction, I felt undeserving of her praise. "My marathon is just an extension of the tireless efforts of others, individuals like Dorit and Jessica who have already made a difference and strive every day to improve conditions for animals. The real heroes are people who work in shelters and we need to acknowledge that and recognize their efforts. It's also not just about saving the lives of cats and dogs; it's about removing the ungodly task of euthanizing from people. I won't stop until the senseless killing stops." I concluded by thanking Dorit and everyone for their kind words and support.

Finally, I was about to take a long awaited step. The day had come when I would be standing at the intersection of my promise and keeping it. My commitment was irrevocable. It was time to put my words into action and my best foot forward. As I set out from there, everyone waved and cheered me on.

It was April 15, 2007 and no longer just a dream to be running across Canada. Today, I found myself actually doing it and on this day my course was set into motion. I was running with a purpose and one clear target: to make it all the way to Vancouver. The first test in my quest was right in front of me, Newfoundland. I embraced the challenge and disappeared into the distance.

While I ran, it was daunting to think that my greatest adventure still awaited me, adventures that can be both fun and scary. With a late start, I would go as far as daylight would take me. I had some security in knowing that Dorit would be driving out to the highway later to meet me before dark.

Almost immediately, the elements of running in foreign territory became a factor. Westerly winds and uphill running were slowing me down. My neck and shoulder muscles ached from the weight of my backpack, but I figured this would all pass once I built up more strength over time.

It was vital that I pace myself if I wanted to run twenty-six miles a day and make it all the way to the west coast. I knew I could run a marathon, I just didn't know if I could do it every day for the next six months.

A man walking his dog was surprised to learn that I was running all the way to Vancouver. "You have a long way to go," he said as I ran by. By the time I reached the exit for the TransCanada Highway, the wind had picked up considerably and it was getting much colder.

Unforeseeably, one of the straps on my backpack ripped off at the bottom. "Oh no," I panicked. "Never saw that one coming." A sewing kit had eluded my survival list and without a secured strap my backpack flopped around. It was awkward, but I held it tight until I could repair it.

Leaving the city limits made me realize how vulnerable I was going to be out here. There was still snow on the ground and my thoughts shifted to setting up my tent later. I had only practiced installing it in my living room at home, never tried it outdoors. "This should be interesting," I muttered under my breath.

Although I had done some camping before, I had never stayed alone in the wilderness and didn't know how I was going to react - it was either going to be in faith or in fear, depending on my focus.

Thirty kilometers from Mile One, I heard a horn beep behind me. It was Dorit and I was very glad to see her. With joints close to being ceased by the cold and driving winds, I sat in her warm car and swallowed the sandwich she brought me.

"How are you doing?" she asked.

I think I was trying to convince myself more than her when I answered, "It's a little windier than I expected, but I'm good. It's going well."

Our conversation transitioned to the turnout earlier in the day. I was grateful for the supporters who showed up, but disappointed in the media. The only coverage came from the radio talk show the night before. We both felt this should improve the further west I went.

Daylight was fading fast and it was time to make camp. My preferred location would be a hundred feet from the highway and sheltered by trees, but not this night. My options were limited to a ridge about twenty-five feet from the road. High enough on a rock, I was exposed but protected from vehicles.

Dorit didn't have to say it but I could see on her face that she felt awful about leaving me there. "Are you sure you want to stay out here by yourself in this weather?" she asked with concern.

To myself, I entertained the idea of going with her and getting her to drive me back in the morning. Instead, I gave her a hug and said, "Don't worry. I'll be fine. Have a safe trip home and I'll see you in Ottawa."

As I watched her drive away, a tiny voice in the back of my mind shouted, "Come back. Don't leave me here." It was too late and she was gone. Silently, I had my own concerns about the night ahead. Could I make it alone or was this bigger than I can handle?

There was no time to stand around and I needed to get out of the cold quickly. I started assembling my tent and as I was fastening the lines, the strong wind was making it difficult. My hands were freezing and they barely functioned, but I managed to get the pegs in the ground and the cover sheet on without losing it. As fast as I could, I threw everything inside, including myself.

I was relieved to be out of the wind and just sat there for a few seconds. "So this is going to be my home for the next six months," I sighed. "It should be interesting. Just me and a tent, alone on the highway." I had to let that thought soak in for a minute.

Then, I rummaged through my stuff as best I could in a confined space and put on some dry clothes. The warmth from my long tights and fleece shirt was exhilarating. I breathed air into a thin three quarter length Therma-Rest pad and it felt good to lie down.

This one-man tent had just enough room for me and to put a few things at my feet. Anything I didn't need, I left in my backpack and used it as a pillow. My sleeping bag was designed for temperatures as low as minus eight and at the time I purchased it, I thought it would be more than sufficient. Tonight, I had my doubts.

I managed to secure a skate lace inside my tent to hang my wet clothing, even though I knew they wouldn't be dry by morning. I wasn't looking forward to putting them on again.

As I settled in, it was hard not to focus on the walls of my tent that were flapping almost ferociously now. I could hear the howling of the wind wailing all around me in every direction causing me to wonder if my Hubba tent was strong enough to withstand its power. If it pulls apart, I'd have to hitch a ride back to town.

Cocooned in my sleeping bag, it took several minutes for me to warm up and stop from shivering. "To think I left all the comforts of home for this," I laughed. It didn't take long for the seriousness of my situation to set in and I began this conversation with myself. "What in the world am I doing out here? Who in their right mind would run across Canada alone without a support vehicle or a sponsor, or a companion for that matter? What was I thinking? I must have slept through something?"

The noise from the traffic was thunderous at times, especially trucks rumbling by. I didn't mind though because it felt like I had some company. It wasn't long before daylight disappeared and the night crept in. Once I was enclosed by darkness, the lure of fear started knocking at my tent with its desire to have me, fear that can overtake you. I didn't think I was afraid of the dark, but the reality that I was out here alone started taking a hold of me.

Fear is so much bigger in the dark. My mind began playing tricks on me, causing me to wonder what every little sound was. I spooked myself with thoughts that the dark was not always empty. I began thinking about things that stirred up my imagination, like being surrounded by wild animals or monsters. Keeping that imagination from wandering away from me was a battle. I had to find a way to keep that monster down, or be overtaken by it.

My thoughts drifted between being in this situation and thinking about my family at home. I worried more for them than I did for myself. Long before now, I had entered into a quiet acceptance that something could go wrong and my journey might have a different ending. There was always the possibility that I may never see them again.

After assuring my sisters that if I ever felt like I was in any real danger I would get on the first bus home, I quickly realized there wouldn't be a bus coming by anytime soon. I was out here for the night and somehow, I had to get through the next eight hours.

Sometime later, I was hoping it would wait until morning, but Mother Nature called and I could no longer restrain myself. It meant getting out of the security of my sleeping bag and tent. First, I had to overcome my fear; it was the kind of fear that paralyzes you and makes it hard to breathe or move.

Out here, I needed some help and I took my battle with fear to prayer. I said words that I had recently come to know.

"When I am afraid, I will trust in you.
In God, whose word I praise.
In God I trust; I will not be afraid."
– Psalm 56:3-4 (NIV)

I repeated that prayer over and over again, until finally I unzipped the flap of my tent. I looked around to see if there were any animals lurking, but without any light I could hardly see my hand in front of my face. A flashlight would have been handy right about now, but it was another item that had eluded my survival list. It was pitch black, with shadows and darkness surrounding me. I quickly reminded myself that I wasn't alone and out I went.

What a rush. My heart pounded so fast that my breathing could barely keep up with me. I was out and in so fast, I thought I was Houdini. "That's one way to overcome your fear," I concluded. Just meet it head on. The fact that I made it back inside my tent safely reassured me there was nothing to be afraid of and I wasn't going to let a little bit of fear get the better of me, even though that was easier said than done.

Eventually, the noise from the highway faded to nothing and the dark hours felt endless. As I tossed and turned constantly, not able to fall asleep, I reflected on the past few days and the people who had signed my flag: animal lovers who understood my motives. It was enlightening to know there were others who felt the same way I did and surely, I would meet many more down the road.

I didn't know what time it was, but I trusted that if I got through the first night, I would never look back. I chose faith over fear. Knowing that the sun would rise again helped ease my mind and I couldn't wait to find out what tomorrow would bring. "Maybe Dorit will surprise me and come back with a warm cup of coffee before she leaves for the airport." Just the thought of that gave me something to look forward to, even though I knew she wouldn't be coming.

Finally, after waiting patiently for daybreak, the inside of my tent lit up with light that changes everything. Having daylight shining through the darkness, my eyes stayed open and the bright morning star rose in my heart once again. I was still alive after my first night and as I lay there, God-willing, I believed I could do this. This is what all that physical and mental training had been about – for the difficult days.

I got out of my shelter and packing up was a bit of a challenge. The more I hurried, the longer it took. There was moisture built up on the outside of my tent and I tucked away wet equipment.

Looking all around me, I was astonished that I had spent the night out here, but jubilant that I did it. Up until a few years ago, my life had been safe and familiar. Now, I found myself in a life-changing battle and uncharted territory.

My secret war was taking me down an unfamiliar path and in front of me was a door enticing me to go through it. On one hand, I believed it was my door of hope. On the other hand, it was risky, full of haunting "what-ifs" and the fear of an unknown outcome. All the same, I trusted my unknown future with the one who was setting my heart free.

Propelled by my passion to make a difference, I harnessed my backpack and made my way to the highway. As I exhaled, I could see my breath. Keeping my stuff dry was already a problem and without the luxury of a support vehicle, I knew I'd be in trouble if the weather didn't change. I needed the sun's help, but today started with a morning mist and bitterly cold winds. Right now, the only thing that was going to keep me warm was to run.

Traffic was starting to pick up and with plenty of shoulder room, I ran in the same direction. As I looked down the highway, I saw 985 kilometers that stood between Port-Aux-Basques and me. My estimated time of arrival was approximately three weeks if all went well. Soon, I would encounter hilly climbs as I run deeper into the rock. I looked up at a cloudy sky and could only pray that the weather would improve with each passing day.

Newfoundland had a bad reputation for weather and someone told me it changes every ten minutes, so you can never be sure of what you're going to get. Kind of like a box of chocolates according to Forrest Gump. Not long after I started running, the mist turned into a light drizzle. The roads were wet and slippery, and I was running right into another head wind.

The wind was so strong at times it tossed me around like a piece of paper and periodically blew me backward. People must have thought I was out of my mind for being out here. Still, I drove myself tirelessly hoping the weather would change. If nothing else, it was great endurance training that would help prepare me for the Rockies.

Drizzle progressed into rain and my feet were swishing in my shoes. On the brighter side, cars started honking their horns. Truckers were the loudest and at one point, an ambulance flashed his lights. Some drivers even waved back at me as they passed. That always made me smile and it was helping to keep my mind off my discomfort.

I had some concerns with the clothing I was wearing, that they wouldn't provide the weather protection I needed even though they were wicking material. Mainly because I'm a heavy sweater and wet skin or clothing on a windy day could lead to frostbite, even if the air temperature is above the freezing mark.

On this cold and soggy day, I ran through heavy rain and after fifty-five kilometers, I met my first angel. "Hop in," he said. "There's a motel just around the corner and I'll drop you off. What are you doing out here anyway? It's dangerous on these roads in this weather."

Sitting in his car, drenched and chilled, I didn't know if I should laugh or cry. I was sure grateful he came along and that he stopped. The clerk at the motel smiled as she gave me the key to my room.

"Would you like me to throw your clothes in the dryer?" she offered.

"That would be great. Thank you. That's very kind of you," I said appreciatively. Thankfully, she also had a needle and thread so I could repair my backpack.

It was such a relief to be out of the rain. The warmth from the shower revitalized my body and then I wrapped myself in a heavy warm blanket. I was so thankful for the sailor who had come along.

Looking around my room, I glanced at everything hanging up to dry and wondered if what I was doing might be too big for me. This was not the start I had imagined and blurred already were the edges of the picture I had so carefully drawn in my head. Why did I ever think I could do this? As much as I wanted to make it happen, I wasn't sure I had the willpower to carry out my steps under these conditions.

After I phoned my sister, Angel, I went down to the restaurant to have a warm meal and hot coffee even though my body complained. My conversation with her had been brief, just to let her know where I was. Not feeling in a talkative mood, I told her I would call again in a few days.

I watched almost numbly as the freezing rain came down. "This is the worst weather we've had in a while for this time of year," some in-landers sitting at a table next to me said.

That night, I fell into bed exhausted not knowing what to expect the next day, except that I would get up in the morning and start running again. There was nothing that could have prepared me for what was waiting for me.

Clarenville was approximately one hundred kilometers away, with nothing in between except the vastness of land and miles of solitude. There was heaps of wide-open space and right now a lot of it was hidden by fog. Since I arrived on the island, there has been little change in the weather and I had to respect that it might stay this way, or even get worse.

Enveloped with dampness, I zipped up my jacket and pulled wool socks over my hands. I took a deep breath and then encouraged myself by saying, "I can do this. All I have to do is take the next step." Despite the threat of disaster, I persisted.

My target was to set up camp in Bellevue Cove this afternoon and then go the rest of the way tomorrow. The road seemed to stretch forever and the land I was venturing into appeared infinitely remote. Newfoundland's nickname is *"The Rock"* and for me that meant some pretty rugged road to cross. My only passage was the highway.

The hills were so long and steep that they became my hills of adversity. At times, I wondered if I would win the battle of the hills. I had plenty of base miles built up, but the weight from my backpack was adding to the challenge. Undeterred by my course, I held nothing back.

People driving by continued to honk and wave, giving me moments of encouragement. I communicated back to drivers with a wave of my own. As self-motivated as I was, I still needed encouragement from time to time. It was making the difference between giving up and going on.

After a pretty somber run, I reached my target for the night. It was mysteriously quiet as I approached the cove and with the landscape shrouded in fog, it had an eerie feeling to it. There was a soft mist as if it had been pumped into the air. Tired and needing to get off my feet, I started scanning for a sheltered area.

Running up a long incline, I came across a flat spot off to the right of the highway. It was about a hundred feet down a hill and protected by some trees next to a stream, as if it had been reserved just for me. "Perfect," I shouted with glee and felt relieved to get off the road.

Within minutes, my tent was up and I changed into my only set of dry clothes. Ravishing with hunger, I ate almost everything I had, except a bagel that I saved for breakfast. Being confined in a small tent had its limitations and I was glad I wasn't claustrophobic. The very essence of the great outdoors has a way of making you feel inferior, especially in a crowd of one.

Darkness fell upon me and there was little noise from the road. This was a different solitary experience than the one I had the first night in my tent. The feeling of isolation was a lot creepier. My mind enjoyed reminding me that if anything happened it would be pointless to cry out for help. No one would hear me. I was out of sight and no one knew where I was. It caused me to wonder if I had overestimated my ability and now my life was in danger. Shouldn't I have known better?

It wasn't long before the changing winds intensified and raced above me. I could hear the falling snow and stepped outside briefly to see what was going on. Trees were shaken and I watched as snow swept through the sky. I was under a storm and at the mercy of Mother Nature.

Returning to the warmth of my sleeping bag, I listened to her vengeance all night long like the sounds of a roaring sea. Each drop from the trees that hit the top of my tent was like a knock on the door.

Feeling lonely and tired, I missed my family terribly. Fear was once again crouching at my door. Quickly, it felt like I was losing control of myself. My night's battle began with that panicky feeling you get when you think you're in deep trouble.

The further into the night I went, the bigger my fear got and the harder it was to cast out that giant. I needed a bigger giant to fight for me and my fear drove me to prayer again. "God help me. I need you to be my giant."

In that moment, I felt God's promise that He would never leave me tumble down from my head to my heart. He was with me. God was bigger and stronger than any giant my head could dream up and I didn't have to be afraid.

At that point, my panic and fear gave way to a calm and peaceful confidence in Him. God protected me the first night and He would do it again tonight. The secret was for me to keep taking my battles to God in prayer.

After some anxious moments and the longest night of my life, I managed to refocus. From that moment on, I felt like I could overcome anything. As I fell in and out of sleep, I constantly reminded myself as sure as the night brings fear, the day will bring hope.

In the morning, after anxiously waiting for daylight, I could still hear the winds blowing intensely. As I peeked out up at the highway, I could see snow blowing vigorously across the road. It was tempting to stay curled up in my tent, but my heart had no desire to spend another night out here alone.

All logic should have kept me from going out there, but with a bit of faith and a wider hope that the ten-minute advice I was given about the weather was true, I packed up and started running.

> *I didn't know it at the time but I had been camped on the small arm that connects the Avalon Peninsula to the main section of Newfoundland, an area bounded by ocean. Trinity Bay was on one side of me, and Placentia Bay on the other. The openness allowed for incredible gusts of wind and freezing rain blowing off the ocean.*

The first couple of miles were miserable. I had wet snow blowing in my face and icicles forming on my eyebrows. The road was slippery with a buildup of ice and being so wet and cold all the time was more than I had bargained for. "What in the world was I thinking," I grumbled. Maybe this is a foolish and impossible thing to do, just like everyone said it was. I was in the middle of nowhere and had no choice but to keep going.

Eventually, I ran my way out of the freezing rain and into a constant drizzle. Pushing through a strong headwind, I was able to keep my focus, but it was taking all my energy. The past couple of days had given me a whole new meaning to choosing your own adventure.

Waving to people as they drove by was something I looked forward to because it gave me some friendship from the road besides my own company, especially truck drivers that traveled the road daily and I saw repeatedly. It amazed me that my perception of time had changed so quickly and days felt like weeks already.

After running twenty kilometers, I was relieved to come across a gas station. It brought me such joy, that I jumped up and down and shouted, "Yes, there is a God!" I stopped to stock up with as much food and water as I could carry. "There's a motel about thirty kilometers down the road," the cashier said.

That felt like such a huge leap from here since it felt like I had already run a marathon, but I made it my new target anyway. Setting goals and then challenging myself to achieve them helped keep my mind off of everything else. It was also helping to rebuild my confidence and to keep me motivated.

Four consecutive days of long distance running was a stretch for me. At best, I ran one long run a week while I trained and mostly on flat roads. In comparison, I had under-trained myself.

Out here, I had to compensate for the different factors every day and make adjustments all the time. There was also nowhere to take cover from the elements except for the odd weigh station. My best defense was to keep running.

The rain continued until I reached the motel where I took a room for the night. I prayed for better weather, but it never came and it rained again the next day. A new day hadn't made any difference and I wondered if I should delay going any further until the weather improved. I argued with myself that it could take days for the weather to break and waiting might put me too far behind schedule.

As the waitress poured me another cup of coffee, she looked at me staring out the window and said, "The rain should stop later this morning." I took it as a sign and would wait for an opening in the sky. If I had to, I would run between the clouds.

At last, the fog lifted and the rain subsided, giving me a window to go. However, the sky quietly warned me there was more to come so I would have to run quickly. As expected, bad weather persisted. Nonetheless, I labored through it and beat the wind and every drop and flake that tried to discourage me.

When I saw the signs for Clarenville, I was elated and couldn't wait to get to a payphone. Out here, the importance of my relationship with my sisters really hit home. They were out of sight, but never out of mind. It was only space that separated us. I have always been able to turn to them, for inspiration and a fresh perspective. I stopped at the first pay phone I found and made my call.

"Hi Angel."

"Michelle, where are you? How are you doing?"

"I'm okay, but the weather has been awful."

"Are you all right?"

"Everything is fine, I just wanted to let you know that I made it to Clarenville."

Not wanting her to worry, I tried not to sound disheartened and changed the subject to hear about something else other than my discouraging start.

"How's everyone at home? Did Mom and Dad make it back from Florida okay?"

"Oh yeah. There was still some snow on the ground, but they got into the campground. They have their phone connected now so you can call them anytime. They're anxious to hear from you."

"Great, I'll call them later. How's Wicked? I can hear him barking in the background."

"He's fine; he just wants some attention," she laughed.

Wicked is her little Shih Tzu dog. In my sister's efforts to make him more lovable, according to human standards, and to be part of the family, I think he forgets that he's a dog and so do we.

She filled me in on any news from home and then said she would call everyone for me. As I hung up the phone, it occurred to me that I had more in my survival pack than a few physical items. It's important to know where you're going, but it's also important to remember where you're coming from.

Having support from my siblings carried more weight than I realized and I thanked Angel for the card she had sent me before I left for St. John's. It read:

> *Hi Michelle,*
>
> *A Dream Come True*
> *Well time sure goes by fast and it is already time for you to embark on a new journey. I just wanted you to know that I will miss you lots. Six months is a long time. But most of all I hope that this journey in your life brings you every dream you have wished for. I hope this will fill that spot in your soul that you have been searching to fill. I pray that your journey will be successful and enjoyable. I want you to know that I am here in every way for you and I will have you in my thoughts and prayers every day. I am sure you will be a big success in this, as you are in everything you do. Remember even though you have your group of supporters who are with you to encourage and help you, I am also sending you encouragement daily. Like you tell me, we may not see each other a lot but we are always in each other's thoughts. Please take care of yourself and show the country what you are made of. I truly wish you a totally successful journey.*
>
> *Take care and Good Luck*
> *Love Angel xxxxoooo*
> *P.S. I am always just a phone call away.*

Angel is a year and eight months younger than I am and only a year and six months separates her from our younger brother. Looking back to our childhood, I recalled the nights when they both would climb into bed with me whenever they were frightened.

"I'm afraid of lightning," my brother would say whenever there was a thunderstorm. We laugh about that today as adults. "If anyone can run across Canada, its Michelle," he said.

Talking with my sisters was like putting the wind back into my sail. "Hi Chris, it's me. I made it to Clarenville," I said excited as she answered the phone. "It's so good to hear your voice."

Christine–also affectionately known to us as "Chris" or "Chrissy"–is the firstborn. As long as I can remember, I put her on a pedestal. Through my child eyes, she could do no wrong. She was the single biggest influence of anyone in my life growing up and the first person to positively shape it.

At a young age, she had the responsibility of babysitting us kids. Most of the time, we played school and she was the teacher. There was always singing and dancing and it was fun to be with her. She also taught me how to catch and throw a ball, and even bought me my first brand new bicycle.

Being insightful and smart, she could have been anything she wanted. Instead, she focused on the family. I've never forgotten the heartfelt words she told me when I left home a long time ago. "There will always be a light on for you," she said, not wanting me to leave. Today, I needed that light to keep my head up and she never failed to encourage me.

"It's amazing that you're even able to do this," said Chris.

"Well, I haven't done anything yet," I told her.

"Yes, but you've always been able to excel at anything you put your mind to."

"It's kind of a blessing and a curse," I half joked.

"Could you hurry up and get here before I have another heart attack?"

At the age of fifty, she had a mild heart attack and I didn't want to cause her another one so to try to lessen her worry, I made light of everything.

"I think it's a lot safer where I am than where you are."

"Yeah right. You're not fooling me. I didn't just fall off the turnip truck you know."

"Well you don't have to worry about me, I don't think I could be in any better shape than I am right now and I feel like I could run around the world. Before you know it, I'll be in Thunder Bay."

"You know it would be a lot faster to get here by plane."

I'm not sure why, but I burst into laughter after hearing her say that. Maybe it was the combination of fatigue and how ridiculous it sounded to take three months to get somewhere when I could be there in a few hours. Or maybe, I just needed to release some of my own anxiety. Whatever the reason, it felt good to laugh and before I hung up the phone I told her, "See you soon."

Marie is the second oldest and we're only thirteen months apart, which makes me the middle child. When we were around eight and ten years old, we spent a fun winters day in the woods with some cousins not telling anyone where we went. At the time, my parents were at a curling event while Chris babysat us. They returned home just as it was getting dark and we were nowhere to be found. "I haven't seen them all day," Chris said. That sent them into a panic searching for us and our fun ended when they picked us up coming out of the woods smelling like smoke.

She also saved my life once, right around the same time. It was summer though and we were visiting our grandmother. We loved to play on the small mountain near her house. "Don't go up there," Grandma used to tell us. Well, we climbed higher than ever one day and decided to take the far side down. It was going well until there was no more footing and we couldn't see passed the steep cliff and void below us. I figured it was still pretty high though, because I was looking down on the tops of the trees. I froze, panicked, and started crying.

Marie managed to get herself to safe ground while I was hanging on for dear life. She didn't leave me behind though. "Grab my hand," she shouted, but it was a couple of body lengths above me–straight up. To this day, I don't know how I didn't fall over the edge and tumble to the bottom. When I felt her hand, she pulled me up and we never went back there again. She too encouraged me with this email:

Good morning Michelle,

Heart of Courage
I just read your blog, just now. I love you so much and am so proud of you. I am printing everything off too so I will send it all to you when you are done. I was just telling my coworkers here about your marathon and cause and one fella is from Newfoundland and they are so impressed you're doing all of this too. We will make some plans when you come through good old Nipigon. Chris spoke to Mom and Dad last night; they are in Montreal and said they would pick you up if you want. Chris also said that Marcel was very impressed with what you are doing and is cheering for you. As long as you stay healthy and are safe we are all backing you. Reading your blog is like being there with you and I am glad you have your angels. The world isn't as bad as we think; it's just the unknown that worries us. Just know Chris and I and families are all thinking of you ALWAYS!

I love you and I'm sending you thousands of hugs and kisses and smiles.

Bye for now. Marie
xoxoxoxooxoxoxoxo

Five days of running over two hundred kilometers under these conditions was a huge milestone for me, it felt like so much more. Speaking with my sisters, along with the comments from my petition and blog, put new life into me and restored some of my deflated confidence. I was encouraged to keep going. From my blog:

Stephanie said. . .
You are such a hero, Michelle. You have left an impression on each one of us who were lucky enough to meet you at Mile One in St. John's, sign the flag,

and wave good-bye as you started your journey. My two young daughters were with me that day, and we talk about you and pray for you every day.

Thank you for every step you're taking.

It was no surprise to wake up to more blowing wet snow. Visibility was extremely poor and this time it forced me to stay put. I took it as an opportunity to visit the local animal shelter. The Clarenville SPCA was located along the flat of the harbor. Hearing lots of praise from the people of St. John's about their shelter, I was looking forward to meeting them.

When I walked into the building, there were pictures and adoption stories covering the walls of the entrance. A young girl said hello and when I introduced myself, an older woman came out of the back office. "This isn't a no-kill shelter," Ann Marie said sternly and looked at me as if I were in the wrong place. This was that moment Dorit had warned me about.

Instantly, my heart sank from rejection and my first reaction was to shrink and crawl under a rock. I tried not to give way to the fear that had come over me; in a split second, I summoned enough courage to speak.

Carefully, I chose my words. "I'm trying to raise awareness about the overpopulation problem with cats and dogs in our country and promote spay and neutering. Shelters are doing what they can to take care of the problem, but people also need to take some of the responsibility for a problem people created. I'm just a concerned citizen trying to do my part."

Then, Ann Marie caught me off guard with her response. "We received an email from Jessica that you want to stop shelters from euthanizing animals." As a result, they had perceived my event as an attack against shelters, which couldn't be further from the truth. I had nothing but admiration for people who work in rescue shelters of any kind. They are far more caring than most of us know how to be and caregivers are some of the most selfless and compassionate people you'll ever meet.

Ann Marie continued charged with emotion. “No-kill shelters stop accepting animals when they are full, but we don’t refuse any. Sometimes we have to euthanize an animal, but it is always a last resort. Isn’t it better to euthanize an animal than to have it live out its life in a cage or left out on the streets to die inhumanely?”

This conception was not uncommon amongst people who worked in shelters. It lurked at the back of many minds, almost always provoking a protest. The mention of no-kill disturbs the tranquility of traditional shelters. Especially for those who feel euthanasia is the only humane way to put down an animal.

The next word I said was crucial. “I’m sure Jessica meant well with her email, but you know better than anyone that the problem cannot be solved overnight. There are too many issues, not to mention that as long as cats and dogs are allowed to breed freely, the problem won’t go away. People need to be educated about responsible pet ownership and that an animal is not a disposable item. It would take some time, but with spaying and neutering the problem could eventually be solved.”

Ann Marie responded more positively. “The problem is too big to solve, but raising awareness about spay and neutering is a good thing to do.” Then, she invited me into her office where we continued this important discussion. After clarifying my purpose, I watched the expression change in her eyes. Her frowns turned into smiles as she began sharing her shelter stories with me and she pulled out the family album like a proud parent. Their unfailing love and tireless efforts to try to save them all was evident as she put a name to every success story.

While she gave me a tour of their building, I met Tina and Jewel. Together, they all spent endless hours of volunteer work trying to give animals a second chance. We walked passed the cages and all the animals entranced me, but their barking was like cries for help. It was as if they were saying, “Please take me with you.”

Freedom appeared to be an innate desire of every creature and in their eyes was the hope of breaking free. It caused me to wonder, if they could talk, would they tell us about the heartless owner who abandoned them? The bewildering truth is that these animals would faithfully, loyally, and lovingly return to their undeserving owners.

I stayed over an hour and then Tina graciously offered to give me a ride back to town. Before I left, Ann Marie said kindly, "I'll send an email to the other shelters and let them know that you stopped here and we enjoyed having you visit us. You're not at all what we were expecting."

My experience at the shelter was humbling and although it ended well, it brought tears to my eyes. People in shelters work in a difficult world and see what the rest of us don't: the heartbreaking effects of suffering animals. Both animals and caregivers go through far too many hardships day after day. What a burden we have put on them.

If shelters have lost hope that it is possible to solve the overpopulation problem, why would anyone listen to me? Why would anyone want to change things, especially if they felt it was going to cost them something? I believed people would listen if the reward outweighed the cost, and saving a life has great rewards.

Facing adversity taught me it does not need to be a reason for discouragement. Some people are disheartened by the enormity of the problem, but what that told me is that the need for change is greater than ever. We can't give up just because we don't have all the answers. As I tried to envision what the future would hold, I was certain I wouldn't waver from my commitment to see this through.

Before I packed up and left Clarenville, I gave Openline an update on my progress. It helped as people continued to acknowledge me on the road. Every time I heard a horn, it made me feel closer to the people of Newfoundland–like I was one of their own.

Despite its remoteness, the natural beauty and rugged hills of Terra Nova National Park gave me a splendid view of the forest that was like a blanket covering the ground, a welcome sight after some sparse vegetation. It was also the home of wild animals. My being out here might result in seeing some of them, but it was fine with me if they kept their distance.

The deeper into the park I went, the more engulfed I became with my environment and not much escaped my senses. There was peace, the quiet, and only the sound of invisible air. Birds followed above me and tree branches clapped whenever the wind passed through. As I ran by, I began thinking of the trees as my cheering section.

Thirty kilometers later, I was excited to come across an Irving gas station. I had reached the turnoff for Port Blanford and was happy to use their facilities, and find something hot to drink. Inside, I met some supporters.

"You're running across Canada without a support vehicle. Wow. What a wonderful thing to do for animals," Sandy, the cashier said. "My sister, Sheri, is going to want to meet you. She'll be right back. We both love animals. There's no charge for the coffee."

"Thank you. Would you like to sign my flag? I'm getting people I meet to sign their name."

"What a great idea," Sandy said.

Both Sandy and Sheri signed their names and looked for names they might recognize. They also gave me a donation.

"Can I take your picture before you leave?" asked Sandy.

"Sure," I smiled and then said good-bye.

"Good luck the rest of the way. We hope you make it," Sandy shouted.

"Me too. Thanks for the coffee," I shouted back and waved.

Not far from there was another gas station. A little boy ran up to me with a donation while his dad filled up his truck with gas. He looked up at me with a big smile on his face as he handed me a five-dollar bill.

"It's for the animals," he grinned.

"Thank you. What's your name?"

"Nicolas," he replied. "I have three fish and two cats. My mom rescued a cat because it followed her home from the highway and she gave him some food and now he lives with us. He didn't have a home."

"Well that's a very kind thing to do and I bet your cats are very happy to live with you." Nicholas shook his head up and down. "Do you know why I'm running across Canada, Nicolas?" I asked him.

In his own childlike wisdom, he nodded his head and said with an expression on his face as if I should have known the answer. "Because you're going to save all the animals."

"Well, lots of people are trying to do that because animals need our help just like your cat needed your help. Do you think it would be a good idea if all cats and dogs had a home with people who love them and take care of them, just like you do with your cats?"

Nicolas nodded his head again and answered, "Yeah."

"Would you like to sign my flag?" I asked him before he could run off.

He shook his head and with some guidance, he signed his name along with his two feline friends, Puss and Matias.

"Thank you Nicolas. Your donation is going to save a life."

His face lit up and he smiled as he said, "I have to go now."

"Bye Nicolas. Take good care of your pets." I waved and watched him run back to his dad at the gas pumps.

Talking to Nicholas was refreshing and impacted me in a way that only a child can. It was his innocence and vulnerability that made me feel children and animals don't deserve to suffer. We can sometimes understand our own sufferings, but not theirs. Maybe that's why it is so appalling to me whenever I hear about or see their suffering–especially abuse. I've tried to make sense out of it, but each time I come away feeling more appalled and justified in saying that the death of a child or an animal is a horrible tragedy.

It's true that animals are unmistakably inferior to human beings. Only people can discern between right and wrong. Animals are incapable of doing wrong; they act on instinct and natural impulses. They are irrational creatures and we don't fully understand them. However, once they learn to trust us, the bond between an animal and a human being is remarkable.

Nicholas responded to his companion friends with his own love. One day, he might be in a decision-making position about an animal, or any life, and I hoped he would make the right choice. We have to set an example for children today. If we teach them well, they will grow up to be moral people.

I continued running for a number of miles and was well into the park when I stopped at Dunphy's Pond. My tent was situated just out of sight from the highway, along a trail that disappeared into the wooded darkness. I hung my food from a tree and settled in for the night.

Not long afterward, the path darkened and night had arrived once again. This time, the experience was natural and serene, with no intrusion from the outside world. I fell asleep listening to sounds from the wild where living things both large and small prowled in the forest; moose calls that broke the almost haunting quiet and squawks from different birds.

In the morning, a loud noise I didn't recognize woke me, but the melody of chirping birds eased my worry. I shook white stuff off my tent and left only footprints in the snow behind me.

The road to Gambo started out partly sunny with little wind, but it was chilly. I enjoyed the sound of "crunch-crunch-crunch" under my shoes and felt free to run the highway. "What is in store for me today?" I wondered.

Just when I thought the hills couldn't get any worse, I came up to Glovertown and began my ascent. Half way to the top, I had to take my backpack off and give my shoulders a rest, as I often did after a long steep climb.

On what I nicknamed "heartbreak hill", I met an older couple walking about and they took an interest in what I was doing out here. "Poor animals, it's just awful that people don't take better care of them," they said and before I continued they encouraged me with, "Don't worry, you won't see another hill like this until you get to Gambo."

From that point on, the hills were less severe, but a strong head-wind challenged me. Just before Gambo, a young cyclist caught up to me and I was happy to chat with her.

"Hello there," I said.

"Hi, you must be the lady running across Canada," Christie said cheerfully.

"Yes I am, but how did you know that?"

"I heard about you before I left St. John's and I wondered if I'd see you on the highway. My name is Christie."

"Nice to meet you Christie. My name is Michelle. Where are you headed?"

"All the way to Vancouver, but I'm not doing it for any cause. I'm meeting up with some friends in Ontario and I have to be back in Saskatchewan by mid-June, where I go to university. It's my first attempt cycling through here and I thought I was doing something brave until I heard about you. I don't think I could do what you're doing," she laughed, almost demoralizing her own efforts.

"Well biking across Canada is no easy feat either. How has your ride been so far?"

"There are so many hills in Newfoundland," she said exasperatingly. "And the winds are incredible. I can't imagine how you're able to do this on foot carrying a backpack. I was trying to figure out where you put all your supplies. How can you run with it? Isn't it heavy?"

"Well, yes. I'd prefer to run without it. It weighs almost thirty pounds when I fill up with water,. But I only carry bare necessities. No cooking stuff."

"You don't cook! You must get awfully hungry? What do you eat?"

"Mostly energy bars and vitamins, bagels, or whatever else I can carry. I don't want to attract any wild animals. You look like you're well equipped. Have you had any trouble?"

"I definitely didn't bring warm enough clothes for this kind of weather and it's too wet to build fires. It's been so cold and rainy. I can't wait to get to the ferry and warmer weather."

"How's your bike holding out?"

"I've wiped out once already when the draft from a transport passing a little too close caused me to hit the gravel and I lost control of my bike. I hurt my shoulder, but I'm okay. That shook me up a bit," she said with a shaky voice.

"How far will you go tonight?"

"I think I'll stop in Gander."

"Well, when you're struggling on those hills and it's getting tough, just think of me on foot and maybe it won't seem so bad," I tried to encourage her.

"I will. When do you think you'll finish?" Christie asked curiously.

"I'm hoping by mid-October, before it snows. You'll be done long before me though," I laughed.

When we reached the exit for Gambo, Christie continued on her way while I headed into town. "Safe travels," we said as we went our separate ways. I watched her cycle out of sight and suddenly became aware of how cold I was. Any warmth left in my body had escaped me and I shook almost uncontrollably, which was normal for me after running.

The town was a lot smaller than my expectations and it made me feel uneasy about what to do for the night. There was a man working on a car just off to the side of the road. I approached him and asked if there was a campground nearby. First he looked around to see where I came from and then said, "There's a bed and breakfast a couple miles down the road, but I don't think they're open yet. If the car starts, I can take you there."

As he tried the engine, I smiled when it started and jumped in the front seat before he could change his mind. While we drove he jokingly said, "I hope the car doesn't stall. It's my mom's and I gave her my car while I'm fixing hers." *What a good son*, I thought.

I knocked on the door of the bed and breakfast, but there was no answer. "I can take you over to Sheila's Restaurant if you like," he said while he kindly waited. We didn't go far and he stopped in front of what looked like a house turned into a restaurant. "Thanks for your help," I said gratefully.

Stepping through the doors of the restaurant felt like walking into a friend's home. There was no doubt I was a stranger in town and I must have looked like a little lost puppy.

"Hello," the waitress said as I put my backpack next to a table.

"Hi," I smiled and asked for a cup of coffee.

"Would you like a menu?" she asked me.

"Yes please. I'm starving," I responded almost desperately.

The waitress's name was Bev and she sat at the table in front of me while I decided what to order. There were four other people sitting at another table, but it wasn't long before they left. I asked for the largest hot meal they had, complete with desert, and then went into the washroom to change into my only dry shirt wrapped in plastic.

Bev's husband, Rob, worked at the restaurant too and he went in and out of the kitchen. They mostly listened while I talked and drank several coffees. During that time, I was unaware that Rob had called some friends and asked them if they would take me in for the night.

Somehow, they knew before I did that I was going to need their help. "They've taken in a few female cyclists in the past," Bev said softly.

I was finished eating when Gerard walked into the restaurant. He looked like an angel to me; tall, handsome and a face you could trust. I went to pay for my meal, but Bev and Rob said, "This one is on the house." I didn't know what to say except thank you and I was awestruck that there were people who could be this kind to a stranger. "Good luck. You're in good hands now," they assured me.

We were within walking distance of Gerard and Paula`s house and on the way there, I must have thanked him a thousand times.

"We were put on this earth to help one another," Gerard said compassionately.

"Bev was saying you've had some cyclists stay with you."

"That was a few years ago. We haven't heard from them since."

Gerard and Paula extended their home to me and offered what they had. Their children had moved away and it was just the two of them now. "If you need to wash your clothes, there's a washer and dryer and you're welcome to take a hot shower," Gerard said.

Afterward, we watched some TV including the news and they shared some insight with me about life in Newfoundland. "The economy has been really affected by disputes in the oil industry and declining fisheries. Lots of men in the area leave their families to work inland and come back on weekends," he informed me.

While I listened to him, I thought, he sounded like such a soft-spoken man who had undoubtedly felt the pains of life and yet there was contentment within him. He himself was recovering from a leg injury and just getting back to work.

The evening went by quickly and it wasn't long before I slipped into a warm bed and fell asleep. What more could I ask for?

In the morning, Gerard made toast and coffee and we carried on our conversation from the night before about hard times people go through. He seemed like such a pleasing man and my new friends in Gambo had taken good care of me. The whole experience taught me that kindness is one gift everyone can give and "thank you" never feels like enough. On my way out, Gerard wished me luck and then closed the door.

Feeling the wind in my hair and the sun on my face was like the feeling you get waking up on Christmas morning. In spite of the cold, the skies were crystal clear with just a slight breeze and today had lots of promise.

After an initial long climb, I enjoyed some fairly level stretches of highway. Running to me had that perfect blend of physical and spiritual well being. To be fit felt like contentment and the fresh air cleared my lungs much to my delight. In one of Canada's most rugged settings, I took great pleasure in a different piece of the road every day and I couldn't help but be awed by the views.

However, in this province of various climates, the sunshine didn't last. About sixteen kilometers east of Gander, the weather quickly took a turn for the worse. This subtle change in weather blew rain mixed with ice pellets and snow at me. Adding to my discomfort was the spray from the highway and strong winds. This was not happiness. With no protection, it was moments like this that I wished I had a support vehicle.

With about ten kilometers to go, a car headed in the opposite direction pulled over and flagged me down. A tall, elderly man got out of the vehicle and crossed the road. "I heard you on the radio and I could never do what you're trying to do. Do you have a place to stay when you get to Gander?" he voiced with concern.

"Well, I have a tent with me so I'll try to find a campground."

To my complete amazement, he handed me a voucher for a room at the hotel he stays at regularly. "Here, give this to the front desk and they'll give you a room for the night," he said. I think I was in shock and my jaw fell to the ground. What do you say to that kind of kindness? "Thank you, thank you so much. I don't know what else to say except thank you," I repeated in disbelief. I was stunned.

Before he left, I gave him a hug and then waved as he drove away. Encouraged to keep going, I shouted as I ran, "Woohoo! Gander here I come." Knowing there was a dry room waiting for me lifted me up and getting drenched no longer mattered.

When I got to the hotel, a woman at the front desk gave me the strangest look as I walked in. I must have resembled something that crawled out of a flooded ditch. Before she could throw me out I told her, "I met an angel on the highway today." As I handed her my voucher, she recognized the name and gave me a key without saying a word.

I proceeded to my room and didn't come out of the shower for what felt like hours. I was so happy to be warm. "That man was a Godsend," I cried. I couldn't imagine what it would have been like to be outdoors tonight. Everything was soaked and my feet were aching so much that I got into bed and didn't move. All the while thinking it was such a luxury to sleep in a bed.

I ordered a large pizza and after arranging to meet with CBC News in the morning, I checked the forecast. The weather was supposed to be sunny and warmer tomorrow, but the gusts of winds were expected to be up to forty kilometers an hour. Intense winds were a normal part of Newfoundland's daily life, but to me they were my winds of adversity. "If only I could ride on the wings of these winds," I imagined, "What a ride that would be."

Early the next day, Leanne let me into the newsroom studio and sat me down. Her cheerful spirit put me at ease right away. Sitting alone in a booth in front of a microphone wasn't exactly entering the public life, but it was never my intention to seek public display. I was just happy to be a quiet voice of reasoning and get other people talking.

The morning talk show host asked me some standard questions, as did Leanne. Before I knew it, the interview was over. My answers seemed to satisfy everyone, but it might have been different had anyone probed a little deeper. Depending on how a question was asked, I wanted to answer as my conscience dictated.

On my way out of the studio, I thanked Leanne and CBC for the opportunity to speak over the radio. Unfortunately and once again, I missed out on hearing any feedback from listeners. My early departure also made it impossible to visit with the Gander SPCA. I was disappointed that it was closed when I called.

It didn`t take long to find my way back to the highway. The winds to Grand Falls were incredible at times and my feet were in need of some attention. There were lost toenails, soreness that had developed on the souls of my feet, and blisters that were getting worse. My first stop in Grand Falls was the pharmacy to pick up some first aid supplies, including Advil for all my aches and pains. I was beginning to feel like the walking wounded.

After I finished nursing myself, I headed for Exploits Valley SPCA. It was also volunteer-driven and covered a big area of the province. Most of the funding came out of their own pockets to keep it going.

I entered their shelter life and was greeted with acceptance by Carol and their shelter cat Captian. Looking at Captian, I could see that he was not your ordinary cat. In spite of his injured hind legs, he managed to get around the shelter just fine. He loved his caregivers.

Carol cheerfully took me on a tour of the facility, where I met other volunteers and animals. One in particular was an older beagle named Kevin. "Our volunteers and staff often make personal sacrifices to make one more miracle happen," Carol said proudly. Kevin was one of those miracles. As I listened to their many stories, it was obvious that Captian and Kevin were extra special to them.

Not much can compare to the selfless act one does for a defenseless creature. Here I was, in the midst of people who willingly and often sacrificially give of themselves with little thanks or praise for what they do. People who care deeply about another life. It`s also not unusual for volunteers, who are exposed to the sufferings of animals, to have a number of abandoned pets living with them. "You can't help but want to scoop them all up and take them home," said Carol.

There was also a circus coming into town this summer that they were trying desperately to band and get the community behind them. When I left, they gave me a t-shirt that read, "Please don't go to the circus. . .ask me why."

As I closed the door to leave, they cheered me on and said, "The animals thank you for helping them," However, it was I who should be cheering them. I felt ashamed that our society put such a burden on them. There was something seriously unfair and wrong about that.

It was my dad's birthday today and when I heard his voice on the phone, I started singing "Happy Birthday". Then, I asked him how it felt to be back in Canada.

"It's a little cold," he said, but quickly changed the subject and conveyed his feelings of concern for my safety. "Do you want to carry a gun with you for protection?" he asked quite seriously.

"Thanks dad, but I think I'll be okay. If something doesn't feel right, I just keep on going. I don't put myself in any vulnerable situations. I'll be careful," I tried to assure him.

"Do you think you can do it–run all the way to Vancouver? Me and mommy were looking at a map of Canada and that's a long way!"

"I'm sure going to try dad. I think I've got my work cut out for me though just getting out of Newfoundland. We'll see how good the genes you gave me are," I laughed.

"We'll come out to meet you when you get to Quebec City for sure."

"That's great dad. I can't wait to see you again. We'll talk about that more later."

Although I was excited they wanted to come, I couldn't afford to peer that far ahead. I had to train myself to think short term so that my task wouldn't feel impossible to handle or that I wouldn't be overwhelmed with how far I had to go. It was just too hard emotionally to let my mind think I had so many miles to do all at once, or to see beyond reaching the next town.

Talking with both my parents helped lift my spirits. I hadn't seen them since last fall and I was looking forward to spending some time with them. "I can't wait to give you a hug mom," I told her.

The forecast was still grim, but I maintained my unwavering belief that every day would get better and I looked forward to crossing the halfway point in Newfoundland tomorrow. I reflected often on the comments from my blog for encouragement:

> *Dorit said. . .*
> *Hi Michelle:*
> *Oh, I'm so glad to "hear" from you. What determination you have. I know what the weather was like in NL. But, it will get better. Spring will come.*
> *Your courage is absolutely inspiring.*
> *(Didn't know one could comment in a blog).*

Take care of yourself, dear Michelle. Don't let yourself get exhausted or sick. Yeah - I know - I sound like a mother.

Anonymous said...
By doing this I believe you will make a difference and give these little guys a voice that can finally be heard. You would have to be an extraordinary person to take on a journey like this. But the rewards will be greater than you could even imagine. So with that may you have a safe journey, good health and lots of love and support. Good luck you are one of the great ones.

Pamela said...
This story made me cry from beginning to end and it's really sad that people could actually have their animal/best friends put down. It's really sad to see that people just throw their pets away as if they were a piece of trash. I'm so glad there are people like you that have the time to help those who can't speak for themselves. The two cats I have now almost went to a shelter where they would only have a week to be adopted, and if not then it was the end for them. I was only expecting to take one but when I seen the two of them I couldn't separate or live with the fact that I would be possibly killing one of them so now, they are happily spoiled kitties. We all definitely need to join together and take a stand against killing our animals. Instead of the government spending on euthanization, why not put that money into helping families getting their pets spayed or neutered?

Headwinds to Badger were as much as thirty kilometers an hour and it felt like I was pushing a wall all the way down the highway. Some areas seemed to take forever just to go a thousand feet. I tried putting my imagination that ran wild at times to better use, like pretending I was running somewhere warm and nice. That never lasted and there was no immunity from the bad weather.

At one point, a snow squall hit and with no protection from the wind and snow, I ran for cover under some trees until it passed. While I sat there, I laughed hysterically thinking, "This is crazy! If my family and friends could only see me now. What would they think? Insanity comes to mind." I was tempted to camp there for the night but decided it was best to keep going.

As I carved my way through the velocity of the winds, all my energy was being depleted. The weather hasn't been perfect and this was not a good day for a run, but I tried to stay positive that things could only get better. Completely exhausted, I stopped at Kelly's Restaurant for something to eat and stayed for the night.

Finally, there was a break in the weather. On my way to South Brook, the warmth from the sun soothed my soul, and for the first time, I ran without wearing a jacket. The sky was like a blue canopy over the ocean and I could see for miles.

Pushed by a cool tailwind, I was making much better time today. My Forerunner was also able to pick up a signal and I was delighted to have my virtual running buddy for company. "Glad you finally made an appearance my friend. You have some miles to make up," I laughed as a digital runner popped up on my screen.

There were fewer hills now and I was delighted, when a family of four going to a basketball tournament stopped to say hello.

"Would you like a bottle of water? You look like you could use it," a woman's voice said after they rolled down their windows.

"Thank you. That's very kind of you," I responded.

"What are you running for?" the man asked.

"To raise awareness about the overpopulation problem with cats and dogs in our country. We euthanize over a million healthy animals a year to control the population. It's not right."

"Wow. That's disturbing. Isn't anyone doing anything about that?" the young girl asked.

"Shelters and volunteers are doing what they can, but it's not enough. We all need to take some of the responsibility. One of the ways we can help is by spay and neutering our pets," I said.

"Not everyone can afford it though," the woman responded.

"That's one of the issues. Low cost spay and neuter clinics would help or possibly a clinic on wheels to go out into the communities. It takes funding, but not anymore than it costs to euthanize."

"We have a lot of stray cats in our neighborhood but no one wants to take them to the SPCA. I couldn't live with myself if I knew an animal I brought there was destroyed."

"I am convinced a national prevention program would go a long way to help solve the problem. Would you like to sign my flag?"

"We'd love to. It's a great cause and we hope you succeed."

After they signed my flag, I wished them luck in their tournament and they drove off.

From time to time, I checked my Forerunner to see how I was doing. I had set it so that I was competing against my digital runner. "Hey slacker, try to keep up will you," I'd say and chuckled as I watched the two of us on my wrist. With the help of technology, I was always ahead and beat the other runner to the finish. "Better luck next time buddy. Get some rest and I hope to see you again tomorrow," I said as I shut it off.

There were plenty of options for a campsite and I found a sweet spot well hidden from the highway. Crossing a manmade ramp over the ditch led me to a clearing and a little road overgrown with grass. As I walked to the end, there was a lot with a locked cabin near the back. There was kind of a horror movie setting to this place, but I laughed it off. It was an ideal location to pitch my tent and air out all my stuff.

The winds were calmer and the early evening was quiet. I nursed the blisters on my baby toes that were bleeding and getting worse. While I lay there, it struck me that I was more than halfway through Newfoundland. Looking at the bigger picture, it wasn't very far, but every mile I ran took me that much closer to the finish line. I still had a lot of ground to cover, but I was up for the challenge.

At that moment, there was nothing else I would rather be doing, or anywhere else I would rather be. No matter how physically tired I felt, my enthusiasm never waned and I believed I could persevere through anything. *"Be relentless"* was my motto and I was completely captivated by the desire of my heart like a fire that consumes everything around it. I didn't know how much was going to be enough, but I was prepared to go as far as my heart would take me.

As the trees cast their shadows and the dark of the night set in, I snuggled into my sleeping bag. His song was with me and I said my prayers. The noise from the highway was faint and I tossed until dawn. Then, daylight and the sounds of birds singing woke me.

What a wonderful way to wake up, surrounded by nature full of beauty and music, birds that sing their little hearts out. Like my little friends sitting among the branches, I too had a melody in my heart and this marathon was an expression of that song. I had become like a bird alone in a tree singing my song all day long. If my life had not changed so dramatically, I would not have been drawn to my quest, my life song would not have returned, and my hope would not have been refreshed.

There was nothing like clear skies to get me in the running mood. One of the things I loved about running, besides the health benefits, is that it challenges you to face yourself and what you think you're capable of doing. Right now, I was chasing a dream, an enlarged vision, and in my own fatigue both my mind and body were being strengthened. To help keep my motivation level up, I visualized success. Every day, I conquered and crossed that finish line.

By now, I had learned not to trust the weather because out here it can turn on you at any time, but this was a good start. Along the way, a mother and her teenage daughter going to St. John's stopped and offered me something to eat.

"What a wonderful thing to do for animals," the mom said.

"I'm hoping to trek across Canada with my dad one day on the TransCanada Trail. Not for any cause, just to do something together," said the daughter.

Hearing the young girl talk about her dream caused me to reflect back on choices I made in my life. Thinking about my own experience, it reminded me that sometimes we are so absorbed by the world that we miss opportunities when we're not paying attention. If I hadn't listened to my heart, I wouldn't be where I am today and we wouldn't be having this conversation.

"That's a great idea. You should do it; you'll never regret it," I encouraged her.

"Have you been getting a lot of support?" her mom asked.

"People in Newfoundland are unbelievable. Cars and trucks have been honking and waving as they drive by and perfect strangers have helped me get out of some trouble early on. It's been amazing and quite the adventure so far. I might have to write a book about it someday."

"Well, we wish you luck."

"Make sure you take that trip with your dad," I shouted and waved as they drove off.

Sometime later, I made a pit stop at the gas station in South Brook. By the time I reached the junction at Springdale, the temperature had dropped and it was overcast. It wasn't long before the drizzle progressed into wet snow again, as I made my way down the west side of Newfoundland.

When I stopped at Junction 410, I had run close to fifty kilometers and my body was so numb that I wondered if it was in shock. "What are you doing to yourself?" it screamed at me and I just sat in the restaurant content not to move.

There was no one else around and as the waitress served me she mentioned, "A young girl on a bike came through here not that long ago. She was so wet and cold that she sat in front of the fireplace in the lounge most of the night, under a blanket. Poor thing." I knew she must be talking about Christie and that she was probably off the island by now.

At this point in my journey, I began questioning myself. If what I was doing even made sense. Was this really going to make any difference, or was I completely disillusioned by what I believed? Could I be fooling myself?

Whatever gloomy forecast I faced, my attitude made all the difference in the world and I needed to get my thoughts under control. Then, I remembered what I told Christie. "When you're struggling on those hills, or you think it's getting too tough, think of me on foot and maybe it won't seem so bad." However, it was Christie who was inspiring me with her determination.

After being held up for twenty-four hours by weather, I packed up my things despite the flurries. Cold rain fell off and on and despite cotton batten between my toes, it wasn't long before my wet feet complained again. I was trying not to be discouraged.

The Valley of Birchy Lake was a nice distraction, sprawling with some of its own natural beauty. As I ran through, I tried to imagine a busy tourist season. Right now, it was deserted and still.

Although I enjoyed the quiet, I often found myself singing songs to help fill the void–anything to keep my mind from getting bored. My favorites were "Listen to Your Heart" by DHT and "By the Rivers of Babylon" by Boney M.

After fighting through forty-five kilometers, signs for a restaurant began appearing and I picked up the pace for another five kilometers. By the time I approached Junction 421, it was pouring rain and my initial observation wasn't encouraging. The stop had an empty RV lot, where I could camp, but the restaurant looked closed and empty. There weren't any vehicles except an old truck on one side of the building.

I decided to try the door handle anyway and thank God I did. It was unlocked and the restaurant was open. I nearly fell on my knees and kissed the ground with joy, I was so relieved. I'm sure there were tears hiding behind drops of rain as I walked in and sat down. I was so happy to be off my feet that you would have needed a crow bar to pry me out of my chair.

"Would you like a cup of coffee?" the waitress asked while glancing outside for a vehicle, but didn't see one.

"Yes please," I replied.

"You're a little wet. You didn't walk here, did you?" she asked bewildered.

"As crazy as it sounds, I ran here from St. John's. I started running on April 15 and I hope to get to Vancouver by mid-October. I'm running solitary across Canada to raise awareness about the overpopulation problem with cats and dogs in our country and to promote spay and neutering. There are too many healthy animals euthanized every year."

"Isn't it dangerous for a girl to be traveling alone on the highway? What if something happens? Where do you sleep?"

"I carry a tent with me and look for a sheltered area off the highway."

"I would be too afraid to do something like that. You must be in good shape to do that much walking."

"Actually, I'm running a marathon a day, not walking."

"How far is a marathon?"

"It's about forty-two kilometers, but some days I've had to go much further. Like today, I ran fifty kilometers to get here."

"That's amazing," Ruby said and went to get her daughter, Laura, who also worked at the restaurant.

Both Ruby and Laura sat with me for a few minutes to hear more about my journey. I appreciated that they took an interest and I was even happier to have them to talk to. Ruby looked at Laura and asked her, "Could you do something like that?"

"Not me," Laura answered.

"Me either," Ruby confessed.

A little while later, a small group of local people came in for dinner. Ruby knew them and introduced me. One gentleman asked, "You're walking across Canada for cats and dogs. Whatever possessed you to do that?"

"Actually I'm running, not walking and there are a million reasons why. That's how many healthy innocent cats and dogs are euthanized every year in our country and it's totally preventable. People need to know that."

"How long do you think it will take you?" he asked.

"I hope to finish by mid-October," I said.

"You don't have very good weather. You should have waited until June."

"That would have been nice. Unfortunately, we can't predict the weather. It was a tossup to start from the east coast or the west coast. I hear they're having snowstorms right now in the west."

After some discussion about the nuisance stray animals can be, they returned to their conversation. Before they left, they wished me luck.

Some time passed and I was still sitting at my table watching the rain turn into heavy snow. That's when an older lady pulled up to the restaurant in her traveling van. As she sat down at a table close by, I said hello. She responded cheerfully, "Hello, I'm Leone and that's my dog K-Cee in the van. We're on vacation from Alberta and it looks like we might be stuck here for the night." That started us talking.

She was astonished to learn about what I was doing and we talked at length how hard it was to comprehend the cruelty owners could inflict on their pets, about the cruelties animals are subjected to. We also talked about how special pets can be to their owners. "K-Cee is such a great companion," Leone said. "I can't imagine abandoning her or putting her down for any reason and it sickens me to think we euthanize healthy animals."

As Ruby poured us another cup of coffee, she too thought it was sad that so many animals were destroyed. To lighten the conversation, Leone shared some of her experiences from her trip with us. She was happy with her camper and thought that was a great way to travel. "That's what you need," she told me. "I'd get one if it came with a driver," I laughed.

My camping experiences haven't quite worked out the way I thought they would. I quickly learned to let go of any expectations I might have had. For some reason, I thought there would be a campground on every corner, with showers and laundry facilities. So far, I haven't seen any and soon I'll have to brave the night again on a wet gravel parking lot. To myself, I entertained the idea of sleeping on the bathroom floor in the restaurant.

Meanwhile, I was unaware that Ruby and Laura had talked amongst themselves about inviting me to stay with them for the night. As I came out of the washroom, Ruby called me over and kindly said, "We talked about it, Laura and I, and we want to invite you to stay with us tonight. We have a spare room where you would be comfortable and dry. We could bring you back in the morning. You'd have to wait until we close the restaurant tonight and then it's about a fifteen-minute drive to Hampden from here. It's a long wait for you, but you're welcome to stay with us if you like."

Their offer warmed my heart and I would have waited all night for them if I had to.

"That's so kind of you Ruby. Wow. I don't know what to say except thank you. It isn't exactly summer out there so I would love to stay with you if you're sure it's no trouble."

"No trouble at all. It'll make us feel better knowing you're safe with us. I'll get you another coffee while you wait."

I couldn't believe what just happened. Here I was, a total stranger that the wind blew in and they were willing to take me home. It was overwhelming and I could have cried right where I stood. "You're an angel Ruby, thank you again."

As I sat down, Leone said to me, "I'm glad they asked you to stay with them. If they hadn't, I was going to invite you to stay with me in the van. You shouldn't be out there on a night like this."

"Thanks Leone. That's very kind of you too."

"Well, I hope you have a good night's rest and we'll see you for breakfast in the morning," she said before heading to her van.

"I'm glad you have K-Cee," I said.

"Me too. Good night!"

After they closed the restaurant, Ruby's son-in-law drove us to Hampden. It was late and dark, and Ruby didn't like to drive in bad weather. Her husband, Malcolm, wouldn't be joining us until later. Sitting in the back seat, I was grateful for their compassion and I couldn't help but feel indebted to them.

Ruby told me this area was a beautiful sight next to the water. Staring out the window, I knew the beauty was out there, I just couldn't see it without any light. When we parked in front of their house, I couldn't believe how much snow had fallen.

Entering their home, the walls displayed a lifetime of family memories and treasures. It was a place where comfort and warmth could be found. They made me feel welcomed and my heart was flowing with gratitude. Upstairs, I peeled off my clothes and jumped into a hot shower, hoping no one could hear my moaning and groaning.

We sat in the kitchen for a short while, talking and enjoying some munchies. The kitchen was the heart of their home.

"We don't usually bring strangers home with us, but we felt this was an exception," Ruby said compassionately.

"I can't tell you enough how grateful I am. Thank you so much for taking me in like this," I replied and after eating a bedtime snack, I crawled into a warm bed for some much needed sleep.

In the early morning, it felt like I had just put my head on the pillow and closed my eyes when the alarm went off. It was still dark outside, but time to wake up. After a late night, my body just didn't want to respond. I was so comfortable that I resisted and had to talk myself into getting up out of bed. "Come on Michelle, you have to get moving or Ruby will be late for work." Half asleep, I rose from my comfort and put myself together.

All was quiet as we piled back into the car. This time, Malcolm drove through the slushy road. On our way there, he told us about the snowfall and then the heavy rains overnight. "When we went back to the restaurant to clean up the garbage, everything was flooded," he said and added, "The rain came down pretty hard."

Hearing that made my being with them feel even more miraculous. We laughed at the thought of me floating down the highway in my tent, had I been outdoors last night. It was a short sleepover, but it turned out to be a blessing for me.

By the time we arrived at the restaurant, morning had broken through the sky. Leone came in for breakfast and she was curious about my night.

"How was it?" she asked.

"Incredible. They took such good care of me. I had a hot shower, washed my clothes, and slept like a log in a dry bed. I still can't believe they took me in like that. I'll never forget it. How about you? How was your night?"

"The rain didn't really bother us. I'm glad you had a good night," she smiled.

While we talked, my thoughts were already running ahead of me. At the end of the day, I would be somewhere else. Leone and I both looked outside at the same time. As I stood up to leave, she asked me, "Are you sure you want to run in this weather?"

I paused for a moment as I thought about how to answer her. The journey of my heart was tugging for me to go and I knew there wasn't a moment to lose if I wanted to make it to Vancouver before winter. "I have to keep going. Besides, I don't want to overstay my welcome," I said.

When I went to pay for my breakfast, Ruby told me they were paying for it. She had already done so much and her kindness seemed to never end. Again her benevolent intentions humbled me and put me at a loss for words.

"Thank you so much Ruby, for everything. I don't know how I can ever repay you."

"Take care of yourself and be careful. We don't want to hear about anything bad happening to you. That's all that matters," she said as we exchanged a hug.

Leone took some last minute pictures and then my heart was on the run once again. As I ran, I thought about how hard Ruby and her family worked and yet they still managed to take care of my needs. "They are such kind people," I thought and it took me a few miles to get over my feelings of attachment toward my new friends. Once more I was "touched by an angel" who had opened up her heart. My gratitude was mounting and becoming a motivator for me to keep on running.

More drizzle hung around and my overworked feet let me know early that they weren't very happy. I slept well, but it just wasn't enough recovery time and I got up way before I wanted to.

Staying motivated over a long period of time was a challenge. While training at home, I'd lose motivation from time to time. Often I had to force myself and push myself to get out there and run even if I didn't feel up to it, or, it seemed like too much of an effort. Just telling myself not to give up wasn`t enough. I had to have a good reason for being out here.

Today was ten times harder than ever to stay motivated and I was badgering myself with questions, "Why am I doing this? What does it matter anyway? Things will never change." It led me to repeat the timeless words from a promise I made and I was going to keep it. A promise that made my conviction far greater than anything I could suffer. It was what I held onto and couldn't let go of.

Deer Lake was such a welcoming sight after feeling like I was never going to get there. While thrusting my fists I yelled several times, "Thank you God!" and I parked myself at the Ultramar after the staff gave me permission to pitch my tent behind the building on the only patch of grass there was. They also had a dryer and a shower for truck drivers, so I made good use of them both.

Hearing the sound of my sister's voice again was like music to my ears. "It's so good to hear your voice Angel," I told her. When you experience what feels like forever without any communication, it's miraculous to get to a phone and hear a familiar voice on the other end. "This is so much harder than I ever imagined it would be," I admitted.

I knew everyone would be anxiously waiting for some news, so we got caught up and then I needed to get off my tender feet. Lying down was such a relief, like jumping in a cold lake on the hottest day of the year. It felt so good. Neither the noise from the trucks nor the rain could keep me from falling asleep.

Early the next morning, the sound of a key unlocking the back-door to the gas station woke me. With every ounce of strength I had, I picked myself up and dusted myself off. I went inside to use the washroom and have a hot cup of coffee. It had rained all night, so I held off leaving for a couple of hours, waiting for dryer conditions.

Meanwhile, I dressed my feet with fresh bandages and put on some dry socks. My energy reserves were getting pretty low now and every little thing I did, on top of running, started taking more effort. Some mornings took me longer than others to get ready. I missed my training days when all I had to do was run.

As I stared down the highway, I took a deep breath and uttered to myself, "How far do I go today?" Corner Brook was fifty kilometers away and there was nothing but wilderness in between.

Knowing your route was half the battle when it came to long distant running. This was like nothing I had experienced before. I could visualize myself running fifty kilometers, but I had no idea what lied ahead of me. I might make it, or I might not. Either way, I had to keep going and reminded myself that every step was a step closer to the ferry.

I took another deep breath and decided to go all the way. My hydration pack was half full to lighten my load. I used some socks as extra padding under my backpack straps that were now cutting into my shoulders.

It took me a few minutes to think of a way to trick my mind into believing there wasn't so far to go. Breaking down my run into small chunks was the answer. I didn't allow myself to look at the total distance and divided it into three stages, with each stage made up of ten miles. As I ran, I started reciting and counting out loud each mile. Like tunnel vision, I focused on one mile at a time.

> *Stage one, mile one.*
> *Finish the first mile then start the second mile.*
> *Finish the second mile then start the third, all the way to ten.*
> *Then I told myself I was a third done! My mind seemed pleased with that. First stage finished, now start the second stage.*
>
> *Stage two, mile one.*
> *Finish the first mile then start the second mile.*
> *Finish the second mile and start the third, all the way to ten.*
> *At fifteen miles I told myself I was halfway done. Then the thought that I was two-thirds there encouraged me. If I can make it this far I can make it the rest of the way. Second stage finished, now start the third stage.*
>
> *Stage three, countdown from mile ten.*
> *Finish at mile one.*

To help with my mental preparation, I pretended I was in the Olympics and going for gold. I visualized myself winning. My mind was completely oblivious of anything else around me, except reaching Corner Brook. I was totally consumed with the desire of making it, and I did.

In spite of the rain and hills, I ran the last couple of miles like the wind. The scenic beauty into Corner Brook was stunning and I marveled at the splendor of the mountains and water. While I approached my target, I clenched my fists and shouted in triumph, "We did it! We did it! I knew we could do it! Thank you God!"

With rain and snow in the forecast, I checked into the Comfort Inn. If you have ever been totally physically exhausted, you will understand what I mean when I say, "I died in my bed last night."

Forced by the weather to stay an extra day, I was grateful to Diana and the Comfort Inn for their support and a complimentary room for one night. My stay in Corner Brook allowed me time to buy a new pair of running shoes and stock up on supplies.

Attempting to visit the SPCA failed as no one answered the door, despite the posted operational hours. It was a long taxi ride there and back. The shelter was too far for me to try again and I was leaving town in the morning. However, I was encouraged by the comments from my blog.

> *Anonymous said...*
> *I think what you are doing is quite courageous and very brave. I hope people along your way realize just how much a feat it is that you have undertaken. It truly is remarkable that you have the determination to battle it out through sore feet, beating rain, freezing snow, and blistering winds. Just remember as each new challenge arises, that someone out here is cheering you on.*

> *Anonymous said...*
> *Mich you crazy chick. I admire your determination and personal sacrifice. Good things do happen to good people. I am sure you will witness this many times during your journey as you already have on a few occasions. Stay safe and healthy. We'll be waiting when you come through Ottawa.*

> *Anonymous said...*
> *Hey Mich...you make us all so proud. I have absolute faith that you can complete this or any other journey you set out to do. The pure light that emanates from your heart will guide you, and your love and dedication will prevent countless senseless deaths. Keep*

God in your heart and courage will live there too. Remember you are not alone my friend; love transcends time and distance. You are in the heart of all who know you. We are all rooting for you back home.

Julia put a map on the website as a visual to track my progress. She had a thumbtack to show my last known location, so I sent her an email letting her know I had reached Corner Brook. She also put this comment on my blog.

Good luck Michelle. It is a wonderful thing that you are doing to bring the idea of a no-kill Canada to our country. It is long overdue and all animals will greatly benefit from your passion, energy and commitment.

I was thrilled to receive this email from the P.E.I. Humane Society. You can imagine the excitement I felt after reading it. It was a huge pick-me-up.

Hi there,

We received information about Michelle's marathon and would like to welcome her to a tour of our shelter (the only one on PEI) when she arrives on the Island. We're located just off the Trans Canada in Charlottetown, very close to the airport, on Sherwood Road.

Can you keep us posted on Michelle's progress and let us know if she'll be able to make a stop to meet us on her journey? If we have enough advance notice, we'd be pleased to contact our local media who have been very supportive of our work.

Thanks!
Kelley
Development Coordinator

Leaving Corner Brook, I could sense how close I was getting to Port-Aux-Basques. I started imagining myself being on the ferry and it was making me anxious to get there. My adrenaline was running high and I was super-charged by everyone's messages of encouragement.

Every time I saw a gas station, I dropped in to engage with people. Beside the Pinchgut Restaurant I met Liz, her son Darren, Nina, Jane, and their dogs. "What a wonderful thing to do for animals," they said as they invited me to join them around their campfire. "I'd go with you but I don't think I could keep up with you," Liz laughed. They wanted me to stay longer and as much as I would have liked that, I had to keep going.

Closer to Stephenville, fewer vehicles stopped and I saw less people. My lonely days on the road felt long except when I was talking to someone.

One night, I shared my camp with the inhabitants of a "Moose Relocation" area and as I walked along the stream of water, I never saw one, but I heard them and there were plenty of tracks. I wondered what they thought of my intrusion.

The evenings were still cold with flurries and fresh snow in the mornings. I often had to kick myself out of my warm sleeping bag to get moving. The trees weren't tall on this side of the island and it made it impossible to hang my food out of reach. Visitors in the night always left something behind to let me know I wasn't alone. They never bothered me in my tent and I'd like to believe we had an understanding, as long as I didn't bother them.

Along the west facing slopes of the Long Range Mountains, I entered an area called the Wreckhouse, known for extremely high winds that can accelerate at speeds in excess of one hundred miles per hour. Warning signs lined the highway and before I could step into its path, an SUV stopped beside me. A man's voice yelled, "Get in. It's too dangerous on foot and it's against regulations" He told me about transport trucks that have faced the fury of the Wreckhouse winds and were blown right off the road. I was grateful for the ride through.

I hadn't seen the sun most days, but the landscaping in Newfoundland was spectacular shaped by mountains, valleys, water and winding roads. Its pristine wilderness environment was unmatched by anywhere I had ever been. The picturesque scenery along the coast was sensational, with mountains on one side and the ocean on the other.

Making it to the town of Port-Aux-Basques was like landing on the moon and I should have been jumping for joy. However, I had just endured an arduous twenty-three-day journey across Newfoundland on foot where I experienced isolation, loneliness, solitude, danger, difficulties, hunger, pain, fear, frustration, disappointment, and little success.

Surviving with bare necessities, my challenges were heightened by rough weather, incredible winds, fatigue, blistered and sore feet, hauling supplies, rugged highway, and dealing with a seemingly endless road.

The early stages of my journey had tested my commitment and my heart. In my mind there wasn't time to process everything and I could only stay in the day I was in. It was all I could handle. Tomorrow, I was looking forward to the ferry taking me to North Sydney and a different province.

May 8, 2007 - North Sydney, Nova Scotia

At the sight of the ferry, I thanked God and was filled with encouragement. The initial view of the ship was emotional as I walked up to it. It was huge. My eyes watered and the lump in the back of my throat just sat there as I fought back the tears. We boarded the Caribou at 10:30am and left port at 11:30am.

I enjoyed being amongst people again and meeting some of the vacationers on board. It made me feel like I was back in the land of the living.

Once we safely left the harbor, I had mixed feelings about leaving Newfoundland. On the one hand, I was looking forward to getting to the mainland and warmer weather. On the other hand, it felt like home, where beauty and solitude had captured my imagination.

Staring back at the island, I could hear the winds whisper as I waved good-bye, "You've had an intimate look at our land and people. Remember them both dearly in your heart and come back anytime."

One of the crewmembers took me up to the bridge for a front row view of the ocean and to meet the captain of the ship. I thought it was pretty cool that he signed my flag.

Docking in North Sydney six hours later and putting my feet in Nova Scotia, was like stepping on to the shores of heaven. While my journey from St. John's to here hadn't been a vacation, I remained faithful to my task. Little did I know that my greatest challenges were still in front of me.

Chapter 2

Cape Breton, Nova Scotia, P.E.I.

With Newfoundland behind me, I pushed on. From Sydney, I took Highway 125 toward St. Peters. While I ran, I was concerned with missing my rendezvous with Julie, a reporter from the Cape Breton Post. After reaching her last night, I was thrilled that a newspaper was interested in covering this story.

Any media coverage would help increase the possibility of this information traveling far. Since the magnitude of the problem wasn't being widely advertised, the more people who took notice and spoke up for these animals, the better their chance for survival would be. I also believed that once people had this information, they would be responsible for their own understanding and accountable for what they knew.

Julie managed to find me and conducted her interview right there on the side of the highway. She asked me a simple question: "Why are you running across Canada?" I shared my enthusiasm with her and made my appeal.

"To help end the killing of healthy cats and dogs in our country; healthy domestic animals shouldn't be killed for any reason, yet every year thousands and thousands of animals are euthanized. I believe we have a moral responsibility to no longer accept the killing of so many innocent animals. Prevention is a much better way to control the population."

After a hearty conversation, Julie wished me luck and I left there with a renewed spirit believing people everywhere would be on board with this. They just needed a little stirring up. Surely, once people had this information, things couldn't stay the way they are.

Although I was pretty happy about being off the island, I had to give myself a reality check. This has been a lot harder than I ever imagined it would be and there was no doubt in my mind that I had dodged a bullet in escaping Newfoundland. I would not have survived "The Rock" without some divine help and the amazing support from people when I needed it the most.

Nothing could have prepared me for something like this and I had no way of knowing if I had what it takes to keep on going if the road got any rougher. Spurring me on were comments from my flag and blog.

> *Anonymous said. . .*
> *Go Mich Go*
> *Amazing adventure and wonderful cause you are taking on. We're all cheering for you and hoping for good weather, healthy feet and lots of kindness from fellow Canadians to help you along your way.*
> *I'll definitely be reading all your posts and cheering you from afar.*
>
> *Anonymous said. . .*
> *Michelle, you awe me with your strength, determination and compassion. May the sun shine warmly for you and the angels across Canada take care of you every step of the way.*
>
> *Kim said. . .*
> *HOLY SMOKES MICH! When you said you'd be away from April to October, I didn't realize it was because you were running across Canada. You go girl. The Rebels are sending you good vibes. . .stay strong. All the best. . .we'll be following your adventure.*

Isabelle said. . .
That is awesome. I've always admired her but now she's my idol.
Way to go Mich.

Anonymous said. . .
Hey Mich,
Keep it up ;) - Good weather is just around the corner. Watching your progress every week and I am so impressed.

Anonymous said. . .
Hey Mich. . .keep it up - you are doing awesome – yahoo. You have endured one of the most difficult parts of Canada and, well, of course you had to experience all kinds of weather. But, that's all behind you now, except for the wonderful memories you have obtained. . .memories that will keep you running in order to be able to catch some new ones. Keep up the great intentions and positivity and only goodness will follow you. Great stuff Mich. . . .we are looking forward to seeing you in Ottawa when you get here. Take good care of yourself.

Their encouragement helped tremendously. It was the boost I needed to get over the hurdles and stay on track. A reminder to focus on the end result and to run straight for the finish line. I was convinced that if I worked hard every day and didn't give up, this run was mine to conquer. No one else could take these steps for me.

By the time I reached East Bay, the temperature had risen to double digits and I was warm. At last, I felt relief from being cold and wet. The summer-like weather revived my soul with a cool and gentle breeze caressing my neck. It finally occurred to me that I was running in just my shorts and a t-shirt.

Passing through East Bay, I met an older woman coming out of the post office. Eastern people are so friendly. "Hello," she said. By now, no one was a stranger to me and I felt like I knew everyone.

After explaining myself, she smiled and responded, "That's quite the adventure you are on. I'm on my way to a ninetieth birthday party. It's my mother's and we're all very excited."

"Wow," I replied. "That's a big one."

As she got into her car, she wished me well and then drove off. Ninety years was a long life to celebrate. After talking with her, I felt homesick and wondered what my own family was up to.

Sometime later, I watched from a distance as an SUV pulled over into the parking lot of an old church. The driver waited until I was close enough before talking to me. "Hi there. My name is Susan and this is my son, Mark. I saw you earlier today and I told my husband that I had to stop and bring you some cold water to drink."

Susan also gave me some homemade cookies that were still partially frozen. They were huge and filled with chocolate chips and smarties. It put a big smile on my face and I thanked her kindly. She was a little surprised to learn that I was doing something like this for cats and dogs.

"What an amazing thing to do, but I don't know too many people who would run across the country for cats and dogs. But I guess we shouldn't be killing them if it's not necessary. How long do you think it will take you?"

"I left St. John's on April 15 and I hope to get to Vancouver by mid-October, before the snow flies."

"And there's no one with you?"

"I'm by myself but I would never have made it this far without the help of some incredible people," I said, without a doubt in my mind. "Easterners are so friendly!"

"Yes, people around here will give you the shirt off their back if they could. Are you getting any media coverage?" she asked as she signed my flag.

"Some local stuff! Getting the media involved is tricky, but I think there might be more interest the further west I go. Mostly, I'm talking to people I meet on the road, like you and stopping at animal shelters along the way."

"Well, we wish you luck and hope you keep getting lots of support."

"Thanks for stopping," I shouted as they drove off. Talking with them gave me a lift and a hope that I would meet many more people like them.

After running another ten kilometers or so, I waved at a man sitting outside on his front porch. He got up out of his chair, gesturing for me to join him.

"Would you like to come up for a cold drink?" he shouted.

Wow. That was pretty friendly I thought and decided to take him up on his offer. "Thank you. I'd love to," I shouted back and made my way up his driveway to the side door. "Come in, come in. Sit down. Take a load off your feet," he insisted.

I shared my journey with him, but he didn't say one way or another what he thought. "People who attempt these kinds of things fascinate me," he said while taking my picture. "If you need to use the phone or the computer you're welcome to them," he offered kindly. Not only did he give me cold water, he made some soup and then a cup of tea.

We talked through lunch, sharing bits and pieces from our lives. He was retired now and his wife was in town visiting a friend. I had the impression they were well connected in the community and that Ivan enjoyed having company.

It was disappointing to leave before meeting his wife and as I waved good-bye, I thought how glad I was to have stopped. If I hadn't, I would have missed out on Ivan's friendship.

Running with a full belly was not a wise thing to do. Thankfully, I didn't have far to go to reach the campground in Ben Eoin. There were a couple of men working in the trees so I shouted at them, "Excuse me, can you tell me if the campground is open? I need a place to put up my tent for the night."

After a brief pause, one of them shouted back, "It's too early for campgrounds to be open. But go ahead and put up your tent. You shouldn't have to worry about your safety around here. We're all harmless," they both laughed. I wasn't quite sure how to take that and mumbled under my breath, "Welcome back to civilization Michelle." I thanked them and then went off to investigate the area.

The campground was empty, but inviting. After scanning for the perfect spot, I put my tent on some grass in front of the water. There is something about being near water that is comforting.

This was more like the camping I had envisioned. As I watched the romance of the sun going down, I felt safe and no longer isolated. My thoughts were full of reflection. You really get to know yourself well and what you're made of when you push your limits every day doing something like this. Things you wouldn't learn or know about yourself any other way.

In reality, I should probably be at home recovering. Instead, I was still out here and the longer I lasted the more compelling my desire became. My surviving was also teaching me to trust in the One who was putting helpers in my path and I believed I was being touched by God's angels.

Tonight, there was *"a kind of hush"* all over my world. As nightfall officially descended, I fell asleep to the sounds of crickets and frogs and a thankful heart.

On the twenty-fifth day into my marathon and after a restful night, I went across the street to Me and the Mrs. Restaurant for breakfast. I shared my hopes and dreams with the people inside, but they were more interested in that I was running alone across Canada without a support vehicle. They wanted something more than the reason I was here.

While I sat there, I calculated how many lives have been robbed by our disposable society since I left St. John's. I wrote with tears approximately 68,000 animals have been destroyed in the twenty-five days I've been running. Even if my calculations were off by a few thousand, it was still too many.

The sad reality is, by the time I get to Vancouver, about 500,000 cats and dogs will have paid with their life for the mistakes people made. The knowledge I carried added to my grief and their deaths were a constant reminder. Shame covered my heart with guilt and each day, these forced deaths accumulated in my head.

There is something morally wrong that affects the way we treat and think about domestic animals in our country. Sadness does not fully convey the emotion I felt. My conscience had been made tender to feel disturbed with the alarming numbers. I couldn't insulate myself from it and what I knew weighed heavy on my heart.

How could I not feel like we were failing our responsibility to care for these animals? It was impossible for me to ignore. I was also coming to the realization that I was in way over my head.

Thankfully, and by the grace of God, I didn't just get up in the morning and think about how many animals died every day. I also thought about how many animals are saved and that statistics can change. It encouraged me to know that prevention saves lives.

In the midst of my adversities, I grasped the importance of every hour. For the first time in my life, I thought about each day as a second chance and that today, and every day I ran, was a gift.

Immersing myself in another day full of adventure, I set out from there believing each step taken would make a difference. All I had to do was endure my journey's trials.

The landscaping of Nova Scotia's northern island resumed with more monster hills to climb. With trees bursting into bloom and silky green grass sprouting in the fields, going from winter like conditions to summer overnight was a welcomed change. There were no clouds in the sky and the sun was brilliant. It was going to be hot and the sun's rays were already scorching my skin.

About fifteen miles into my run, there was an older couple working in their yard. As I waved the lady asked me, "Would you like a cup of tea?" This was déjà vu from yesterday and since that worked out so well, I gladly accepted.

Once again, I climbed a steep driveway and joined them on their balcony. "What a gorgeous location and such a beautiful view of the Bras d'Or Lake," I said as I looked out at the scenery with awe. "We retired here eleven years ago and we love every season," they said.

As we sat down, they introduced me to their two beautiful dogs. Logan, a Golden Retriever and Roo, part Collie. "I can't understand why anyone would want to harm an animal. They're such loving creatures," Ruthie said bewildered. Then they asked me questions about how I was managing and tea turned into lunch.

They shared some of their history with me and I couldn't help but fall into their lives, they seemed so fulfilled. Talking with them was like a breath of fresh air–I just wanted more.

Today was going to be exceptionally hot. Arriving in St. Peters early, I filled up with water and made the assumption I could replenish my supplies at the next gas station. My decision to carry less weight would prove to be a mistake. I would discover there was nothing for miles.

By noon, I was out of water and the only food I had left was an apple and an energy bar. After running twenty-six miles, I couldn't take the desert-like heat anymore and needed to get out from under the sun. Soon after, I found a shaded area off the highway.

While I was unpacking, I startled something big just beyond the trees. It put me on guard but whatever it was moved on. Once my tent was up, I hung my clothes out to dry and in this heat it didn't take long. Even though it was hot, I had to wrap everything in bags overnight to keep them from the morning dew.

Lying down, I fell asleep but woke up from more stomping noises in the woods. Flies were buzzing around trying to invade my tent and I watched as some rabbits hopped by. Lifted high above the quiet, birds sang and to me they were a symphony of joy conducted by the Creator. My ears never had their fill of hearing their song.

Early in the evening, hunger and thirst set in. I ate my apple, but saved the energy bar for morning. The apple tasted like honey in my mouth and I was grateful to Lester for giving it to me. However, it also left me wanting for more.

Under the stars, I waited patiently for morning to come. My struggles always felt worse at night, but with every new sunrise, there was hope. Hot weather loomed in the air and rising was my faithful sun.

As I got up, I remembered the water I took so freely from my kitchen tap at home, the food I could get from my fridge and my shower whenever I wanted one. Water is so precious, like breathing in air. Out here, there were no faucets. I had taken water for granted and now I had none. In this heat and direct sunlight, I needed lots of water and constant nourishment.

The sun beat down on me mercilessly and the temperature was rising. There wasn't even a breeze. To make matters worse, any exits off the highway were too far for me to go on foot and there would be no help from the road today. "I've got to be getting close to something soon," I cried while panting for water.

My throat was dry and my tongue parched and sticking to the roof of my mouth, like a dry stick. My face felt flushed and my body dehydrated. The longer I went without something to drink, the more desperate I became. Willpower and tears were my only food. Without enough fuel and too much exposure to the sun, heat exhaustion was close to shutting me down.

Until finally, Port Hawkesbury came into sight. What a beautiful sight it was. I sighed with relief and ran into the nearest store. My body had been deprived long enough and now I needed a couple of drinks. I downed a Mountain Dew, and then another one. They tasted so good.

Outside, I sat on a bench eating and drinking until it brought me back to life. "How in the world did I make it here?" I said in disbelief. I had been careless and it was a lesson I would never forget.

Once I felt refreshed, I continued to Port Hastings where I checked myself into a motel room. After my experience, I was in need of a hot shower and a good night's sleep. Speaking with Kelly of the P.E.I. Humane Society was uplifting.

"I bet you're enjoying the hot weather," said Kelly.

"Yes, it's a little warmer than Newfoundland," I replied.

"How are your feet?"

"They're a bit stressed but happier since I started wearing shoes one size bigger."

"That's great. Everyone is looking forward to meeting you. You're an inspiration to us all. We're trying to get accommodations for you when you get here and see if we can arrange for the media to interview you. There's an election going on right now so any media coverage will depend on what happens with that."

Kelly's cheerful heart was contagious. She wished me well until the next time. When I got off the phone, her enthusiasm stirred me up and I was eager to get there. Encouraged by our conversation, I went over to the public library to update my blog.

While I was explaining why I needed a computer to the librarian, another lady joined our discussion. "It's wonderful to hear about someone trying to help these poor creatures. It's shameful that people don't take better care of their animals," she said.

Listening to her explain this to her two young children and the impression it made, brought tears to my eyes. "Maybe it will be their generation that will change things," I thought as I sat at a computer. When I opened my email, I was happy to see these messages waiting for me.

> *I just read your blog, congratulations on making it to Nova Scotia. And finally the weather will improve for you. Now you will need sun block. Ha-ha! Reading your blog I feel I am going to miss Newfoundland too. My heart is with you and I hope to hear from you soon. The kids all say hi and send their love and are routing for you.*
> *Love, hugs and kisses, Marie*

> *CONGRATS! I just read that you made it through and out of NFLD. WOW. You must be sore and exhausted. I sent your link to Francine and Chantell (N's newphie friends who live in TO - Fran got you the runners - they wanna know if you are crazy. . .lol..they are from there and know that province and can't believe you've crossed it on foot - they're amazed). . . . As for me, I admire your passion and courage, and just ask that you please promise you'll do everything you can to be and stay safe and if at any point along the way your body tells you to take a break or stop I hope you will listen to it. Your longterm health has to be a priority. We're proud of ya (and worried too - of course, but that's to be expected I'm sure). I just wish I could be there to follow you. If you need anything let me know and maybe I can send it out to my friends that live in Fredericton - Carol and Dave are good friends, I asked them to keep their eye out for you. I hope you get to connect with them, as I'm sure they'll offer you a warm bed and hot shower. Way to go bud*

> *- you've already accomplished more than 99.9999 percent of the population would even fathom as a consideration - so you should be very proud. I hope you will meet many more angels along your path and that they will make your journey all that you want it to be. Enjoy the warming weather. I'm sure you'll be glad to get some double-digit temps. Angel has been awesome with keeping me posted when you call in to her or your mom, which has been great because lots of yours friends are calling me to make sure you're alright, especially if it's been a few days since you added to your blog. Take good care my friend and please stay safe. May there be footprints in the sand along your route whenever you need there to be. Your proud (and allowed to be concerned) roomies. We all miss ya,*
> *Sharron, Mannie and Kali*

On occasion, Dorit and I played telephone tag. Sometimes my timing was bad. The last message I left her was while I passed through St. Peter's to share my excitement about the newspaper article. I appreciated her support.

> *Got your message. Thanks so much for calling. I'm sorry I didn't have my phone on. This morning was weird. Not only did I not turn my phone on, I forgot to bring it with me, AND I forgot to close and lock the doors of my house before I left. I'm really losing it. Anyway - my dear, you sounded tired. Are you OK?*
> *Dorit*

Dorit was always concerned about my well-being. She told me Julia would post any news articles on the web site, where it would be accessible for others to read. Back in my room, I was thankful to have survived my day.

That night, a storm blew in off the ocean. The sound of heavy drops hammering down on the roof woke me. There was a constant stream of rain that made visibility out the window very poor. The unusual force and large raindrops caused me to reminisce about my training days when I would purposely go out and run in bad weather to help build up my mental toughness. It didn't matter if it was rain or snow or forty below, I ran.

Sometimes, I stayed out there too long and would be in tears by the time I got home. However, I always had a home to run back to. Out here, I never knew where I would end up or what I would run into. I was flirting with the unknown, but everyday convinced me I was right where I should be.

The phone rang early in the morning.

"Good morning Michelle, did I wake you?" said my sister.

"You can wake me anytime Marie," I said, happy to hear her voice.

"How are you feeling?" she probed.

"I feel pretty good. I'll have a good breakfast and then get going again."

"Did you get enough sleep?"

"Yes, I did. It's a good thing I was indoors though, because a heavy rain storm blew in overnight."

"Maybe you should take a few days off and rest."

"I'll have lots of time to rest when I'm done. Right now, I have to get moving. I'm pretty excited about getting to P.E.I. and visiting with the shelter there. They sound like a great group of people."

"Well, we're all very proud of what you've accomplished already and no one would think any less of you if you stopped now," she said hoping I would get on the next bus home.

"Stop? I can't stop now; I'm just getting started? I know everyone is worried, but I'm fine, really."

"You don't want to end up crippled or worse, dead on the side of the road somewhere, do you?"

"You've been watching too much TV."

"Well, you know how much you love your sports and if you permanently damage your feet, you may never be able to play again."

"That's not going to happen. I'm listening to my body and if it gets to be too much, I'll stop. I won't let it go that far."

"Well, we all know how stubborn you can be, you've made your point. So, if you need to come home, you can always finish next year."

"I'm not ready to give up yet, but if the time comes to stop, I will."

"It's just hard for us to read your blog and not be worried."

"I know and I love you for it, but don't worry, I'm fine."

My sisters must have been talking to each other because the phone rang steadily. It bothered me terribly that they worried so much and that this was stressful on them. Nevertheless, I had to push back their fears and keep reassuring them that all was well. For me to quit, there would have to be no doubt in my mind that I couldn't continue.

When I opened the door to step outside, the force from the winds threw me back into my room. "Woo! What was that?" I chuckled with surprise. Wind gusts were as much as sixty kilometers an hour as I fought my way to the Canso Causeway.

The causeway was constructed with tons of rock to allow for crossing over the strait. Traffic was stopped at the swinging bridge while a ship was passing through. As I waited, I hung on to the fence to keep from being swept away. That's how I met Harold. He was about four vehicles back when he got out of his SUV. Dressed in blue jeans and a black jacket, he walked up to me and said, "These winds are pretty strong and even stronger out there. It's not safe to walk across the strait. I can give you a ride to the other side."

I made a quick assessment of my situation and decided he was right. These winds could easily blow me into the water or traffic. Since he was so concerned for my safety and had such a kind face, I accepted his offer. I threw my bag in the back of his truck and then hopped into the front seat.

We had several conversations about life in the short time I spent with him. However, the one I'll always remember is when he showed me his gratitude rock. "I always carry it with me," he said. "It was for everything in life I am grateful for," he told his grandson. He loved his grandson and their times together, especially when they went fishing. His son lived on the other side of the causeway and that's where he was headed.

When we reached the other side, he pulled over to let me out. Then handed me my backpack. "That thing weighs a ton. How do you run with it?" asked Harold.

"You get used to it. Besides, I don't have much of a choice," I said.

Harold gladly signed my flag and wished me luck. It always amazed me how some people could make you feel like you've known them all your life when you first meet them. Harold was one of those people.

Overlooking the strait, I was mesmerized by some of the most breathtaking scenery in eastern Canada. Its beauty was staggering. "Wow," came out of my mouth more than once as I enjoyed the tranquil perfection of the views all around me.

However, the two-mile climb from sea level up wasn't without some challenges. It was a battle against the forces of nature. Oh the winds. At the top of the hill, I had to give my back a break and sat against a signpost hoping there wouldn't be another one like it. However, there was, and each time I got to the top, I looked at my climb behind me and thought I must be out of my mind. Under normal circumstances, I would never attempt this.

The more distance I put between the causeway and myself, the less wind I encountered. Each climb that came into view, I looked skyward with dismay and wondered how many more I would have to endure today. Surprisingly, I never cramped up enough to have to stop. If the hill had a gentle climb, I was okay. On the other hand, with a steeper grade, I made it half way and then walked to the top. It was more about survival at this point and less about triumph.

With the hills leveling out now, the worst was behind me. Along a flatter area of the highway, I approached a car off to the side of the road where two young girls were trying to fix the passenger window that had slipped off its rail. I offered some assistance, but there wasn't much that could be done.

Then, they looked at me as if to say, "What are you doing here?" They were put at ease once I explained myself.

"That's terrible that so many animals are killed. Isn't there a law against that or something?" one girl asked.

"Laws are only as good as they can be enforced. People's attitude toward animals are a bigger problem," I responded.

"I love dogs. We have three of them and sometimes there are as many as nine or ten in the house at one time. We could never give them up or have them euthanized; that's just wrong; shame on people who do. More people should speak up for these helpless creatures and there should be stricter laws to protect them," said the other girl.

After they signed my flag, I thanked them and wished them luck with their window.

Passing through Havre Boucher captured my imagination. My eyes never tired of looking at the coastal landscaping and rolling hills. Around every bend was a piece of heaven and I could see the beauty of God's creation in everything.

In Monastery, a librarian named Mary was on her way home and decided to stop when she saw me.

"It's disturbing the way animals are mistreated in our country," said Mary.

"Yes it is. Is there anywhere I can camp for the night?" I asked.

"You're welcome to camp in our yard if you like. We live right there off the highway," she pointed.

"That would be great. Thanks."

Mary and her husband lived in a beautiful bungalow home. We were greeted at the door by her two dogs and three cats. Mary loved animals and nature.

"You must be hungry. Would you like something to eat? I can heat up a bowl of vegetables for you," she offered kindly.

As I was eating a delicious dish, she talked about each one of her pets. They were all special in their own way and friendly. You can always tell when an animal is well cared for. Life is pretty good for them.

When I finished eating, Mary invited me to join her for some bird counting. Her face was beaming when I accepted. "We'll drive out to my favorite spot along the coast for a bit of sight-seeing at the same time," she smiled.

While we drove out there, we were on the lookout for birds. Among some of the birds we saw, was a young bald eagle perched on a rock. Observing the ease and grace of an eagle mastering the skies is mesmerizing and fascinated me.

I could see why the coast was a happy place for Mary. I fell in love with it too. The view was splendid and the shoreline delightful as we took in the vastness of the ocean. Remarkably, we didn't get stuck in the soft, beach-like sand as we cruised on by.

Mary's husband, Alain, was at home when we returned. He was a tall, dark, and handsome man, and well dressed. At dinner, I discovered he was an accomplished musician. They both shared a concern for the mistreatment of animals.

"Unfortunately, there are people who don't think that an animal has much value," said Alain.

"Our country is a little behind when it comes to laws protecting them," Mary added.

One of the most important considerations in the debate on pet euthanasia is whether or not, as a society, we embrace the belief that an animal's life has value. Why is this so important? It's important because it's about life and death.

How we have allowed animals to be put to death for being homeless is beyond comprehension and should violate the conscience of every human being. What our country needed was to act with more compassion. I was thankful that God did not treat us the way we treat our animals.

> *Dictionary Definitions:*
> *Euthanasia - the act or practice of killing individuals (as persons or domestic animals) that are hopelessly sick or injured for reasons of mercy.*
>
> *Compassion – pity for the suffering or distress of another (as persons or domestic animals), with the desire to help or spare*

After a hot shower, I was grateful to Mary for letting me stay in one of the spare bedrooms for the night. There was a big double bed, covered with pillows and lots of blankets. With a dry roof over my head, it didn't take long for me to slip into a deep sleep.

Early the next morning, my wakeup committee consisted of Tam the Golden Retriever, Weaver the mixed Husky and Lab, and Alister the cat. Tam greeted me with a wet dog kiss, while Weaver landed on the bed and put his head right under my chin. To complete the ensemble, Alister jumped up, plunked herself under my armpit, and began to purr. Talk about an invasion. "Good morning everyone," I said happy to see them all.

After returning their affection, I let out a sigh and said, "Okay, you guys are pretty convincing. I'll get up." As if to understand me, they all jumped off the bed at the same time. It was quite the wakeup call.

While I was putting myself together, I could hear noises coming from the kitchen. Mary was up early to volunteer at a kennel for a friend. When I walked into the living room, I found her gazing out the window through binoculars. "Would you like to take a peak?" she asked me quietly.

Mary loved to watch the birds. She knew everything about them. Looking through the lens, I saw what she saw. Beautiful birds in the trees and rabbits hopping about. Their home was surrounded by plenty of wildlife for her enjoyment and peace.

After some toast and porridge, Mary sent me off with a care package consisting of raisons, cheese, an orange, and some contact numbers. "Thank you Mary," I said one more time as I closed the door. In a short time, Mary had been a good friend and I found some tranquility being with her quiet spirit. "What a kind and gentle soul," I thought of her.

Another two-mile climb up a mega hill, and I was glad to get it out of the way early. The scenery continued to be spectacular and there was more sun to enjoy.

Today was Mother's Day. There is nothing that touches a child more like a mother's love. Our family was traditional in celebrating every occasion and I was disappointed to miss this one. On this special day, I couldn't be there but I honored my mom in my own personal way. "Today's run is for you mom," I said and then ran my little heart out.

In the beautiful town of Antigonish, I stopped at the Oasis Campground. It was closed but the owner allowed me to camp anyway and at no charge.

"I remember the day Terry Fox ran through here in 1980," he shared with me. "His van stopped looking for water and money, but Terry didn't come in. It was his brother I think. I never heard of anyone running across Canada without a support vehicle though. You must be the first female to do it. And to do it for cats and dogs, I don't know anyone who would do that. You can have your pick of any site you like. The water is running up there too. It's nice to have met you and good luck the rest of the way," he said as he pointed me in the right direction.

Once I was settled in, I went across the street to the gas station to use the pay phone. "Happy Mother's Day mom," I said, happy to reach her. "Sorry I didn't send you a card or anything, but I've been thinking about you all day." Mothers always know the right thing to say.

"A phone call is better than a card," she thanked me.

Hearing everyone in the background made me feel a little homesick. I think my Mom could sense it in my voice. "Your dad and I will drive out to meet you in Quebec City. Angel's coming too and we'll bring Buddy. Just give us a call when you get there," she said.

It was her day, but I was the one receiving a gift. "That's great mom. I can't wait to see you again and give you a hug. Well, I should get off my feet and let you get back to your party. I just wanted to tell you I love you."

As I heard the dial tone ringing in my ears, my mind kept repeating the last words she said, "Take care of yourself and don't forget we love you." I hung on to every word she said.

My attempt to contact the local media failed. It was Sunday and hard to reach anyone, but I was able to connect with Betty of the Antigonish Animal Shelter.

"I'm pretty far from the highway and I don't have a car to come out and meet with you. But I think what you are trying to do is wonderful. If animals are going to have a fighting chance, the public needs to be made aware. I wish you all the best," said Betty.

Before I left the gas station, Judy the cashier told me an interesting story that sparked a stimulating discussion.

"I've been trying to find homes for these two abandoned dogs I took in but I just found out that one of them is a mom when she suddenly gave birth to a pup. Surprise, we had no idea she was pregnant until there it was," Judy said, as hard as it is to believe. "I'm not sure what happened but someone forgot to tell us she was having puppies. Now, I don't know what we'll do with them all?"

"People don't understand the consequences of not getting their pets fixed, or why it's so important," I said.

"It would help if pets were spayed and neutered before they are put into the hands of an owner," Judy added.

"That would help. As long as pets are allowed to breed freely, the problem won't go away," I told her.

"Something needs to be done about all the stray animals too."

"We need a ban on breeding cats and dogs other than legitimate breeders until the overpopulation problem can be resolved. That would help shelter animals find homes."

"And prohibit pet stores from selling cats and dogs and shut down the puppy mills and shelters for profit. If people abuse their responsibility to care for a pet, it should be taken away from them."

"These are great ideas if they can be enforced."

Our thoughts were so aligned that I asked her if she wanted to come on the road with me. "Sure, as long as I can make it back in time for my next shift," Judy laughed. We wished each other luck and then I went on my way.

After stopping for something to eat at the nearby restaurant, I went back to my tent. I delighted in the cool air and quiet, except for the faint sound of traffic from the highway. The only thing that crashed was me.

However, sometime that night I was abruptly woken by something heavy that fell on my legs. Then, it clawed at me from the side of the tent. It happened so fast that I barely had time to react. Whatever it was didn't return. So I rolled over and went back to sleep thinking it was probably a directionally challenged raccoon.

In the morning, I checked my tent for damages but found nothing. It made me wonder if I had imagined the whole thing.

Before I left Antigonish, I called Mary of the *Guardian* newspaper in Charlottetown. Kelly had given me her number to let her know my estimated time of arrival.

"We're currently working on an article about spaying and neutering. I'll see what I can do about an interview when you get here, but it will depend on what happens with the elections," said Mary.

Although soon being in P.E.I. encouraged me, every day was getting a little tougher than the day before. As I ran, my stressed feet reminded me that I was breaking just about every running rule in the book. It went against all logic, but it wasn't technique that was getting me through each day. My body might have been weakening, but my determination was getting stronger.

At the end of my run, there were plenty of doors to knock on in this part of the country. Houses had big backyards and plenty of room for a tent. From a distance, I watched a young boy playing outside and thought a home with happy kids should be a safe place for shelter.

I tried getting his attention by shouting and waving my arms, but the noise from the traffic was louder than my voice. As soon as I stepped onto their property, dogs came out of nowhere and started barking. I stopped in my tracks and gestured for the boy to come to me.

Then, his mom came out of the house to see what all the commotion was and saw a strange figure standing at the end of her driveway carrying a flag. She sent the boy to investigate.

Watching him march down the long driveway, he was a handsome young lad and couldn't have been more than nine or ten years old. He halted in front of me and greeted me with a big smile. I couldn't help but smile back at him and then introduced myself.

He relayed my message back to his mom and dad and returned once again. "You can setup your tent at our other house so it won't upset the dogs as much. There's an older lady living there, but she won't mind."

Matthew then showed me the way. He took me through the backyard and across a road to a driveway leading to June's house. An elderly woman and her dog answered the door. We had just finished some introductions when Matthew's dad, Darryl, came over to invite me for supper.

"We're about to sit down to a steak and lobster dinner. You're welcome to join us," he said kindly.

Sitting down for a proper meal wasn't always going to fit into my schedule so I gladly accepted.

"Wow. It's not every day I get an offer like that. Thank you. I'd love to." June didn't mind so I left my bag and followed Darryl back to his place.

The entrance to their home brought us into the kitchen where the table was already set with an extra plate. Other members of Matthew's family included his younger sister Megan, and his mom, Mary. They were already sitting at the table.

Their mood was very much alive with everyone talking and waiting to be served. Darryl made sure everyone had plenty to eat.

"I tied the dogs up outside. They're good dogs, they just get protective and a little anxious when new people come around," said Mary.

"Well, it's nice to see they are loved and well taken care of," I acknowledged.

"Are you running across Canada?" Megan asked.

"Yes I am, to help save the lives of healthy cats and dogs in our country. Do you think that's a good idea?"

"Yes," she answered and spawned a big smile.

Eating lobster turned out to be quite the experience. I think Darryl could feel my pain trying to crack open the shells. He decided to help me and that got everyone laughing. Watching him was entertaining. He was the kind of guy everyone loves–jolly and charismatic.

Feeling right at home, I sat there and thought how much Matthew and Megan were a reflection of their loving parents. Truly wonderful children. They were full of laughter and stories to tell. In addition to enjoying their company and sharing some family time, they had their own special way of capturing my heart.

Megan colored a picture for me and Matthew wanted to give me a stuffed animal that I regret not being able to take with me.

"Will you come over again tomorrow?" Matthew asked.

"I'd like to, but I might be on the road before you get up," I said with disappointment, "but I have a blog online where you can follow me across the country if you like."

Upon hearing that, Matthew smiled and appeared to think that was a good idea.

After we had coffee, we took some pictures. Darryl worked truck driver hours and had to leave for work. Mary and the kids had their evening routine ahead of them and I didn't want to overstay my welcome. It was time for me to head back to June's house.

"Thank you so much for a wonderful meal," I said gratefully.

"It was our pleasure," said Mary.

"Good luck the rest of the way," they all encouraged me.

June was like a grandmother to Darryl. Now eighty years old, she lived alone with her dog Rosie. She was outside in the yard when I arrived.

"It's terrible the way people mistreat animals," she said.

"Yes it is June," I agreed.

"Would you like to see my pet cemetery?"

The first thing that popped into my head was the Stephen King movie, *Pet Cemetery*. Not knowing June well, I wondered what I had gotten myself into.

"Sure," I answered and proceeded to follow her around.

We walked along her backyard and paused at each gravesite. I listened to their stories and related to her pain. "They were all very special in their own way," she said tearfully.

Once we finished our walk about, June wasn't quite ready to go inside. "Would you like to take a drive through town with me?" Again, I found myself wondering what I had gotten myself into as I hopped into her car.

Driving through the streets, we waved at people she knew. "It has changed so much since I grew up here," she said. Thorburn was her hometown, but she had lived most of her life somewhere else.

We made a connection when she found out I served in the Canadian Armed Forces. She was a nurse in the war and I enjoyed her many stories.

"What did you do in the military?" June inquired.

"I was a photographic technician posted to 434 Tactical Fighting Squadron in Cold Lake Alberta. Best five years of my life," I said.

Back at her house, she invited me to stay indoors for the night. "It's not very big but you're welcome to sleep in the spare room. Unless you want to spend the night in your tent," she grinned.

There was a bit of humor underneath her exterior armor after all. She also revealed a caring side of her. "I don't imagine you have pajamas in that backpack of yours," she said as she handed me a pair of old flannelettes to wear. "You can change into them after you take a bath." It had been sometime since I put on some PJ's and it felt rather good.

June brought out a late night snack of pop and chips. We were watching Law and Order on the television, but it was all I could do to stay awake. Especially after taking a hot bath. I was only able to watch the first half hour and then needed to sleep.

"I hope you don't mind June, but I don't think I can stay awake any longer."

"Heavens no dear, you go off to bed anytime you're ready. You must be exhausted."

"Thank you June. I'll see you in the morning."

I don't remember falling asleep and I thought I was dreaming when I heard a loud knock on my door.

"Are you awake in there?"

It was June. I jumped out of bed and answered, "I'm up, thanks." For a moment, I thought I was back in boot camp. It must have been all that military talk.

While I was sitting on the floor bandaging my feet, she knocked a second time. I guess I was taking too long.

"Everything okay in there? Your tea is ready."

My morning routine was somewhat of a process. I swung the door open and began explaining it to her. She observed me for a minute and then said, "That seems like an awful lot of trouble to put yourself through. Be careful those blisters don't get infected." Then she disappeared again.

There's nothing like the fresh aroma of homemade muffins and tea brewing to captivate your sense of smell. It was making me hungry. I took in a deep breath as I followed my nose into the kitchen like an ant going to a picnic.

"Something smells really good," I said.

"I made muffins and there's some butter to put on them if you like," June responded. It made me wonder if she had slept at all.

With Rosie close by her side, I think June enjoyed having some company. "A friend calls me every day to check on me," she stated and looked at the clock. "If one of us doesn't answer the phone, we know to send for help. At our age, we have to watch out for each other."

June had been kind to me and I was glad there were people around to look out for her. Before I headed out the door, she gave me some Tim Horton certificates to take with me. "I don't use them," she said. "Someone might as well."

After I hugged her and patted Rosie, I disappeared from her sight. I felt exceptionally good today. My lungs never ran out of air and I ran tirelessly, all 112 pounds of me. With not an ounce of fat left on my body, I was in the best shape of my life, doing something I loved for something dear to my heart. If it wasn't for sore feet, I think I could have run forever.

Chugging right along, someone tried to get my attention by beeping their horn. It was Mary. She drove passed me, honking and I could see Matthew and Megan waving vigorously through the back window. The smiles on their faces stretched from ear to ear and I could only guess what they were trying to say to me. "What great timing," I thought to myself as I waved back at them.

The school was right off the highway and I looked for Matthew and Megan playing in the schoolyard. I didn't see them but Mary was waiting for me at the intersection.

"I didn't think I would be this late leaving or I could have stopped by this morning."

"That's okay. Mornings are pretty crazy at our house anyway. How was your night with June? Did she show you her pet cemetery?"

"Yes, she did. It's not every day you meet someone with a pet cemetery. We had a good evening. She took me for a tour of the town and let me sleep in the spare room."

"I'm glad," said Mary.

Under different circumstances, I would have liked to stay longer and hang out with Mary. She had a wonderful personality and was one of those people who makes you feel good just being around her. Instead, we went our separate ways. One day, I hope to return for another visit.

I thought a lot about Matthew and his family all the way to New Glasgow. Their down to earth hospitality made my being with them extra special. They had been my angel family and I'll be forever grateful to them. Darryl drove truck on these highways and I hoped our paths would cross again too.

The main exit into New Glasgow led me in front of a veterinary clinic. I went inside and met Amy and Marilyn. They were intrigued by what I was doing.

"Educating pet owners about spay and neutering is so important," they agreed.

"What an amazing thing to do," said Amy.

Amy was heading over to Tim Horton's for a coffee, so I joined her. I thought about June when I used the certificate she gave me. On our way back, Amy shared her desire to become a veterinarian.

"Owning a pet shouldn't be just for the privileged. There are very caring people who love animals but can't afford the costs. It would go a long way if veterinarians and/or students could donate some of their time to spay and neutering pets," I said and appreciated that she listened.

From there, I stopped at the Irving gas station and called the New Glasgow Evening News. A reporter named Lana came out to meet me for an interview. "We don't get many females running solitary across Canada without a support vehicle," she said astonished. I was happy that another article would be published. In my mind, that equaled another small victory for our companion friends.

Along the coast of the Northumberland Strait, I marveled at the scenery. It was breathtaking. However, the change in weather was a shock after some pretty hot temperatures. The forecast for the next couple of days was five to ten centimeters of snow mixed with rain. It was a chilly, north wind that I was feeling.

When I reached Pictou, the ferry to P.E.I. was in sight. I stopped to give my feet a rest when a car pulled up. "I saw you earlier today," Kelly said. "You run a long way. Hop in, I'll give you a ride to the door and save you a few feet."

In that narrow window, Kelly told me he had traveled across Canada himself several years ago and enjoyed the experience. "Good luck to you," he said. It felt like a long wait for the ferry.

After a short boat ride across the strait, we arrived in P.E.I. and docked at Wood Islands just before dark. The terminal was closed. All bundled up, I stood in the middle of the road not knowing where the road would take me. Everyone from the ferry was already gone. Looking around, I could see a building in the distance and signposts where the road branched off. "Start walking Michelle," I said.

Any doors I tried were locked tight and I ended up standing at a fork in the road. "It's not the first time I've encountered a crossroad in my life," I chuckled. One of the signs pointed to a campground one kilometer away, so I followed it.

After a couple of miles, I figured something was wrong when I didn't find it. The skies were getting darker now and clouding over. I needed to pick a campsite soon while there was still some daylight. A little panicked, I turned around and headed back to the fork in the road.

This time, I decided to go in the direction of Charlottetown, even though it was forty-four kilometers away. I reassured myself that every trial I faced made me that much stronger and I was ready for anything. However, I didn't have to go far when the Meadowlands Motel came into view. It was closed for repairs but the owners gave me permission to pitch my tent in their backyard. Night had fallen by the time I zipped up.

That night and into the next day, snow and rain fell holding me captive. The heavy rainfall made my tent sound like being in a tin cup. I was thankful that the terminal had a restaurant where I could get something to eat. Then, I waited anxiously to leave.

Finally, the time had come for me to visit the shelter in Charlottetown and I didn't want to miss it. I was glad that the highway to town was relatively flat and it made running a little easier, despite the wet conditions.

On the outskirts of the city, I ran through a downpour. A kind man and his dog rescued me and dropped me off at the Tim Horton's where Kelley agreed to pick me up.

While I sat there waiting, I had no doubt that my survival on this journey was only possible with some help. There was no time for me to be fooled into thinking I could do this on my own. My position was such that I had to trust the people who were taking me in.

Through the window, I watched a vehicle with "Humane Society" printed on the door, turn into the parking lot. I made my way outside and walked up to the van.

"You must be Kelley?"

"And you must be Michelle?"

"It's great to finally meet you."

"Well congratulations for making it this far, hop in," she said cheerfully.

"Thanks, it's great to be here."

"Sorry the weather couldn't be better for you."

"It brings back memories of Newfoundland."

"Poor you. We've been following your blog and hopefully we can provide you with at least one night of comfort before you leave. Everyone at the shelter is anxiously waiting to meet you. How are your feet?"

"They're okay, a bit stressed but somehow every morning they're ready to go again."

"Well, the ShipWright Inn has arranged for you to stay with them tonight so you won't have to be in your tent. I think you're going to enjoy that."

"That's fantastic Kelley, thank you so much."

"You can thank Trevor and Judy when you see them later. They're huge supporters of our shelter and donated the room."

"Wow. That's very kind of them."

"You'll also be able to take a hot shower when you get to the shelter. Allana, one of our shelter attendants, has been working very diligently this morning to clean and have the shower ready for you."

"Wonderful. That's awesome. That'll help take the chills away. I have to apologize for my wardrobe, but it's a little thin at the moment. I've been wearing the same clothes for a while."

"Perfectly okay. I think Allana might even have some dry clothes for you to change into too."

"Great. I think she might be my new best friend."

I wasn't really sure what to expect coming here but Kelley's super personality quickly put me at ease. She had thought of everything and the amount of effort they were putting into my arrival was heartwarming.

Entering the shelter, I found acceptance and safety and I was charmed with my reception. As staff members stopped what they were doing to say hello, I nervously shook their hands. Their attention bolstered my confidence and I was calmed by their hearty welcome. Everyone fascinated me.

"This is Heather, Lesa, and Elizabeth," said Kelly.

"Hi, it's nice to meet all of you," I said.

"How are you doing? You probably need to get off your feet," said Heather.

"They're not too bad right now." All the excitement made me forget about my aches and pains. Somehow they disappeared with our time together.

"Hello, I'm Allana."

"I'm really happy to meet you. I heard you're the person to see about a shower."

"Yep, and it's almost ready."

"Thanks so much Allana. I really appreciate it."

"I'll show you where it is and then come back and get you," Kelly said.

They all kindly let me hit the shower and get out of my wet clothes. The heated water brought me back to life and after toweling off, I put on the scrubs Allana left me. I thought the Newfoundland t-shirt was a nice touch and all that was missing were the words "I survived Newfoundland".

Wearing them proudly, Kelley took me on a tour around the shelter. Everyone was so friendly and happy that it made me wonder what his or her secret was. This was the first shelter I was in where the morale of the staff was so high. It was also evident that the animals were well cared for.

As we passed by cages, they all appeared to say to me, "Pick me! Pick me!" Entering and leaving their environment, their voices sounded like desperate cries for attention and someone to love them.

The more abandoned animals I saw, the easier it was for me to think less of people. I found myself asking the question, "How could we? How could we allow this to happen?" For every homeless pet, there was someone responsible for that.

My tour ended in the staff room where Erin, another volunteer, made me a cup of hot chocolate. Two students from the local veterinarian college, Ashley and Chad, joined us. Others came in and the room was lively in conversation and laughter. It was great medicine and exactly what I needed to take my mind off of everything else.

Lastly, I met Dr. Cawthorn, the shelter veterinarian. I appreciated she took the time to speak with me.

"We have students from the local veterinarian school performing various volunteer works with animals as part of their training. Their works go a long way to help reduce problems," she said. "Myself, and a couple other volunteers have started a new program called the SpayAid Assistance Program. One of the other members will try to stop by the inn before you leave to meet with you. We all want to do what's best for the animals."

Time went by too quickly and my visit came to an end. They wrote on my flag, "Thank you on behalf of all the animals" and then everyone gathered outside for a couple of pictures.

As we drove away I thought, "What a delight it had been to connect with people who cared so much." They were an amazing group and I said to Kelley, "You have a wonderful team. In our world of animal abuse, working in a shelter is not always a happy place to be but you've managed to build a good morale here."

When I asked what their secret to success was she proudly replied, "We have the support of our community and we love our animals. We believe we make a difference every day. It's not always pleasant, but we're a close group and we support each other."

My new friends were an inspiration and reflected the words of Marion Wright Edelman: *"you really can change the world if you care enough."* Their positive attitudes and encouragement refreshed my hope that change is possible everywhere if we don't give up trying.

The ShipWright Inn was an old Victorian home built in the 1800's by a local shipbuilder and then restored into the best bed and breakfast on the island. From the outside it has an elegant Green Gables style structure and on the inside the owners, Trevor and Judy, were able to retain its heritage using a nautical theme with antiques and artwork collected from the same period of time it was built.

I was about to become the beneficiary of some of their island hospitality and pampering. "Welcome to the ShipWright Inn," Trevor said like the captain of a ship extending a friendly greeting. "We're all cheering for you and happy to have you with us."

He gave me a grand tour complete with some background on the inn's history and then wowed me with a luxury suite.

"It's all yours for the night. We hope you enjoy your stay and we're happy to support you any way we can. Make yourself at home," he offered kindly as he gave me the key to my room.

"Wow. This is fantastic! I don't know what to say except thank you," I said, thrilled beyond words.

The apartment style retreat had a king size bed, sitting room, TV, kitchenette, tub, fireplace, so I couldn't help but be overjoyed with spending the night here. I could tell Kelley was happy for me too by the look on her face.

After they left, I didn't know if I should laugh or cry. Behind closed doors, I was a little lost. My suite left nothing to my imagination except how to enjoy it. However, all I could think about was sleeping in this gigantic bed full of pillows later in the evening.

Out of curiosity, I wandered the halls taking in some of the inn's history on display and delighted myself with some afternoon tea and cakes. They had access to the Internet and after some blog updating, I sat down to a relaxed dinner. Trevor and Judy were incredible hosts, always ensuring their guests were well taken care of. Their wonderful service included great food and conversation.

Back in my room, I felt like I had won the lottery. My first thought was to call my sisters to let them know I was having a great day. They were always relieved when they knew I was somewhere safe.

Not wanting the morning to come too soon, I tried prolonging the night by staying awake as long as I could. I turned the TV on to see what was playing. There was a man talking who appeared to know an awful lot about God. He got my attention when he said, "God wanted to give me a new heart." That was good news to me.

That night, I relished in the comfort of the inn and I was thankful to spend one less night in my tent. Waking up the next morning, it took me a few minutes to remember where I was and what I was doing here. When it all came back, I moaned and groaned about the task in front of me. It was tempting to stay under the blankets, but instead, I kicked myself out of bed.

Everything was dry again and I packed up. Then, I went downstairs for breakfast. "Good morning. I hope you slept well," Judy said cheerfully.

"The world could have come to an end last night and I would have never known. I slept like a baby. I can't thank you enough for your kindness."

Trevor and Judy's attempt to make my visit a unique experience, as they did with all their guests, was successful. It was an evening I would never forget and be forever grateful for. As we said our goodbyes they said, "We hope you've enjoyed your stay with us and that the rest will help you to continue. Good luck the rest of the way."

Before I left, I had a visitor. Joy from SpayAid dropped by to meet with me and find out more about my plans. We discovered our goals were similar. SpayAid is dedicated to eliminating the pet overpopulation on the island with a non-lethal solution. She saw the vision of a national program across Canada but said, "It will be an enormous task to bring shelters under one umbrella, if it's even possible."

Our discussion was all too familiar and my conversations were consistently the same with everyone I spoke to. She encouraged me though by saying "raising awareness could only help" and I acknowledged that SpayAid should be an example for the rest of our country. We exchanged a hug and then wished each other luck.

Bob, one of the shelter animal protection officers, had arrived to take me to the bridge. This time Kelley wouldn't be coming with us but she was there to make sure everything went according to plan.

"Thank you for everything Kelley. It has been a privilege to meet all of you," I said, humbled by their kindness. All of their efforts were appreciated and I was running out of ways to say thank you.

"Be careful and we'll be following your blog. Hope the weather gets better for you too."

As I waved back at Kelley, I was instantly overcome with the same emotions I felt when I left Newfoundland. "I won't forget you," I whispered to myself and my gratitude was deepening with every kind hand I was extended, a reminder of what truly matters.

Bob drove down a road where I could get a good look at the Confederation Bridge from below. The fog made it look monolithic and the view was impressive, leaving an imprint in my mind. When he dropped me off at the terminal, I thanked him for going out of his way to give me such a lasting impression. It was a memorable way to conclude my visit on Prince Edward Island.

Only vehicles were allowed on the bridge. While I anxiously waited for the bus to take me across, I thought about what a roller coaster ride I was on–up one minute and down the next. When I was flying high it was wonderful, but nose-diving was tough. On the way down, my emotions were like riding a runaway train that was about to crash.

I was publicly strong and able to hold my composure. However, in those quiet private moments, it was a different story. Any feelings of despair I had, brought on by fatigue would set in. My inner journey was life-changing and every mile demanded more.

Making this kind of conscious effort day after day to sustain my enthusiasm was draining. The effort to get ready to push myself again and again was tenfold after leaving the company of others. Discipline and self-control was the only thing keeping me from a train wreck. Not far from there, I was about to come face to face with a piece of reality.

Chapter 3

New Brunswick and Quebec

When I stepped off the shuttle bus, I could hardly believe my feet were in New Brunswick, or that I was even here. I found cover from the heavy rain inside the terminal and thought, "There are just some things in life we have no control over and the weather is one of them."

Peering through the window, I began scouting for a possible campsite. If the rain didn't let up, I would have to find shelter for the night. Then, something prompted me to call Peter and update him on my whereabouts.

Peter and Corinna ran a cat rescue operation called CA-R-MA somewhere in the area. As I dialed the number, I wasn't expecting anyone to answer the phone but then, I heard Peter's voice. Without hesitation, he said he would be right over to pick me up. He was a lot closer than I thought and I was excited about meeting him in person. This was his response to my email before I left Ottawa:

> *Michelle,*
> *This is great to see. I can just hear you say the words as I read them. I know that you will inspire thousands and make a real difference in the policy of our society toward the unnecessary killing of cats. Perhaps people will one day think differently about our relationship to animals in the same way that*

> *many are now realizing that our environment has been treated cruelly.*

While I waited for him, I quietly reflected on the question he had asked me before I left on this journey. He wanted to know how committed I was to the idea. The implication of his question was understandable and I understood skepticism. Most people say things casually and have a hard time keeping long-term commitments, or staying motivated. Lots of people start well, but never finish.

To him, I was a stranger. How could he know that I wouldn't cling to my goal unless I was completely inspired to finish it? However, right now, I wasn't all that sure of myself. Although my heart has been fully in it since the beginning, I was struggling. After a month of running, I didn't know how much longer I could keep this up.

Peter is also the founder of Triad Film Productions that actively produces documentaries. He contacted Dorit about the possibility of including a piece from my journey with a documentary he was working on. He too wanted to raise awareness using the media, but CTV failed to support him and passed on his proposal. They said:

> *Hi Peter - I think you were close with this idea – cats obviously appeal to a mainstream audience. We just weren't confident that the approach and this particular story would attract a large CTV audience. While we know the subject is dear to your heart, we weren't fully confident that this way in would be enough to bring in a million viewers. Certainly people who know about the issue might watch - but maybe not even all cat lovers would be open to an hour on cat abuse? Tricky I think.*

The project was put on hold until he could find another broadcaster. Breaking the barrier of reaching the larger public was a challenge. It was disheartening that the media didn't feel enough people would watch Peter's documentary or that it wasn't dramatic enough to show. The thought that the broadcast market is so driven by ratings that social conscience takes a back seat is very discouraging for people trying to improve the world we live in.

I admired Peter for trying; he cared so much about life and social issues. Both he and Corinna were making their own difference with CA-R-MA by transforming broken animals into happy creatures. Then, finding a loving home for them, something that can take a long time and money. It takes a special kind of person to do that: a selfless person.

They, and others like them, have a more than ordinary compassion for not just cats, but for all life forms. Somehow, I just knew Peter wasn't going to give up on his story. I was also about to find out what else we had in common.

Peter embraced me with a hug. In my mind, I had etched an image of what a documentary producer should look like and as it turned out, I wasn't that far off. He wore a black leather jacket and resembled Nicholas Cage; at least I thought he did.

Here I was, in the presence of a successful filmmaker and I wasn't dressed in my best Sunday clothes. I was glad it didn't matter to him. Under different circumstances, I might have been more intimidated by meeting him, but I had reached a point where I was beyond feeling discomfort with anyone.

We arrived at his house and meeting Corinna was equally as lovely. I wasn't there more than a few minutes when she whispered to me, "Do you want to see a mom and her babies?" They were in a bedroom upstairs. When she opened the door we peaked in and there were "oohs" and "aahs". The kittens were only a few weeks old and adorable.

The mother appeared fine with us fussing over her young. While we held them, Corinna said a cat is one of the most misunderstood creatures in the world. "The evidence is in the way they are disposed of," she stated sadly.

There were also several other cats in the house and a beautiful gold brindle Dutch Shepherd dog named Timber. "These breeds are often used for rescue and police work," Peter said. He was so obedient and focused on Peter; it was fascinating to watch them together. Timber never made a move without Peter's approval.

Sometime later, while we were sitting down for dinner, Peter and Corinna shared with me how CA-R-MA. began. A few years back, they lost a cat while traveling in the United States. They met with some caring animal people who joined them in their search. The cat wasn't found, but through this experience they learned how enormous the overpopulation problem was.

They returned home without the cat. However, about a month later, these same people thought they had found their missing cat and shipped it to them. When it arrived, it wasn't theirs, but they decided to keep it anyway. That's when they decided to rescue cats themselves and gave life to another startup shelter to fill a gap animals fall through.

Then our conversation led to questions I wasn't fully prepared to answer. "What prompted you to run across Canada?" they asked curiously. Whenever someone asked me that question, it shattered my own illusion that all was well with me because there lays the mystery behind my reasons.

My answer could have easily opened up scars that tell a different story. However, I didn't want to look back where my trials began, or shift the attention from cats and dogs.

"I wanted to do something to help animals and I think this is the right thing to do," I said.

"But there are lots of ways to help. You could volunteer at a shelter or write letters to the editor. Why run across the country?" Peter asked.

"Anyone can do that and the problem doesn't just exist in Ottawa or New Brunswick, its Canada wide. There are a lot of people, like yourselves, bending over backward and practically standing on your heads to make a difference. Running is something I can do and sometimes it takes drastic measures to send a message."

By now, I was fully aware that it was going to take more than a marathon to fix a problem of this magnitude. I had come to the realization, I wasn't going to win this battle and I was facing a near impossible situation. Not that I felt defeated, just that the problem was so much bigger than I imagined and it would take a miracle to move this mountain.

In spite of this truth, my commitment did not change. My soul was like a tree bending under the weight of the wind and I desperately needed to find freedom from my guilt. In the midst of my altering life, I was never going to rest until I found peace. Making up for the mistake I made was the only way I knew how.

That night, I lay in bed thinking about what Peter had said to me earlier in the day. "It must feel good to act righteously." I wondered what he meant by that. If what I was doing appeared righteous, it was only because I was eager to do what I felt was morally right. How could it be wrong for me to expect others to do the same?

"The senseless killing/mistreatment of animals are circumstances that you did not determine - but now you are part of - in your journey to make others aware and act according to your beliefs."
- Peter d'Entremont

In the morning, Peter dropped me off on the highway and said, "I'll be back to pick you up later." He inspired me to run that day. I could have easily taken the day off, but he was there to give me the push I needed. Even before I left Ottawa, he worried about how my training was going.

What a joy it was to run with little weight on my back. I felt lighter and ran faster than ever. However, I didn't pace myself well and slowed down considerably near the end of my run.

Peter swung by a couple of times to check in on me and each time, I felt like I had barely moved. My legs were like lead and my body felt like it could seize up at any moment. "This must be what runner's call 'hitting the wall,'" I thought. I struggled through the last six miles, but I got through it and with three provinces behind me, I had hit another milestone.

Over the next couple of days, Peter took care of everything while I ran. He fed me meals fit for an Olympian, organized an interview with local media, and arranged accommodations for me when I got to Moncton. He was such a great encourager. Corinna even pitched in and picked up my parcel at the Amherst shelter.

> *Kirsteen, who worked at the shelter in Amherst, had also replied to my email announcement. If I hadn't taken the ferry in Pictou to P.E.I. and come out at the bridge, I would have passed through Amherst and stopped at their shelter. Before I left Ottawa we had pre-arranged shipping my parcel there that contained a supply of vitamins and energy bars. Peter and Corina had a connection with them and were able to arrange pickup. I was grateful to Kirsteen for her help but disappointed that I didn't get to meet her.*

On my last morning with them, Corinna let me in on a little secret. In my room on the wall, was a picture of a marathon runner. It was Peter. I had no idea he even ran. No wonder he knew exactly what I needed.

When you travel the road of long distance running, you understand the language of encouragement. His support was making all the difference in the world and it came at a time when I was wrestling with doubt and uncertainty about my being able to finish.

Peter and Corrina dropped me off for the last time and then continued to Moncton. Everything was pre-arranged for me to stay with friends of theirs, Madi and Dave. After they relayed my stuff, they headed back home.

On the return trip, they stopped when they saw me and I was glad they did. Peter even ran a few steps with me and gave me some last minute words of encouragement. I didn't let on that I knew his secret. This time, we said good-bye for the last time and I would be forever grateful for his help. He didn't disappoint me and I didn't want to disappoint him.

Sometime later and to my surprise, a vehicle pulled over and it was Madi and Dave. Madi was also involved with cat rescue and they embraced me like family. We sat in their vehicle drinking Tim Horton's coffee and eating the muffins they brought. What an unexpected delight.

After an exchange of conversation, I had to return my attention to running. Their heartfelt support re-energized me and meeting my new hosts was both encouraging and welcoming.

Eleven miles went by pretty fast and before I knew it, I had reached our rendezvous point. As planned, Madi and Dave were right on time and picked me up at the junction for Highway 2. When I saw them, my face lit up like fireworks on the first of July. You would have thought I'd known them all my life the way we greeted each other. I was happy to be with them.

While we drove to their house, I considered how much trouble people were going through to help me. Every little thing someone did, no matter how big or small, may have seemed insignificant to others but to me it was monumental. How could I not love them for it?

Later, we had a wonderful homemade chicken dinner and then it was all I could do to stay awake. I had my own room in the basement and a washroom. "Watch out for the feral cat," Madi cautioned me. "He's hiding in the bathroom."

After I brushed my teeth, I sat on the bathroom floor talking to the rescued cat. He had taken refuge in a corner. I told him how much easier it was to talk to animals about people, than it was to talk to people about animals. He never moved and just stared at me. Finally, I said goodnight to the frightened critter and slid into my bed.

The next day, Madi brought me back to the junction. She sent me off with snacks in the same way a mother would send her child off to school. Strangely and progressively, the more kindness I was shown, the lonelier I felt about being on the road by myself.

On my last night, Dave warned me that it would take three days to get to Fredericton on foot. "There's nothing along that stretch of the highway," he worried for me. "We want to give you this gift calling card so you can let us know how you're doing." I was moved by his genuine concern and at the same time I wondered, how bad could it be?

Madi tried to have the media catch up with me, but we never connected. She also arranged for me to stay with her sister, Flo, in Fredericton. "She's a foot specialist and can look at your feet when you get there," Madi said. This kind of support was so uplifting and without it, I don't know where I would be.

In the morning, Madi stopped at Tim Horton's for coffee on our way out, she was so thoughtful that way. She also told me about another feral cat she was planning to trap that day, something she was concerned about.

At the split to St. John's or Fredericton, I got out of the van. When Madi pulled away, I was overcome with feelings of separation. An emotion I wasn't expecting, or able to control. Both Madi and Dave had touched me in a way that could only come from their caring hearts. Every tear I shed inspired me not to give up and my heart was expanding with every tear I wiped away.

While I ran, I encouraged myself by saying, "I have the best relay team in Canada. By far the best in the world." I found inspiration from their help getting me through this part of the country. Bit by bit, I took a piece of everyone with me and it felt like we were all in this together.

Running with the full weight of my backpack again was a lot heavier than I remembered. Quickly, I felt pain in the arches of my feet and struggled. My tolerance level now softened, I stopped frequently because of the throbbing. It was only after popping several Advil that I felt any relief.

Halfway through my run, I understood what Dave was talking about and I felt the loneliness that comes with isolation. This section of highway was boring and running it felt endless.

The monotony of the road and not being able to run my best was disheartening. To top it off, one person stopped but lost interest when I mentioned cats and dogs. He shook his head and got back into his car. Whenever someone reacted that way, it stung as hard as if it had been a slap in the face.

Of all the days, today I did not want to run more than forty-two kilometers. However, there was nowhere to put a tent out of danger and the ditch was never an option. Deer fences lined the highway and the grounds were flooded from rain.

The sky was gray and my eyes a fountain of tears. By now, my feet were screaming at me and my mind was a mess. Today, I had to face my highway of adversity with perseverance. "God give me strength," I cried in distress and ran another sixteen kilometers.

After a punishing fifty-eight kilometers, I finally reached Young's Cove. When I saw McCready's Motel, I had to pull myself together before going inside. It had been by far the most painful day of my running experience.

Inside, I met the owner and asked him if I could setup my tent in the back. I don't know what he saw in my face but for whatever reason, he kindly gave me a complimentary room for the night. There are no words to describe how grateful I felt. When I got into the room, I collapsed from exhaustion.

Standing in the shower, there were a few tears mixed with the water that fell on me. Water that hit my skin like little beads massaging my body. I didn't stand there long before sitting in the tub sobbing, "Maybe this is far enough."

Sprawled out on the bed, I popped a hand full of Advil to take the edge off the pain in my feet. Then more throughout the night and again in the morning. I was eating them like candy now.

Stepping outside, the temperature had dropped below zero and I was glad to have been indoors overnight. Walking on my feet was tender as I made my way to the restaurant for breakfast. I knew then that my days were probably numbered.

Earl, the motel owner, came in just as I finished eating. I must have thanked him a dozen times for my room. Before I left, I called Madi and Dave from the pay phone. Dave reminded me to call Madi's sister when I got to Fredericton. After yesterday, I wasn't sure I would make it that far. "Thanks Dave, I will. Thanks again for everything," I said and hung up the phone.

It was starting to amaze me that my body was able to keep going like this. No matter what happened the day before, I got up and ran again. It was as if my feet had a will of their own.

I wasn't breaking any speed records, but I settled into a nice easy pace after a few miles. The morning air was cool and dry much to my delight. It warmed up fairly quickly and my face basked in the warmth of the sun. Not wanting an encore from yesterday's performance, I asked God to help me.

Later in the afternoon, a white van pulled up with two guys in it.

"Do you know Sharron from Ottawa?" the driver asked.

"I read an email from Sharron saying she had a friend named Dave in New Brunswick and that he was going to keep an eye out for me. You wouldn't happen to be Dave, would you?" I smiled.

"Yup, that's me. You know Sharron, when she says look out for someone you better do it," he smiled back.

"That sounds like her. It's a small world isn't it?"

"It sure is. You're making pretty good time. I saw you yesterday but I was going the other way. Should we give Sharron a call and let her know I found you?"

"That would be great. I haven't talked to her since she dropped me off at the airport in Ottawa."

He placed a call from his cell and it was nice to hear her voice.

"I'm going to kick your butt when you get to Ottawa," she said half joking. "Some of your friends can't even follow your blog because they are so worried."

"Well, tell them not to worry and that I'm fine."

"We're all very proud of you. Just get home safely."

"You bet. See you soon," I said.

Dave kindly gave me some apples and oranges. If I hadn't already had accommodations in Fredericton, I was welcome to stay with him. "I'll look for you again tomorrow," he assured me. Before he drove away, he warned me about some moose sightings up ahead.

Just knowing there was someone watching out for me, made me feel a whole lot better. If something were to happen, they would know where to start looking.

Jemseg River was a great location to camp for the night. I hung my flag on a branch to claim my territory and to act as an aid, should anyone need to find me. There were animal droppings everywhere, so I parked myself off the trail.

The air was thick with black flies and they were feasting on me. I hurried to get inside my tent and didn't want to go back out there. Bugs tried to invade my space and the sound of buzzing was amplified by the quiet. Watching them crawl around the outside, trying to find a way in was my source of entertainment.

While I lay still, I thought how well this tent had worked out for me so far. Then, it occurred to me how small it really was. I was beginning to think that downsizing wasn't such a bad idea. In fact, my struggles getting this far have helped me distinguish between necessities and luxuries.

Living in a tent, I was discovering that our basic needs are few and there is a lot of waste in our country. We live in such prosperity and yet we are always wanting more. When we don't get what we want, we do a lot of complaining. Like a spoiled child. This journey was teaching me to loosen my grip on things I once held so tightly. Right now, all I wanted was to lie down and sleep. My body was feeling like it had been through a war.

Wide-awake, I watched the coming of dawn and the rays of the sun break through the sky. There wasn't a breeze in the air and it was hot early. It took longer than usual for me to pack up and I fought myself with every moment.

My pace was slow and each step I put forward with agony. The combination of running and the weight on my back had taken its toll. My bruised feet were way over stressed and it felt like I was standing on twigs, ready to snap. Advil was no longer effective and I was hurting.

By early afternoon, Dave pulled up and his timing couldn't be better. While I leaned against his van, I felt like I could pass out.

"Hello again," said Dave. "I had strict orders, from Sharron, to bring you some water and snacks," he smiled.

"Thanks Dave. That's very kind of you."

"No problem. How was your night?"

"Good. I found a great spot to camp, but I didn't see any moose."

"That's probably a good thing. They've been known to attack people. How are you feeling?" he said with concern.

"Well, your timing is perfect. I'm out of water and my feet are cramping so bad I can barely stand on them. I think I'm done for the day. Is there a place nearby where I can get some first aid stuff?"

"There's a pharmacy in Oromocto. I can take you there."

I humbly accepted his offer. I'm not sure what would have happened if he hadn't come along, but I was grateful that he did. He was every bit the friend Sharron said he was. I was disappointed to not see him again after he dropped me off.

Outside the pharmacy, I sat there for a while collecting my thoughts. Of all the things that could go wrong, I never considered my feet to be one of them. My knees yes, but not my feet. It was so painful to stand on them, that I didn't know how I was going to take another step.

Feeling discouraged, I walked with mounting frustration to the Days Inn. I needed some time to figure out what I was going to do next, before calling anyone.

That night, I chewed on Advil and had my own little pity party. My dream was being threatened and I didn't want to accept that it could be over. To me, that would equal failure.

However, new every morning was an opportunity for change. When sunrise comes, it's like getting a second chance for a comeback. You take it and you run.

While I was having breakfast, I saw someone with a baby stroller. That was it–I could trade in my backpack for a running stroller and get rid of the weight on my back. That would relieve the stress on my feet.

The wheels started spinning in my head. "Surely Fredericton would have something to meet my needs," I thought confidently. It was the spark I needed to re-ignite my enthusiasm and keep my hope alive.

"Don't ask for a light load,
but rather ask for a strong back."
– Anonymous

Hope is never really gone as long as you are willing to believe. "No more pity party," I said. Time to move to "Plan B" and at least make it as far as Ottawa. I could live with that.

Excited to continue, I dialed the number Madi gave me. After a couple of rings, a woman answered the phone.

"Hi Flo. It's Michelle the runner. Madi gave me your phone number."

"Thank God you're all right. We thought something terrible must have happened to you," Flo said with relief.

"No, I'm fine. Why would you think that?"

"Stan and I drove up and down the highway yesterday afternoon looking for you and when we didn't find you we started to worry. We thought we should have heard from you by now."

"Oh no! I'm so sorry Flo. I've had a rough couple of days and I spent the night in Oromocto. I should have called you sooner," I apologized.

"That's okay. I'm just glad you're all right. Where are you now?"

"I'm on my way out of Oromocto. It's going to get really hot today. Would you be able to pick me up around noon?"

"Of course. Where should we look for you?"

"I probably won't get much further than Fredericton so you don't want to go too far west. It's easy to miss me if I'm off the highway for any reason. However, I'll make sure I stay on the road around noon. You're sure it's okay?"

"Of course. We'll start looking for you then."

"Thank you Flo and again, I'm really sorry for not calling sooner."

"Not to worry. We'll pick you up later."

After hanging up the phone, I felt terrible for putting them through that and I was upset with myself. In the future, I needed to be more sensitive to the people trying to help me.

Under a hot sun, the reflection off the pavement made it feel as hot as you know what. High temperatures had swept the area and the heat was incredible out in the open. "Slow and steady Michelle," I kept telling myself.

It wasn't a very impressive run, but I managed to get passed the exit for Fredericton. By the time Flo and Stan found me, I don't think I could have taken another step. They had no idea what a relief it was for me to get off my feet. It puzzled me that my feet hurt more to walk on them than it did to run.

Once more, I apologized for being the cause of so much worry for them. They were so forgiving that it made me feel even worse. Before I could say another word, they kindly offered to bring me into town.

"We'd like to take you for lunch and if you need to pick up anything, we can drive you around," said Flo.

"That would be great. I could really use a new pair of shoes if there's a sports store nearby," I replied.

"Stan has to stop at the bank and I think there is one on the way. We'll drop you off and then come back to pick you up. After that, we'll go for something to eat."

It didn't take long before we were sitting in Subway having a sandwich. While we sat there eating, I asked them if they knew of any store that might carry running strollers.

"If I can find a stroller, I could push all my stuff instead of carrying it. I've been having some trouble with my feet and I think if I take the load off my back it will help," I said.

"That sounds like a good idea. There are a couple of stores we can try and later, I'll take a look at your feet," Flo said kindly.

So we began our search. The first two stores came up empty, but then we found the perfect fit at Ski Wolf. It was called "The Shuttle". Made to carry a small child, it had just enough room for all my stuff, with a little extra space for more water and food. The color even matched my flags.

Feeling immensely pleased with my find, my heart was encouraged. After forty days and running a thousand miles carrying a twenty-five to thirty pound backpack over some rugged terrain, I was relieved to give it up. The store supported me with a discount and receiving this kind of help, renewed my enthusiasm.

Fortunately, everything fit in Stan's car and we headed out of town to their home. There's nothing like being in the country to regenerate and renew your spirit. What a difference a day was making.

As we drove into their driveway, there were piles of wood to be stacked, new plants ready for planting lined up along the flowerbeds, and grass that needed to be cut. Being surrounded by greenery fed my love for nature and I savored every smell.

Inside, Mini and Charlie, their two rescued cats, greeted us. They loved it when people came to visit and were not shy to show their affection by rubbing their furry bodies up against my leg.

The kitchen table was covered with more plants. "I haven't got around to planting them yet," Flo said as she started to sort through them.

After I took a shower, I joined Flo and Stan in the basement where it was much cooler. The room was filled with collectables and I enjoyed looking around at everything.

"I just got off the phone with Madi. She had an accident the day she dropped you off," said Flo with concern in her voice.

"Oh no. What happened?"

"The feral cat she was trapping scratched her arm up pretty bad."

"That's terrible. Is she okay?"

"She's all right and resting. She'll be fine."

"Wow. Poor Madi. I remember she was pretty worried about that. Cat scratches can be nasty. I'm glad she's okay." However, I wondered what had gone wrong.

Stan had just finished cutting the grass when he came in. He was concerned about a bird nest he uncovered with the lawnmower.

"I didn't see the nest until it was too late and I'm afraid I exposed it and the babies," he said with great concern for them. "I tried to shield it again but I don't know if it worked. They may not be hidden well enough anymore from the cats." Stan felt bad and worried about it constantly.

I went to lie down for a short nap before dinner and woke up from the smell of Flo's cooking. We sat down to another wonderful homemade chicken dinner and afterward Flo took me for a personal guided tour of Fredericton.

Flo knew everything about the city's architecture and heritage. She fascinated me with stories about interesting patients she had cared for as a nurse before retiring. As we drove in and out of the streets, the view and nightlights were spectacular.

The tour ended at one of my favorite places - the DQ. We stopped for an ice cream treat and I enjoyed being in Flo's company. However, I could feel my head bobbing as I tried to stay awake. I was glad when she suggested we go home.

Sitting in her living room, Flo caringly examined my feet. She gently pampered them and I was moved by what she said. "If I had known sooner about your marathon, I would have traveled part of the way with you." My eyes welled up after hearing that.

Flo's treatment included filing down calluses, foot powder, some first aid stuff, two pairs of new socks and some tips for the road. All to enhance my foot comfort. By the time she finished, I was humbled by her compassion and selflessness. She was one of the kindest people I had ever met and her care was like a mother's love; it made everything feel better.

That night, I didn't recall falling asleep, but I remembered waking up and feeling refreshed. We loaded up the car and on our way to the highway, we stopped to pick up someone they knew. They reminisced about how their community had come together in the past to help families in their times of need. Something our world could use a lot more of.

Standing on the side of the highway again and saying good-bye was a lot harder than I thought it would be. "Thank you for all you've done," I managed to say as my eyes watered. The last words I heard were, "Take care of yourself."

As they drove away, their departure grieved me. I just stood there for a few minutes looking at all my stuff and wondering, "What is with the tears?" It was getting harder emotionally not to feel attached to people after being in their care. So much of my being out here hinged on their efforts and I needed them to survive. They were my lifelines.

In my pursuit for change, I had become my own casualty. Like a lost and found person, found by people who weren't looking for me and lost by people who were. "You have to pull yourself together Michelle," I said.

The Shuttle was my new running buddy. Although I thought it was pretty innovative, it put me closer to the danger I was trying to avoid. Wheels needed pavement and being so close to traffic, it made me more vulnerable to vehicles zooming by, sometimes within inches. All of a sudden, the possibility of getting hit by a car became more real to me. However, considering the alternative, I made the adjustment.

Running with a stroller was challenging at times. Pushing it up some of these hills was a workout in itself, like lifting weights. Going downhill, I had to constantly restrain it from getting away from me. There was some ease on flat stretches when I barely had to navigate her. Without the weight on my back, I felt light on my feet and I was making much better time.

King's Landing was my target and about half way there, a truck pulled up in front of me. A maintenance patroller from MRDC Operations Corporation had seen me a couple of times and decided to stop and ask me what I was doing out here.

"Where's your support vehicle?" said Tom.

"I don't have one," I answered.

"You're kidding me, right?" he said, astonished.

"No, there's just me."

Fascinated that I would do such a thing, he took my picture. He couldn't believe it. Once he found out I drank coffee, he said he'd be right back with a "double double". Sure enough, he returned from Tim Horton's and we sat on the tailgate of his truck, drinking our coffee. Before he drove off, I thanked him for his thoughtfulness and that he took the time to stop.

It was a beautiful day and breathing in the fullness of my natural surroundings stimulated my running pleasure once again. The skies were clear with not a single cloud in sight and being outdoors reminded me that everything is beautiful in its time. With seemingly less effort, I reached King's Landing and I was so encouraged that it restored my hope about making it to Ottawa.

There was a gas station and restaurant close to the information centre. It was lunchtime and I was hungry. Before I went inside, I met some interesting people. There were four young adults, two guys and two girls, filling up with gas. All at once, they all got out of the car to meet me. They were so full of energy that I could barely keep up with their questions.

"We saw you running on the highway. Are you doing this for a cause or something?"

"Has anyone ever run across the country without a support vehicle before?"

"You must be the first female to run across Canada?"

"Do you think you can make it?"

"You must be in great shape to do something like this. How did you train?"

"What's it been like?"

"Have you had any trouble?"

I think they were more excited about me running across Canada than I was. Their words of encouragement and support gave me a much-needed boost. Before they left, they shared the location of a secret swimming hole with me.

While I made my phone calls, I also met a couple of cyclists and other vacationers coming and going.

"Is there a baby in there?" they'd ask as they looked inside my stroller.

"No, there's no baby, just all my supplies," I assured them. It was kind of funny how many people thought I was running with a baby.

Overall, having a running stroller solved most of my problems. However, it also created some new ones. I couldn't leave it unattended and if I wasn't able to bring it inside with me, I had to make sure I kept it in sight.

After enjoying a meal, I explored the area for a place to camp. Near the information centre was King's Landing Historical Settlement, but it was closed. I strolled up and down the streets and came across some roof coverings in a field. It made a great shield from the road. Up went my tent and inside I went. All the while, taking in the fragrance of flowers in bloom.

With the remains of the day fading, I let out a sigh of relief to be resting. Except for some black fly bites, I was comfortable. "Maybe now my feet can recover," I hoped not knowing how much damage had been done.

The twilight I longed for and the quiet made for a peaceful night. One last kiss from the moonlight and I was fast asleep.

Sunrise broke my eyes at the crack of dawn and I was on the road early. With the gentle brush of cool air on what would be another hot day, I came across my first deer and then another one. These were moments that took my breath away and enhanced my joy. As I watched them run through the fields, I was awestruck by their beauty.

Someone told me once that I ran like a gazelle. "If only that were true," I thought. With feet like a deer, I'd cross this country in no time. Right now, I was just holding onto my running stroller, pleased she carried my load. She had become my new best friend and I was already yapping at her.

She heard all about my frustrations. There were the stubborn drivers who hogged the right lane when there was no oncoming traffic. Even with two lanes open, they stuck to the shoulder. It made me wonder if their hands were frozen to the steering wheel. If they ever hit me, it would probably be fatal.

However, even more annoying than that, were the pebbles in my shoes. It always baffled me how they got in there. I constantly had to stop and shake them out.

Meductic is a little village along the St. John River with a small population. I love little towns because life appeared so much simpler and slower there. People were usually friendly, open, and made you feel like family.

I stopped at the Irving gas station and went inside. There was a little café area where I sat down with a sandwich and a drink. The cashier was an older lady who was cautious with me at first. There were a few people that came and went. As I paid for my food, we struck up a conversation.

"The mayor lives in the house next door and if you knock, he would probably chat with you about your run," said the cashier.

"Great, I'll do that on my way out. Is there somewhere nearby that I could camp for the night?"

"There's a park just around the corner, next to the river. Kids play there, but it should be okay for you to put up a tent and no one should bother you."

"Great. Thanks for your help."

"Good luck to you."

I knocked on the mayor's door several times, but no one answered. Heading toward the park, I observed a playground on one side and a parking lot on the other. There were two small buildings, but they were locked. I put my tent behind one of them and out of sight. So I thought.

Lying there, I could hear children's voices boisterously yelling in the playground. Periodically, motorbikes used the parking lot to turn around in.

Sometime later, a car drove up. Three guys and a girl got out. Their behavior suggested they were drinking. When they spotted me, it suddenly became quiet. Then, rocks started shelling my tent like I was target practice. They continued laughing even after I shouted, "Hey stop it! There's someone in here and I'm coming out." By the time I put on my shoes and got out of the tent, they had run off on foot.

Relieved that I didn't get hit in the head with a rock, I decided it was time to move camp before they came back for the car. However, it was getting dark and it had started to rain. I had to move quickly.

Concerned about being on the road at dusk, I was glad I didn't have to go far when I came across a church and a house. The sign read "Meductic Baptist Church" and I thought this should be a safe place.

There was a light on and a car in the driveway. I walked up to the front door and knocked. A man and his wife answered.

"Can we help you?" asked Pastor Charles.

"Sorry to bother you, but I've run into some trouble," I said a little desperate.

"Oh? What kind of trouble?" he asked.

"I'm running solitary across Canada and I was camped at the park by the river. Some teenagers started throwing rocks at my tent. They ran off, but I didn't want any trouble. So before they came back, I packed up and left."

"Sometimes the kids party under the bridge, but they're usually pretty harmless," said Shirley.

"You have a huge yard. Would it be okay if I put my tent up somewhere in the back?"

"Come in out of the rain," Pastor Charles said considerately.

That invitation became my refuge for the night. Over a hot cup of tea, I shared my hopes and dreams with them. I found comfort in their words and a warm bed to sleep in. Once again, I thanked God for bailing me out of trouble.

Charles and Shirley had to get up early for a trip they were taking. They had two very curious cats and on my way out the door, they tried to hitch a ride in my stroller. Although I would have enjoyed their company, I had to leave them behind. I left there, grateful to my rescuers.

Under a gray ceiling, it was a pretty gloomy run to Woodstock. The highway was crowded and it was near impossible to avoid being splashed by cars and running through puddles.

When I finally arrived, I stopped at Leah's Salon for a much needed haircut. She took me without an appointment and I think she was glad because it took her away from some cleaning. I was a little short on cash and appreciated that she accepted what I had.

From there, I went to the public library to use a computer and I was encouraged by this message on my blog:

> *Julia said. . .*
> *Our thoughts and prayers are with you throughout your journey.*

The librarian contacted the local newspaper and they sent a couple of young reporters to meet with me. Even though I would be long gone before the article was published, I considered it another little victory for our companion friends. My night in Woodstock was uneventful and in the morning, I was anxious to move on.

Just west of the city, I came up against some strong headwinds and the winds of Newfoundland I remembered. As I ran up a long steep hill, a gust of wind hoisted my flag in the air and whisked it away. Without thinking, I let go of my stroller and chased after it. One quick jump up and I was able to grab it.

Turning back, I watched with shock as my stroller rolled down the side of the hill. At that same moment, a transport truck was passing by and the driver laughed while shaking his head. I just shrugged my shoulders and started laughing too. What else could I do?

After I picked it up and dusted it off, I resumed running. I ran and I ran, winding my way through New Brunswick's heartland.

While enjoying the natural beauty of the landscape, my eyes were drawn toward something out of place. It was a discarded beer bottle. Then, there was another one and another one, along with other trash.

In this setting, the ugliness of litter stood out like a giant stain on a freshly laundered shirt. It was a visual reminder that people's messes are not confined to cities. Ashamed of some of the things I saw, it frustrated me that people disregarded their responsibility to clean up after themselves. It really is a simple principle. If you make a mess, clean it up. It was disappointing to see so much litter on the side of the road.

The further inland I went, the less interested people seemed to be and mostly people just ignored me. Traffic was progressively getting heavier. I tried to remember the last time anyone waved or honked at me and I had to go all the way back to Matthew and Megan. Then, I smiled as I remembered their faces from the back of their van. It was comforting, if only for a moment.

On the days when no one else was around and I needed inspiration, somehow it was always there. These were times when the aesthetic side of me delighted in the stunning scenery I was discovering around every bend, or a landmark I wasn't expecting.

With the scenic backdrop of the St. John River Valley, I got a glimpse of Hartland's signature attraction. Amid the natural beauty of the country, was the longest covered bridge in the world, The Hartland Covered Bridge. Also nicknamed the "Kissing Bridge" or a "Wishing Bridge". It was another one of Canada's great treasures and historical sights. Its very existence revealed something about it and if you listened carefully, you could hear its whisper.

I continued west until I came upon the River Country Campground. It was located right off the highway and immediately became a place I adorned and could have easily disappeared in.

My campsite was situated close to the water, surrounded by pine trees and a breathtaking view. I enjoyed the exchange of conversation with seasoned campers and then a hot shower before crawling into bed.

With what was left of a gentle night, I savored the experience. Some things just can't be rushed. I held on to these incredible moments while I was in it, because they evaporated quickly.

Morning was coming and every day now looked like a giant. The odds of me going all the way were getting slimmer by the mile. Even if I could run like the wind, my chance for success would be next to impossible.

Carrying that reality added to my challenge. However, my endurance was inspired by hope for something better. Sometimes, holding on to that hope was like reaching out into the darkness. I could never be sure if I would get through, especially on days when I didn't feel up to the task.

Mile after mile, my battles grew bigger. In front of me was my Goliath and it felt like forever to reach my next destination. Baird Campground was several kilometers off the highway and not well marked. Every minute, gained or lost, was vital to my recovery time at the end of each run. Especially for my feet. It felt like I was walking on marbles.

When I finally arrived, the campground was more like a parking lot for RVs. "Not many people camp with tents anymore," they said. I was thankful to have a safe place for the night, but glad I didn't have to stay.

In the morning, I woke as I always did. The sun was rising and I packed up without eating. I stopped at the gas station along the river to grab a coffee and a pastry. The taste of my coffee did not disappoint me.

Before I continued, I paused to take in some of the peaceful sights and sounds of the early morning. Like a wind-blown leaf, or ripples running on the water. The beauty of my surroundings satisfied me. Then back over the bridge I went. It was a short climb up a hill leading to the highway.

Someone must have turned up the heat. The temperature rose quickly and it was almost unbearable. Halfway to my day's target, I came up to a big Irving gas station in Grand Falls. Instead of filling up with gas, I filled up with food.

Inside, I met a couple of friendly workers, Kevin and Richard. They took an interest right away and bubbled up lots of questions. However, an older man eavesdropping on our conversation made a disturbing remark. "They should make dog food out of all the strays," he said heartlessly on his way out.

I was sorry he felt that way and couldn't believe someone could say such an obscenity. "Thank God the destiny of animals are not in his hands," I said, troubled by his comment.

Then, Richard pulled me aside and asked, "Would you like to take a shower before you leave? We're only supposed to let truck drivers use the showers, but I can make an exception for you." Since I never knew when my next shower would be and that cooling off would be refreshing, I gladly accepted his offer.

While I was in the shower, Richard phoned a campground near St. Leonard. They confirmed it was open and gave him instructions. It was roughly another twenty kilometers away and I had already covered about thirty. Richard gave me the directions and his cell number in case of an emergency.

Feeling regenerated, I ran the distance and followed the signs to the campground. When I passed through some trees and entered the park, I thought I had hit the jackpot. It wasn't paradise, but compared to where I stayed the night before, it was sweet. Like my own little hideaway hidden from the world.

There were no other campers around and I selected what I thought was the perfect site along the Grande River's edge. The washroom was close by and I had my own picnic table. It was peaceful and the environment was just right for resting.

After a short nap, I woke up to find a fisherman sitting right in front of me. He was as quiet as a mouse. Under his hat was an aging face. It was picture perfect, with the water and shore for a backdrop.

"Have you caught anything?" I asked him while rubbing my eyes.

"Nope," he replied.

"Any bites?" I inquired after a brief pause.

"Nope."

"Have you seen anything?"

"Nope."

"Well, good luck," I said and fell back to sleep. When I woke up again, he was gone and I wondered if he had been there at all.

Later, the sun came to rest. The night was thick with sounds of crickets and frogs. I was almost beside myself with the thought of being home soon and how far I've run. Exhausted, I slept through the night till dawn.

The next day, I set out for the province of Quebec. My day's run began with encountering a baby moose. It was a precious moment I wished I could have bottled to take with me.

I saw him just off to the side of the highway. He was about the size of a small horse. "Wow. Would you look at that," I said, fixated. The sight of him fascinated me. I had never seen one in real life before.

Once he caught wind of me, he stood motionless in the overgrowth of brush. He tried "staring me down" as I approached him and I don't think he wanted to play. "Where's your mama?" I said as I stared back.

Getting within fifty feet of him, I moved cautiously forward blowing my emergency whistle several times. My whistle was my defense weapon of choice.

Finally, the mighty moose thrust its body and disappeared into the wooded darkness. "Stay away from the highway little one," I shouted as he ran away. Maybe our crossing paths prevented him from getting hit by a car.

The day was bright and beautiful and the sun was warm to my face. It was exciting to think I was almost through New Brunswick. After a stopover in Edmundston, I was thrilled about crossing the border into Quebec.

However, spoiling the moment was my brief encounter with an elderly man walking his dog near the town of St. Jacques. I waved, but he didn't wave back. His dog did what most dogs did and barked. I was appalled by the actions of his owner.

The man yanked the leash so hard that the dog tumbled a couple of times. He dragged him in the dirt to keep him moving. Remarkably, the dog didn't break his neck. However, the yelp that a dog makes when its hurt sent shivers down my spine. "Hey, how would you like it if I did that to you?" I snapped at him. The man just kept on going.

Seeing any act of cruelty always disturbed me and left a bitter taste in my mouth. "People like that shouldn't have pets," I thought as I tried to shake it off.

Visiting the information centres became a routine stop for me at towns and provincial borders. They were helpful in finding campgrounds and learning the status of any wildlife in the area. There were usually plenty of people to meet.

In Notre Dam du Lac, I was back on Eastern Daylight Time and welcomed an extra hour of sleep. As I continued to run, I started to sense how close I was getting to Quebec City. Knowing I would be with my parents soon kept me motivated. However, it was also making it hard for me to keep from getting over anxious.

At times, I could feel my heart racing a hundred miles an hour and pounding in my ears. I couldn't get there fast enough. It seemed the closer I was, the longer it was taking. At the end of the day, they might as well have been a million miles away. "Just stay in this day Michelle," I kept coaching myself.

Suddenly, I became aware of so many large dogs chained in their yards and how extremely agitated they were as I passed by. The exposure of their teeth as they barked was frightening and I thought if they ever got loose they would probably tear me to pieces. "Thank God for fences," I sighed.

I reached the edge of St. Antonin county and came up to a motel almost in the middle of nowhere. I stopped and asked the manager if I could setup my tent in the back for the night. She looked at me as if I was out of my mind. "We get lots of wild animals around here, but you can camp at your own risk," she said. I wasn't sure if she was referring to the four legged or two legged kind.

There was a gravel road between the motel and the bar restaurant, leading to the backyard. It extended from one end of the lot to the other. The grounds were rough and only cleared to the edge of the tree line. I picked a spot along the back wall of the motel and used it for some protection.

The day was but a shadow and night had fallen. Sometime later, I woke up to the sounds of footsteps approaching my tent. Instantly, the hair on my body stood on end. Overwhelmed with fear, I was suddenly reminded of my fragile existence.

Sensing the presence of danger, my heart began pounding as if it was going to leap out of its place and run off. I lay still, but my imagination ran wild as I thought of the seriousness of my situation. Closing my eyes, I began to pray. "God help me."

Whoever it was stopped for a few minutes. Then, for some reason, they turned around and walked away. They didn't return and I felt the fear that had crept back into my mind begin to subside. It was the longest few minutes of my life. I tried not to think the worst, but that was way too close for comfort.

Thank God for His mercy and nothing bad happened. However, it cautioned me that disaster could strike at any time. I wasn't invincible. The only reason I could go back to sleep was because I believed God was protecting me.

In the morning, when I thought about what could have happened, I was a little shaken. Quickly, I finished eating and I was happy to leave that place.

I made a westerly swing past Riviere-du-Loup, but it wasn't without incident. Just before the junction, a downpour snuck up suddenly and I had to sprint a few kilometers to get to a rest stop for shelter. I was soaked by the time I got there and chilled from being wet. As far as rest stops went, this was the "cream of the crop". There was a sitting area and a pay phone.

While I waited out the storm, I called my sister.

"Angel, you'll never guess where I am right now," I laughed almost hysterically. Maybe I was losing my mind from being on the road too long, but just the idea of being stuck in a washroom made me laugh.

"Wherever it is, it sounds like a lot of fun," said Angel.

"I'm at a rest stop and it's pouring rain."

"Oh no! What are you going to do?"

"I might be stuck here for the night if it doesn't stop."

"Well at least you're out of the rain."

"Yeah, but it reminds me of a movie scene where someone gets stranded after their car breaks down and then gets murdered by a serial killer."

"Well, at least the phone is working and you can call 911," Angel laughed.

"No way; I'm making a run for it as soon as the rain lets up," I said convincingly.

That's what watching too many thrillers and horror movies does to a person. There was no way I wanted to be here alone at three in the morning. Not with so many shady characters coming and going. Thankfully, the rain cleared long enough for me to make a run for it.

From there, cyclists and pedestrians were prohibited from being on the main highway. As soon as I made the loop, a patrol officer stopped me. "You can't go any further," he said. "You have to turn around and go back."

Once I explained myself, he suggested Highway 132 but it would be several miles for me to back track and switch roads. He kindly drove me to the junction in his police cruiser. It wasn't the police escort I had envisioned.

Highway 132 was an alternate route that followed along the St. Lawrence River. It was a rough road with little shoulder on either side. Often, I had to pull over and wait for cars to pass as the two-way traffic left little room for all of us.

At the St. Alexander junction, I climbed a hill to get to the gas station. Off to one side was a parking lot and motel rooms. There was an area amongst the trees where I could put my tent. I went to have a closer look and then followed the roar of running water. There was a stream nearby and I settled in just above it. I could tell I wasn't the first to be here.

The night was long, with strong winds and rain that lasted well into the morning. I was pleased to have a washroom nearby and I enjoyed meeting travelers inside. It was close to noon before the weather cleared.

Returning to the junction for Highway 132, I watched as a young man on rollerblades cruised up to me. There was a camper following close behind him.

"Hello there," I said.

"Hello. I'm Rich Ralph," he said as he slowed down.

"What brings you out here?" I asked.

"I'm rollerblading across Canada for cancer. Those are my parents in the camper."

"Wow. That's quite a trek. It must be nice having your parents with you and a support vehicle."

"He had to bring his mother along to cook his meals and wash his clothes," Rich's mom laughed.

"Where did you start?" I asked.

"St. John's NL and I'm going all the way to Vancouver," Rich answered.

"Good for you and it looks like you're well equipped for it," I said.

"We have a computer, cell phone, camera, food, and everything he needs. Where's your support vehicle?" asked Rich's dad.

"I don't have one. It's just me."

"You're running across Canada without a support vehicle? That's amazing! Can we take a picture of you with Rich?"

"Sure."

As we stood posing for the picture, I asked Rich how his journey was going so far.

"It's been great although this road is a little rough. Good thing there's not a lot of traffic," he said, displeased.

"Have you had much media coverage?" I asked.

"Easterners were great but we're not having any luck in Quebec."

"Same here," I said.

Before they left, they kindly gave me some water and fruit. We wished each other safe travels and I watched as they disappeared over the horizon. Although it was a pleasure meeting them, it made me feel isolated and alone again. A traveling companion would have been nice.

Shortly after that, I encountered two male cyclists heading east. They had trailers attached to their bikes for hauling their equipment and they were dressed like road warriors. I was glad they decided to stop.

"Hello there, where are you guys headed?" I inquired.

"I flew from St. John's Newfoundland to Kingston to ride with my friend here back to St. John's. Then he's going on to Africa," the first cyclist said.

"I'm trying to raise funds for education in Africa," said the other cyclist.

"He's leaving me behind in St. John's when we get there," the first cyclist laughed and then added. "I saw you in Newfoundland before I flew to Kingston."

"Really? What are the odds of us running into each other out here?"

"I also met a female cyclist named Christie going across the country. She had an accident and her bike needed some repairs. She was okay, but I lost track of her after that."

"What a small world. I met her near Gambo, Newfoundland when she passed me on the highway. I wondered how she was doing. Did you see the young guy on rollerblades?"

"Yes we did and stopped to chat with him. He covers a lot of ground on his blades," the first cyclist said.

The cyclists appeared to get along well with each other and they made me laugh more than once.

"Do you guys always have this much fun?" I asked.

"You gotta have fun and enjoy life," the first cyclist smiled.

"You should get a bike. It would be a lot easier and faster, and, someone to go with," said the other cyclist.

"Maybe I'll try that next time," I responded. Then, we wished each other safe travels and went our separate ways.

The landscaping along the river was captivating. However, most of the villages were too far off the highway for me to get to. I had little contact with people until a beat up old van passed by. He didn't pull over right away, which led me to believe he must have thought about it before he decided to stop.

As I got closer, all I could see was an arm covered with tattoos hanging out the window. There hadn't been a lot of traffic and as I looked up and down the highway; I couldn't see anything or anyone for miles. This was that scenario where parents tell their children not to stop and talk to strangers. Or the scene in a movie when you know the girl is going to get it.

I'm not sure what the statistics are, but I think violent crimes to women traveling alone happen every twenty-two seconds in North America. My being abducted, assaulted and/or killed was always a real danger. However, I tried to keep things in perspective.

The driver had dark hair tied in a ponytail and his appearance could easily give anyone the wrong impression. He waited until I reached him before saying anything, "What are you running for?" he asked.

My thoughts quickly tried to assess my situation and reason with myself that most people have a soft spot for animals. I knew enough French to be understood and I think he appreciated my effort.

As he responded, there was gentleness in his voice and a kindness in his eyes that put my mind at ease. He told me how much he loved his dog and wouldn't give him up for anything. Then, he handed me a donation and drove off.

A few minutes later, he returned to tell me about a breeder nearby who had beautiful White Mountain dogs. "If you would like to see the puppies, I could take you and bring you back," he offered. Anyone who loves animals couldn't be that dangerous I thought. I gladly hopped in his van and closed the door.

Inside, the floor was littered and the back of the van was empty. Relying on a total stranger to treat me well was a risk, but at this moment it was one I was willing to take. Under normal circumstances, I wouldn't put myself in such a vulnerable position, but this was different. I prayed he was the good man I thought he was.

He backtracked a few miles and then turned off the highway. Driving up a dusty road, I was relieved to see the breeder's house. Stepping out of the van, the panoramic view was breathtaking and perfect in beauty. From up here, it was a wider view than from any other point in the area. We could see for miles in any direction at the gently rolling terrain, broken with farming and wooded sections. It was all parallel to the river.

Then, I was struck with delight at the sight of several dogs. They were all white except for their black eyes and nose. "What beautiful creatures," I said in awe. After a few minutes, they brought out the most adorable puppies I had ever seen. We watched them, entranced by their playing as they chased each other all over the yard. This was another one of those unexpected pleasures.

After a few minutes, my attention shifted to the breeder who commented on a recent article in the Montreal newspaper. It was about crowded animal shelters. This is an excerpt from that write-up:

> *Mon Jun 4, 2007*
> *Animal shelter packed with abandoned pets as Quebec July 1 moving day looms*
> *By Nelson Wyatt*
>
> *"Cats are piling up," says Pierre Barnoti, executive director of Montreal's Society for the Prevention of Cruelty to Animals as he surveys his feline charges in the society's west-end headquarters.*

The tabby tide is being blamed on Quebec's annual July 1 moving day, when the province becomes the one part of the country where moving vans outnumber Canada Day parade floats.

In 1973, Quebec law was amended to make all leases end on July 1, presumably to prevent families' lives from being disrupted by moving during the school year.

Besides resulting in a cacophony of straining, grunting movers, the July 1 moving day also means a flood of animals being dropped off at shelters or being left to fend for themselves.

Recent arrivals at the SPCA have jumped to 60 to 80 animals per day from about 20 to 30 animals per day - about 65 percent of them cats.

"Montreal landlords are extremely difficult in accepting people with pets," lamented Barnoti. "I believe in Ontario it is forbidden to discriminate against pet owners. In Quebec, it is practically a standard clause in every lease - no pets allowed.

"A lot of people who have given notice to move discover they cannot find a dwelling that will take their pets so the animals are sadly dumped at the SPCA."

In previous years, moving vans have even made pit stops at the shelter to drop off animals.

But Martin Messier, a spokesman with the Quebec Landlords Association, acknowledges many landlords don't allow pets but that trend has some roots in how people look after their furry friends.

"You have to understand that when (the landlord) does accept pets the problem is never the pet itself, the problem is with the owner of the pet," says Messier, who is himself a pet owner.

Sometimes when pets are left alone, they disturb other tenants, he said. As well, owners do not properly clean up after them when they take them outside in some cases.

Messier also pointed out landlords tell people of their pet policies before they sign their lease.

"You can still shop and find units where you have the right to have animals," he said. "This is still available."

Barnoti says the SPCA scrambled to accommodate new arrivals this year and quickly pressed 300 foster families into service. A mobile home is being brought in to handle more cages.

"But we know it's a very short-lived reprieve before we are flooded again."

So far it's mainly cats and dogs. In the past the SPCA has had to deal with exotic critters like parrots and iguanas - and even a black panther. The organization spent $14,000 to save the sleek jungle cat, whose owner had its teeth pulled and claws removed. He decided the big cat wasn't for him when it urinated on his sofa. It now lives in a zoo.

Barnoti acknowledges there's still a lot of educating to do about pet ownership. The amazement is still evident in his voice when he recounts the tale of the man who came in and wanted to rent a dog for two weeks to amuse his children on a camping trip. The man left the SPCA empty handed.

People have to realize that they're in for a long-term commitment when they adopt an animal because the animal will always be dependent on the owner.

"If you are not prepared to devote the time, the energy, do not adopt," he said, pointing out the stress of abandonment can cause 75 percent of an animal's immune system to shut down and make it sick.

The factors that contribute to the problem are many and there are more questions than answers. Why do we allow pet owners to give up animals so easily? Whatever happened to preserving life? How many animals have to suffer or die needlessly before people realize we are the problem?

By the time I put up my tent in the campground of Riviere-Ouelle, it was dark. Tall pine trees and an overcast sky surrounded me. My walk from the shower back to my tent was like walking through a black hole. Without a flashlight, I could have walked into anything. Somehow, I managed to find my way without hurting myself.

Before entering my tent, I always shook it and brushed myself off to remove any unwanted hitchhikers: bugs. It was another sleepless night with heavy rains and rolling thunder. Keeping me motivated was the thought of being in Quebec City in three days.

Over the next two nights, I stayed at Camping des Aulnaies and then Montmagny where I met a young cyclist camped beside me.

"Hello," I said.

"Hi, I'm David," he replied with a heavy French accent.

"Where are you headed?" I asked.

"I go to Gaspe and come back to Montreal. What about you?"

"I left St. John's April 15 and I hope to get to Vancouver before winter. I didn't realize there were so many people who biked the highway."

"Yes, lots of bikes. It's not my first time I go to Gaspe. I go every year."

"Have you had any troubles?" I asked him.

"Some drivers come too close and run me off the road a few times. But I wouldn't change my way. You should get a bike, it goes faster."

"That's what people keep telling me."

Talking with another road warrior who understood what it was like to be out here was comforting. It was a small circle of people who traveled the highway in this way and I was one of them. Up until now, I had no idea we existed.

Under the shade of a small tree, I slept. The distant night gave way to another early sunrise.

Levis, QC - June 9

Finally, after anxiously waiting for this day, it had come. My destination was a small town across the water from Quebec City. The thought of being with my parents was all the motivation I needed to get me there. Conditions for running were perfect. All systems were a go and my sight was locked on Levis.

As I ran, my heart beat so fast that it felt like I had a drummer pounding on it. My mind picked up speed with every step. Remarkably, my resistance to pain increased and nothing about my body hurt.

I was no longer conscious of myself running and kicked into automatic pilot. Completely oblivious of my surroundings, the terrain passed me unnoticed. It was as though I had tunnel vision and everything around me zoomed out. I was so stimulated I ran on pure adrenaline for thirty-eight miles.

However, it was not without effect. The trip down from such a high was going to play havoc with my emotions. It was either going to be a positive or a negative reaction and so far on this journey, I've experienced both.

With the sun still high in the sky, I stopped to call my mom. "Hi mom, I made it to Levis," I said excitedly.

"You're in Levis? Hang on and let me get your father. You know me, I'm no good with directions."

My dad was working in his shed and I could hear my mom shouting at him. Then he picked up the receiver.

"Michelle, you're already in Levis?" he said, surprised.

"Yep, I made it."

"And in record time. We weren't expecting you for another couple of days."

"Well, I couldn't wait to get here, so I just kept running. If it wasn't for my achy feet, I think I would have run all the way to Montreal today."

"Well, we'll take a drive and meet you. Where will you be?"

"I'll be at the Comfort Inn at the main exit for Levis; they allow pets there."

"Okay. We'll leave first thing in the morning after we pick up Angel and we'll bring Buddy too."

Buddy was a little Bishon and I called him my little "bro". We joked about how they had replaced their kids with a dog.

"That's great dad. I can't wait for you to get here."

"We should be there by noon."

"I'll be waiting," I assured him.

When I got off the phone, I don't know why, but I began to cry. Things that didn't normally make me well up with tears did now and for no reason. I think I was feeling the effects of a mild depression. After such an intense effort to surge here, I crashed and I was completely drained from elevated levels of emotion.

Pushed to the point of exhaustion, my body moaned most of the night and it wasn't the restful sleep I was hoping for.

In the morning, I spent some time on the guest computer. At first, I was thrilled with the new messages I read.

> *June 1*
> *Hi Michelle: sorry I missed your call last night. You sounded really good. Please do call me again when you have a chance. The Ottawa group has a few questions I need to ask you. All the best, Dorit*

Followed by:

> *Just occurred to me - I can pose the q's here and you can think about them and get back to me when you can:*
>
> 1. *They're wondering if you have any plans for Montreal - they would like to give you a police escort as you go through.*
> 2. *We're looking at 12:00 noon on the 25th for the rally on Parliament Hill - OK?*
> 3. *They're wondering if you would like to visit a couple of high schools while you're in Ottawa.*
> 4. *How long will you be in Ottawa?*

Can you imagine the lift it gave me to learn some rescue shelters in Ottawa wanted to get involved? Everything was progressing well until I read this message. It was a setback, but I was encouraged to hear about other options.

> *June 1*
> *I missed your call last night. And I need to talk to you. I was wiped out, went to bed early. Ottawa is not working out. Because of preparations for Canada Day, no rallies on Parliament Hill will be allowed that week or the weekend before. The Ottawa group has several options that I need to talk to you about. I'm so sorry that I turned my cell phone off.*
> *Dorit*

> *June 5*
> *Hi Ladies:*
> *I talked to Michelle twice today. First time, I gave her the news and the options. We talked but I encouraged her to think about it and get back to me. She called me later in the afternoon and here's what she would like to do:*

Re: Ottawa - hold a media conference and that's basically all - on the 25th at or around noon. So that would require booking some public place - not too large - to which the media can easily come. For this, we probably don't need a banner, just three flagpoles to display her flags. She also would be delighted to speak to High School groups anywhere. She will be staying a couple of days in Ottawa since that is her home.

Montreal - Her parents are going to meet her in Quebec City and then sort of hang with her until Montreal. They will not be driving with her but catching up with her in Montreal again. Montreal is their home. She has been bounced off the TransCanada Highway onto Hwy 132. Apparently nothing but cars and trucks are allowed on this stretch. A police escort in Montreal would be most welcome, especially if they can escort her through Montreal to Hwy 20. As I'm checking the notes I took while speaking with her, and looking at a map of Montreal, it's not clear to me. Anyway, she has a preferred route that apparently might be easier if she has police escort. Most likely you all know what she's talking about better than I. She is in Quebec right now and finding drivers VERY unfriendly. She's anxious for a brief time with family and friends.

Hope that helps.
Dorit

Coordinating a media conference in Ottawa wasn't without its challenges. However, the ideas were flowing and full of possibilities.

June 6
Hi Dorit,

Here are two suggestions where Michelle could hold a press conference in Ottawa:

1) The Charles Lynch Room, Centre Block, Parliament Hill
Details: LLC can have a maximum of 7 LLC members/supporters in the room (including Michelle) - so the good thing is that we wouldn't have to worry about low numbers
-advanced passes would be needed for each of the invitees
-Michelle and the other 6 invitees would have to go through a security check (this is done for anyone visiting the Parliament Buildings)
-it's free of charge
-unlimited number of journalists can attend
-stationary camera for CPAC - the parliamentary access channel, which would be seen in MP's offices and journalists offices
-30 minute maximum for the room - Michelle could talk for 5-10 minutes and then the floor would be opened to questions

Contact person is Joyce (sorry, I don't have a last name) at phone: 613-992-4511 or fax: 613-995-5795

2) Press Gallery, 150 Wellington Street (across the street from the Hill)
Details: it has to be booked by a Member of Parliament, who then has to host the press conference - I can't remember if you do not want to involve an MP at this time; if this isn't a problem, who is the MP who is pushing the new anti-cruelty bill? (sorry, I have forgotten his name)

-Michelle and as many LLC members/supporters can attend
-will have to go through security, but I don't think that advanced passes are required - need to confirm
-the positive thing about this space is that many journalists have their offices at 150 Wellington so it makes it even easier for them to attend

My partner, Len, who has organized many press conferences recommends that you try holding the press conference by 10:30-11:00 is often the best time to hold one so that media can carry the story at noon, and then it will hopefully be picked up in the 6 pm and 11 pm news.

If you decide to go with one of these venues, Len also suggests that LLC call or fax the request. If needed, I am happy to be a contact person but I will not be in town for the actual event. Len says there are several flags in the room, but he doesn't know if there are extra poles. When you call or fax, be sure to say that you would like to put up several flags.

Press Kits:
-I am still prepared to put these together and deliver them to the media the week before the press conference. I will need:

1. *if possible, several good photos of Michelle on the road or meeting supporters in communities in Canada*
2. *any good newspaper stories/press clippings to demonstrate that this is an important story that the media should cover*
3. *you sent us a previous media release - I will make sure that I can copy and paste the LLC logo for an Ottawa release*
4. *any letters of endorsements*

5. *if possible, a statement from Michelle about her Ottawa visit - if she can't send one, I will prepare one*
6. *info on the draft legislation/private members for the anti-cruelty bill?*

As soon as I have the press release ready, I will send it to you for your approval.

We should put out a media advisory about a week in advance (Who, What, Where, When) to let journalists know that Michelle will be arriving in Ottawa for the 25th.

In terms of my schedule, I just found out that I have to research and write a fairly large presentation for first thing Monday morning. As a result, I am going to be busy with this over the weekend - there is no way that I'll be able to finish it by Friday.

Therefore, in terms of my commitment I can help organize the press conference and media releases, but I don't have time to organize school presentations. Is there anyone else involved with LLC from the Ottawa area who could arrange school talks?

As for the Montreal leg of Michelle's marathon, I am also unable to assist with this part. However, my friend who has the amazing email media list covers Montreal journalists.

I hope that one of these two venues meets Michelle's approval, and that they are available on the 25th. If they are OK with her, I would send a request to book them immediately. If they aren't OK, I don't know what else to suggest. I don't think that any community centres would be appropriate and if the conference is held mid-day, the numbers of supporters probably won't be that great.

I'm heading out for a few hours and will check my email later this evening.

Thanks,
Beth

This was the last correspondence I read before meeting my parents. Seeing them again was like eating comfort food that is so good and familiar–you can't help but smile. Having their arms wrapped around me was like a security blanket and I didn't want to let go.

"You've lost a lot of weight," my sister Angel said after hugging me.

"Look at you, there's nothing left of you," my mom said in shock.

"Well, there's not much fat on me, but I'm in the best shape of my life. If it wasn't for my feet, I think I could run around the world. But don't worry mom, I'm not planning on doing that," I laughed.

Sitting around just caused my body to complain and I needed to keep moving. We spent some time at the river, walking along the waterfront and watching boats go by. Gazing across at the magnificence of downtown Quebec City, it was a city of contrast, with old and new buildings jostled side by side.

Being together was just what the doctor ordered. However, there was also something surrealistic about it. It felt like I was in a dream and could wake up at any moment and they would be gone.

On our way back to the motel, we picked up Chinese food and ate in our room. Then, we sat outside for a while and met a friendly couple from Ontario. They were walking their two dogs.

"We're on our way to Moncton for a holiday," the woman said.

"My daughter just came from there. She's running across Canada by herself and she's doing it without a support vehicle. We're up from Montreal to spend the day with her," my dad said proudly.

"I'm trying to raise awareness about the overpopulation problem with cats and dogs in our country and that prevention is better than euthanizing for animal control," I said.

"Wow. That's a great cause. It's terrible how people treat animals," responded the woman.

"I think our country can do a much better job of handling the surplus with prevention," I replied.

"I wish our country would do something about the puppy mills. It's horrifying what those animals go through," said the woman.

"There are lots of issues, but it's like opening a can of worms that no one wants to touch," Ii said.

"Well, good luck the rest of the way and our pets thank you."

"You too. Enjoy your trip out east."

Once they left, we moved back into our room for some card games. While playing, a funny story happened over eating some cheeses. Out of the blue, my dad seriously looked at my sister and said, "If you eat two at a time, it'll go faster."

There was a pause for a second and then we all cracked up over that one. We laughed so hard it was painful and brought us to tears. From there, it just got worse and at times we were out of control. We couldn't say a word without bursting into laughter.

Being with them was the medicine I needed. With lots of laughing and TLC, I was happy they were here. It was a time of renewal in ways that mattered and I had a sense of belonging that comes from being part of a family. In difficult times, it is so important to have family bonding because they help you get through some of the tough stuff.

After the lights went out, we continued talking for a while. Then Angel said goodnight and she was going to say her prayers. That prompted me to ask my parents an important question.

"Do you believe in God?"

"Yes," they both answered and I was glad.

"Me too," I said, "and I've started reading the Bible."

"I don't know if I believe everything in the Bible," said Angel.

"Why not? It's the Word of God," I responded.

"Yeah, but it was written by people."

"But they were inspired by God and they couldn't have known these things any other way," I acknowledged.

Silence filled the room and eventually everyone fell asleep, except for me. As I lay there in my own thoughts, I listened to the sound of their breathing. Even Buddy was snoring, but I didn't mind. For fifty-eight days, I could never be sure this moment would ever happen. I reflected on every night I spent alone in my tent when I missed my family terribly. There were moments when I would have given anything to be cradled in my parents' arms. Right now, I just wanted to hug them and tell them I loved them.

The next day, we tried to drag out the morning as long as we could, but our time together went as quickly as it came.

"Are you sure you don't want to come home with us?" my mom asked.

"It's tempting, but I have to finish this," I said.

"Okay. If you're sure that's what you want."

"I'm sure."

They knew me well enough to know that once I had my mind made up about something, there was no talking me out of it.

"Call us when you get to Montreal and we'll pick you up," said dad.

"As long as the weather stays good, I should be there in four or five days."

"Take care of yourself and be careful. We love you," Mom said.

"I love you too. See you in a few days," I said as we exchanged hugs.

Traffic along this section of the highway was much heavier. It was progressively getting more dangerous. There were stretches of road without any shoulder and my running stroller didn't push well in gravel. The most annoying thing of all was constantly picking stones out of my shoes. I was not enjoying my environment and I couldn't be happier when I reached the town of Deschaillons.

The night before, I stayed at the Ste-Croix campground. It was so overcrowded with people trying to escape the heat in the city that campers were crammed into every empty space. Today, I was hoping for a quieter refuge.

For some reason, I was drawn to the Motel de la Rive. The setting of cabins next to the river lured me inside the office to have a look around. I started talking with the owner, Claude, and I was stunned when he offered to give me a cabin for the night at no charge.

Shortly after being in my room, I heard a knock at the door. It was Claude and he had a tray in his hands. On it was a plate of food and a drink.

"I thought you might be hungry," he said kindly.

"Wow. Thank you so much Claude. How much do I owe you?"

"Nothing. Enjoy your meal," he smiled and then left. I couldn't believe it.

After taking a refreshing shower, I sat outside on a swinging chair overlooking the St. Lawrence River. The rays from the sun warming my face. It was peaceful and quiet. I spent some time reflecting and my thoughts drifted between being at home soon and the lack of interest by the public. The feeling I had was much like the feeling you get when someone forgets you.

Back in my room, Claude surprised me again with a great meal and then another in the morning. It is humbling to be the recipient of such generosity that stems from someone's heart. There are no words to describe it.

I don't know if Claude realized it or not, but he was a tremendous encouragement to me. The valleys came at night and as low as I felt, his kindness lifted me up. He didn't ask for anything in return and it reminded me of every helping hand I'd been given on this journey. I was deeply grateful to him and would never forget my stay here.

Quebec was famous for aggressive drivers. Most of the time, I don't think they paid attention to what they were doing. People were passing cars before hills and corners. The worst part was that if anything ever happened, it would probably be fatal. There wasn't much room for oncoming traffic, let alone me. As traffic intensified, I had my share of near death experiences.

Arriving at St. Gregoire, I had to take a detour along a bike path to get around the Ville of Becancour. It wasn't well marked and I had to guess my way through the countryside. Then through some construction under the bridge to Trois Riviere, which took what felt like forever.

The information centre was helpful in finding me a campground. It was one of the few that allowed pets. The owners, Rolland and Terese, had a dog of their own. They didn't charge me for camping and said, "It's terrible how people mistreat animals in this province."

Some curious campers came over to talk while I setup camp. Their reaction was either shock or disbelief. Few people knew how to respond to this kind of passion. Once their curiosity was satisfied, they left me to myself. Snuggled in my sleeping bag, I fell asleep to the crackling sounds of a campfire.

The next morning I slept in and through most of the miles I ran. Before I knew it, I was in Pierreville trying to find another campground. It wasn't well marked and I stopped to ask for directions. There was an older man cleaning his soft-top camper trailer in his yard. "Bonjour," I shouted.

At the sound of my voice, his bulldog ran out from behind the camper, tail wagging.

"Don't worry. He won't bite you," the man said as his dog began licking my hands and legs.

"He's quite friendly, that's good. What's his name?" I asked.

"His name is Gambi and my name is J.P."

"Nice to meet you Gambi," I said and then wiped his saliva on my shirt before shaking J.P.'s hand. "My name is Michelle and I think I might be lost."

"Where are you going?" J.P. asked.

That question translated into a conversation and friendship I wasn't expecting. We sat outside on his patio talking and a glass of cold water turned into wine and pizza. J.P. didn't speak English and my French improved with the more wine I drank.

Mostly he talked about Gambi, his best friend. "I don't know what I would do without him," he kept saying as he wiped up more of Gambi's saliva off the deck. "He comes with me camping and I wouldn't go without him." J.P. was retired now and tomorrow they were leaving on another trip.

Nighttime swept in and I never did get directions to the campground. I was in no condition to walk and J.P. kindly invited me to stay in his camper for the night. "Make yourself at home," he said with glossy eyes and a grin from ear to ear.

Not long after J.P. went inside, I could hear the sweet sound of music coming from the house. Without any effort, I fell asleep listening to inspirational native songs.

The morning after, we both got off to a rough start. Feeling the effects from the night before, I quietly said goodbye to J.P. and then sluggishly made my exit. I ran in the heat thinking, "I should have stopped after two glasses."

Suddenly, it dawned on me what day it was. At the end of this one, my parents would be picking me up once I reached the edge of Montreal. Suffering from cumulative fatigue, I was ready for some TLC and a campground was a perfect place to relax.

It would have been more exciting except I was trying not to get myself killed on the way there. "These drivers are insane," I grumbled under my breath. They weaved in and out of traffic with no regard for the safety of others.

I almost didn't make it when a truck pulling a long high and wide trailer brushed up against my shoulder. "That was way too close," I thought as my life flashed before my eyes. I was more than happy to reach Sorel-Tracey and get off the suicidal road.

Sitting in the van with my parents once again was another surrealistic moment. I had to pinch myself a few times to make sure I was really present. It had been less than a week since I saw them, but my emotional roller coaster ride made it feel so much longer.

Heading north, we took the Terrebonne exit. Driving along the river road, we passed by our old house and my dad slowed down so we could get a good look at it. Selling it was part of their retirement plan when they became empty nesters. Now, they spend winters south of the border and summers at their favorite campground nearby, Camping au Plateau.

As we drove through the gates, the owners waved. Friends of my parents came by to express their congratulations and support. I think my Dad had done some bragging.

After a time of socializing, I jumped on the computer to update my blog and to catch up on any messages.

> *Hi Michelle, just wanted to say that we're all proud of you and keep it up. Just so you know Karine came in second place last week in the provincial games. Well you really are going all out for this cause, but you're the person to do it because when it comes*

to determination you got an overdose of it. Well Michelle keep it up, and we will be watching for you. Don't forget we all love you, bye for now.
Marcel

Well done. You have marched your cause through 5 Canadian provinces. . .we will look for you when you cross into Ontario,
KYHU
The Octostars

Then, I read a series of messages between the Ottawa group and Dorit. At this point, I think it's important to introduce the Ottawa group. Joanne, of JazzyJo Havenly Felines, is also known as Jo. She runs a cat shelter outside of Ottawa. I met Jo before I left for St. John's. More about that later. She offered to help in any way she could and contacted Beth and Heather, who are also involved in animal rescue. I was disappointed to learn of a crisis that had been brewing.

Four days ago, Jo sent a message to Dorit and copied the rest of us.

Hello Dorit,

After speaking with Michelle on Sunday night, and given the limited time we have left to do anything at all, and, Beth's intense work schedule with a sick partner to tend to, I decided this morning to write to Talk Ottawa. It was through my contact at Rogers Cable TV that he received all the info and e-mails which describes Michelle's plight.

Michelle said she would call me Saturday upon arriving in Montreal. However in light of this interview which is a sure thing, I am hoping that if she contacts you beforehand would you ask her to please call me due to the other interviews I would like to book:

a) Nicole Joncas is contacting CJAD tomorrow and will let me know if they will interview Michelle in Montreal (it can be taped).

b) I must call the local newspaper here and must know the exact time she will arrive here at my shelter and MUST NOW advise Talk Ottawa to send their camera crew when she arrives so to do this I must talk to Michelle; she said she was flexible from Saturday on for whatever interviews are planned.

c) I have had a very difficult time re inquiring for any type of police escort; I spent 2 hours on the phone with the Quebec and Ontario Ministry of Transportation yesterday as well as speaking with 8 or 9 different police detachments; apparently Michelle CANNOT run on Highway such as the 40 or 20 and they suggested to take a parallel route BUT I must talk to Michelle as I have to request an escort for wherever and whichever distances by various detachments. This seems almost impossible for me to coordinate at this time but would like to let Michelle know about this now so that we can schedule those VIP interviews.

d) Can you please confirm if you yourself will be in Ottawa for this Talk Ottawa show and/or you might wish to send them a media release, however they do have all of the pertinent information I believe.

e) I would like to then ask Beth if she has time, before she leaves this weekend, to send out a general press release for you as her list is extensive; also she has direct contacts with reporters of the Ottawa newspapers therefore would you please write Beth or send a press release to her for this now and copy to me, if this is 'kosher' with you as she mentioned to me that she needed a few days to do this. (Flash: Beth just wrote and said she would do this now - is that o.k??) She will probably not answer tonite as she is off to bed.

f) Given the time and this interview and possibly a few more (will try BOB FM in Ottawa) and CJOH TV, I believe we have enough and will not pursue further re high school talks as this also is not feasible due to exams now and students leaving after they write.

g) I would also ask Michelle now if she wishes to visit the Petstore/SOSCAT/DOG SPAY/NEUTER contact in Montreal while she is there and maybe we can have her interviewed by CJAD there; Sylvie, the store owner and founder of the program is agreeable to this but of course she would like some advance notice to prepare her time/employees etc.

*h) Michelle had also indicated she would like to visit one of my vets *(who does not euthanize healthy pets) located nearby and must set a time with this very busy vet and also get that local newspaper to cover the story.*

Hoping that this is some good news. I will negotiate with the local newspaper also, (I have met the owner) to cover the story. I will do anything to continue to help with this project and know that I am going out on a thin limb.

Regards,
Jo
P.S. Heather is out of town until Friday late and gone again on the 24th.

Jo then sent this email to the host of Talk Ottawa.

Dear Mr. Hendricks,

Let Live Canada, a national animal welfare organization focused on raising awareness re the importance of spaying and neutering companion animals, would like to request an interview at your studios in Ottawa on June 25th or June 26th, 2007 with Michelle Jameus, cross-Canada Marathoner and Dorit Girash, President of Let Live Canada.

Michelle Jameus began her cross-country marathon from St. John's, Newfoundland to Vancouver, British Columbia on April 15, 2007. Ms. Jameus mission is to also raise awareness regarding the massive numbers of "healthy" cats and dogs that are euthanised in Canada every year and to join other Western Nations in converting to a compassionate No-Kill country.

Every dollar raised by this endeavor will support and facilitate low-cost or free Spay/Neuter Programs across Canada to be accessible for all Canadians.

Michelle is scheduled to arrive at my shelter on June 19th and can be contacted here on that date in the evening or on the 20th morning before continuing on to Ottawa.

Michelle has informed me by telephone 2 days ago that she would greatly appreciate the opportunity of a live interview and would be willing to prolong her stay in Ottawa by a day or two to accommodate, if needed. I will be in contact with Michelle again by phone Saturday, June 16th therefore you can contact the writer, Jo to inform us if this is a possibility.

I have attached herewith added information for the Marathon.

Thank you for your consideration in this matter,

On behalf of Let Live Canada,
Joanne

Reading the response from Talk Ottawa was exciting.

Hello, Joanne:

Funny you should ask, because I had an interview request for Michelle on my "to do" list this week. You beat me to the punch.

It would be ideal if we could have Michelle on "Talk Ottawa" on Monday, June the 25th, from nine to ten p.m. The program airs live from our studios here at 475 Richmond Road, and we'd want to make sure she was in our green room by about twenty-to-nine.

Please let me know if that works for you; also, please let me know if you have any visuals connected with Michelle's work or the marathon that we could use as b-reel during the show. Oh, and I wonder if you would give me a heads-up just before her arrival at the shelter so we can have a camera out there to record her arrival.

Many thanks!
James Hendricks
Host/Producer
Talk Ottawa
Rogers Television 22

One of the great things about living in the computer age, is the speed of the Internet and instant messaging. However sometimes, miscommunication can happen. I'm not sure at what point things started to break down, but there was a storm brewing at home. When frustration set in, I found myself caught in the middle.

> *Joanne and everyone:*
> *Whatever media attention can be arranged is good. Please note that, I have booked my flight so that I can be there for a media conference in the Parliament Building on Monday morning as we had all agreed. I have also arranged with an MP to get us the Charles Lynch room for that media conference as Beth had suggested.*
>
> *So, I sincerely hope that this is still going to happen. Otherwise I've wasted a lot of money, since my ticket is non-refundable. I held up booking my flight until there was something definite in Ottawa, and we had decided that there would be a media conference on the morning of the 25th in the Parliament Building.*
>
> *I will also have made a fool of myself with my MP friend and his staff.*
>
> *I don't want to jump to conclusions, but it sounds like we're back to promoting the Ottawa shelters and Let Live Canada is again out of the picture.*
>
> *I HAVE LITERALLY MOVED HEAVEN AND EARTH TO GET TO OTTAWA FOR A MEDIA CONFERENCE ON THE MORNING OF THE 25TH. THE MP IS DOING THE SAME.*

Followed by this message addressed to myself:

Michelle, it looks like everything that we had negotiated before has been changed. I was hoping that I didn't have to, but I now have to tell you that this has been a mess. One of the group (who has since dropped out) was quite hostile toward Let Live Canada and insisted that it not be mentioned and that all promotion be for the local rescues.

Now we're back to that, aren't we?

Throughout it's been difficult negotiating with them, I was initially buoyed by their enthusiasm, but realizing that they didn't have much organizational experience, I continually had to do what I could to keep them focused and not diverging into a thousand different directions. This one woman was really difficult; with regard to Joanne, she sees it as a way of making money for her shelter. They don't see the big picture, and now have destroyed any hope of the country seeing it.

It's now been converted to a local story, promoting local shelters, not a national one, promoting the No-Kill Canada marathon.

The woman named Beth who clearly had some professional and organizational talents became the leader. You might recall that she gave me a series of proposals with regard to the Ottawa situation, I proposed them to you and you chose which one you thought was best - namely the media conference on Monday morning. She and I then set out to arrange that - and I booked my flight based on that.

Now we're into a whole lot of disorganized things at the shelters, not the national cause and no media conference.

I know that my efforts don't compare to what you are doing, but Michelle, but, I have literally moved heaven and earth to get to Ottawa for Monday morning and that was eliminated without any consideration whatsoever.

This lack of disorganization and consideration is going to hurt Let Live Canada's image, as well as my personal finances. When I travel, I always pay for it myself, but cannot afford to waste money (or time).

Dorit then sent a second message to the Ottawa group:

In thinking about this some more, I am getting more and more frustrated.

The last plan we had was for a media conference in Parliament Building planned for Monday morning to promote the No Kill Canada Marathon and Let Live Canada - BECAUSE IT IS OTTAWA, THE NATIONAL CAPITAL. Where did you get the idea that you could unilaterally change that to a local story?

Obviously, I am not going to fly to Ottawa for a local story. Shall I hold you responsible for the cost of my plane ticket?

How could you do that?

Followed by another message to myself:

Hi Michelle:

I am really sorry that this has happened. When the other fiascos happened, I told them that I wasn't going to sadden you with the negativity, but since this happened, there is no choice but to make you party to the correspondence.

I am furious. This is nothing short of a hijacking of our national project for their own gains. That's what they started to do, then with Beth's help, we refocused it, now it's back to that.

I was looking forward to seeing you in Ottawa, but unless there is a national media conference in the Parliament building on Monday morning, there is no point in my flying up.

We had hoped that with a national media conference, we would get national sponsors as well as donations coming in from across the country. The disjointed local stories they have planned on behalf of their own shelters won't do anything for us. ZILCH.

Had there been one media conference, we could have presented a unified message to the whole country.

I am absolutely devastated by this turn of events.

Dorit

Followed by another message to the Ottawa group:

Just one more thing, then I am going to shut up.

As I have attempted to emphasize, the purpose of the Ottawa media conference was to focus attention on the national project. To get national corporate sponsors, to get people from across the country to donate, to enlighten the whole country about the plight of animals and to stimulate some federal action to solve the problems.

We are trying to raise funds to help set up spay/neuter programs across the country - not just in the OTTAWA community!

Kindly reinstate the national media conference in the Parliament building on Monday morning.

Dorit

In the midst of these emails, Jo was corresponding with Talk Ottawa.

I am so sorry to not have gotten back to you earlier however, the Let Live Canada people have had some changes in their schedules and we are also now waiting for Michelle to call us.

She is supposed to be arriving in Montreal tomorrow and call me. If she does I will forward her your e-mail so that she herself can respond, if it is not too late, on when she can be in Ottawa.

After inquiring with Quebec and Ontario Min. of Transports and the police detachments along the route from Montreal to my town, it looks like she will have to take alternative roads and Michelle will be the only one to decide which route she will take and how long it will take her.

If I do not hear from her tomorrow I will forward this to the Let Live people in Windsor immediately. They did not yet answer whether there were any visuals but I will request this again.

I apologize for any inconvenience for the delay in responding and will contact you the moment we hear from Michelle.

Much appreciated,
Regards,
Jo

Then I read this email from Jo.

Hi Michelle,

Hope you are well and still holding on. You should get a nice well-deserved rest now.

I am forwarding you these e-mails tonite hoping you will see them soon because as you can read, I am at a standstill without any go-ahead from anyone. I certainly also wish to stay in the good books of Rogers.

I hope you can call me tonite or tomorrow. I must step out tonite but not for long so you can keep trying or please can you leave me a number and I'll call back. I'm up very late and mornings late so best time is late at night or after noonish, so I can get some shelter work done.

There have been some mix-ups, difficulties, to say the least with scheduling anything with Dorit. Beth worked so very very hard and I also from the start. We just don't get it anymore.

So right now, unless Dorit has her own concrete plans for getting you some media attention, this Talk Ottawa gig is or was solid. As you see I did not respond until late last night due to another change in Dorit's plans, etc. Beth and I had our hearts, souls and full-time energy in this not to mention our hope that this was the launching pad for changing the lives of these poor animals.

I must run now as I've not seeded my garden yet and it's the only darn thing I do for myself, and it's also backbreaking work, but I need the veggies.

Hoping you can reach me as I would like to 'save face' with Rogers as I have a good contact/supporter there and she was the one who pushed for this. Just to give them a final definite reply.

I think, if you can, we should talk. I so much admire your bravery, to say the least.

Also I contacted both Ministries of Transport Quebec and Ontario and about 7 polices detachments between here and Montreal and they say you just cannot run on the 20 or 40. There is a parallel route and I've printed it out to relay to you.

I can also get you to meet one of my vets nearby for 10 min. but I must call on Monday to book it for the next day.

Have a good rest,
Jo

Life is full of reversals. Plans discussed just a short time ago had fallen beyond recovery. Hopes were high; the downward turn of events had dimmed everyone's enthusiasm. Without harmony, the challenge was too great and there was little time left. I couldn't bring myself to talk about it with anyone and quietly excused myself to be alone.

Sometimes, life can feel like a storm and nobody cares. It was times like this that made it difficult to sustain my motivation.

Shooting so high to make a difference, I felt myself caught up in an attitude of defeat. Sadness invaded my soul and left me feeling empty. Every obstacle I faced was taking its toll, but it's the disappointments and discouragements that make us want to quit.

After viewing the circumstances, my mind raised up another fear. It was the same fear that could have easily stopped me from ever trying something like this in the first place. Why did I ever think I could do this? At that moment, my vision felt hidden and my goal was almost forgotten.

Sometime later, I sat quietly with my mom. When you're tired and not thinking straight, it's overwhelmingly tempting to whine and complain. However, we didn't say much. As adults, my parents rarely got involved in our lives or conflicts. Instead, they opted to be sounding boards if needed. Good or bad, it helped us to think for ourselves.

"You look tired," mom said with concern.

"That I am, mom, and I feel it in my face."

"Why don't you go to bed and get some rest?"

"I will, soon."

"What's wrong with your feet? They're all swollen," she alerted me. They were so puffy it was hard to tell where my toes were.

"It's just from sitting too long. Putting my legs up should help. I think I will go to bed now."

"Well you sleep as long as you like sweetie."

"I will. Love you mom," I said and then kissed her goodnight.

As I lay in bed, my mind was like a recorder replaying through every day of my journey. You can't really know the depth of your own character until you see how you react under adversity.

This setback could have easily led me to give up my march for something better. Instead, my inner fight wanted to keep going. Right from the beginning, I understood there was a price to becoming involved in this cause and I would have to become vulnerable. It wasn't going to be without costing me something personally. Finding a way to fight through it was an important lesson for me to learn.

Things always looked better after a good night sleep. My struggles were worse at night, but life was so much brighter under the sun. When sunrise came, it never failed to bring with it new hope and my desire to continue. In the morning, my thoughts were a whole lot clearer.

It was time to call a friend, Sharron from Ottawa. She worked at the RA Centre and might be able to help.

"Hi Sharron," I said.

"Hey buddy, congratulations on making it to Montreal."

"Thanks. It's great to be here."

"How are you doing?"

"I'm good, but I have a bit of a problem I'm hoping you can help me with."

"What is it?"

"We've had some challenges organizing a media conference in Ottawa. Plans to have it at Parliament Hill didn't work out. I know this is really short notice, but does the R.A. Centre have a conference room available on the morning of June 25?"

"I can't promise you anything but I'll look into it for you and call you back."

"That's great Sharron and if there's something great, but if there isn't, that's okay too. I appreciate you looking into it."

"I'll see what I can do."

The rest of the day was filled with activity. From walking around the park, to playing ladder golf and lawn darts, I was soaking up all the attention and pampering I could get.

As we sat outside, my brother and his family stopped by for a short visit, as did other campers periodically. Then later that evening, everyone in the campground delighted in a corn roast and listening to music.

At dusk, we sat by the campfire. It was one of my favorite parts of camping. One strike of a match is all it took and my dad had a fire blazing. We watched as flying embers floated in the air and listened to sparks popping. Flames flickered and coals glowed as we witnessed the dramatic consequences from the fire's heat.

Then once the fire was burning strong, my dad added a garden hose inside a copper pipe that gave the flames some added colors. There were "oohs" and "ahs" from the effects making it even more enjoyable until the fire sputtered out.

Inside, we delighted in playing card games. As I watched my parents, they were like two little kids constantly, but playfully going at each other. After fifty-four years of marriage, they were still together and it made me happy to know they had each other. I thanked my dad for taking care of my mom and mom for taking care of dad, and God that they were still with us.

The next day, Sharron called with the good news. They had a room available and she put it on reserve for us. I called Dorit to let her know and her response was favorable.

> *June17*
> *Excellent. Michelle, I have a 10 minute video entitled "The Humane Solution" produced by Alley Cat Allies - it documents the financial and humane benefits of TNR programs and has convinced everyone that has seen it that's the way to go. What do you think about showing it at the press conference?*
>
> *I can bring a laptop, but could we get hold of a digital projector somewhere? Actually, it would be good if we could also get a laptop, because it's a real pain to get them through airport security.*
>
> *Dorit*

. . .and again.

> *I also have a whole bunch of PowerPoint presentations that I've given to numerous groups. I can put one together for this. I will also revise my big document on Cat Overpopulation for the national media and bring those with me.*
>
> *NOW, I'm getting excited about this!*
>
> *SYS*
> *Dorit*

Finally, after being in repair mode, I was able to relax and put aside any disappointments. If I was going to continue and remain positive, I had to store them away in the parking lot of my mind.

It was Father's Day and we gathered at Angels' house. After missing Mother's Day, I was glad to be a part of the celebration. I found it interesting how we all fell back into our family order whenever we got together. We were all character extensions of our parents and even though things have changed since we grew up, I embraced the comfort of feeling like a daughter, a sister, and an aunt again.

The evening flew by with a blink of an eye, as it always did. I stayed at Angel's that night and would leave from there in the morning. After saying goodbye to everyone, I was happy to learn my parents would see me again in Sudbury. They had planned to visit with my mom's twin sister who lives there. "We'll time it for when you're passing through," they said.

In the quiet of my last night, I checked my email one more time to find this message from Dorit to Beth.

> *Good Morning, Beth. I hope this finds you well on this Father's Day.*
>
> *Beth, Michelle called me yesterday and she arranged to have the national media conference at this location:*
>
> *June 25 @ noon*
> *Confederation (Curling) Lounge*
> *R.A. Centre*
> *2451 Riverside Dr.*
> *Ottawa*
>
> *She also loved the media release that you wrote and we ask that you revise it to reflect this time/location and then forward it to the national media. What are you thinking of including in the media kit?*

You could add to the media release that we will be showing a short film (9minutes) on "The Humane Solution"; it's a video that has persuaded everyone who's seen it to go the no-kill way.

We both really appreciate your help with this. I understand that you won't be there, so we won't meet you, but I am very glad that you have come forward to help us with this.

Thank you again,
Dorit

The next day, Angel dropped me off on Highway 158. I was forced to take an alternate route again because of restrictions on the main roads. It was another two-way highway with gravel shoulders.

"There are a lot of trucks that take this road," Angel cautioned me. "Be careful and we'll see you in Ottawa at your conference."

"Tonight, I'll be staying near Hawkesbury with an animal rescue friend.

I'll call you when I get home in a couple of days," I said.

Meanwhile, Talk Ottawa and Jo were awaiting my arrival in Hawksbury.

Hello, Jo:

I now have confirmation from Michelle that she'll be able to make the program on Monday, June 25th; also that she'll be in Hawksbury this afternoon. We're ready to send a shooter out for that, so I wonder if you could get back to me with the right address and the approximate time she's expected to arrive.

Thanks again!
James

Jo replied with:

> *Hi James,*
>
> *Just left you a phone msg. re leaving shelter about 2ish to pick up Michelle in Grennville QC just across the bridge from Hawkesbury around 3ish. I have to call the local papers for a short interview when she arrives there and then I will be taking Michelle back to my home/shelter therefore not sure exactly what time we should be back, maybe 4-5:30 p.m.*
>
> *Of course she is available this evening at any time, maybe time for her to have a quick shower before you got here if it's this evening. Other option is tomorrow morning when she leaves from here. I will be driving her back to Hawkesbury to Hwy 17.*
>
> *Thanks a million!*
> *Jo*

After two days of rest, my body felt a little rusty. I had to work through some stiffness before settling into a rhythm. It felt good to be surrounded by familiar country. Increasingly, I became more aware that home was just around the corner.

Running through Lachute felt a little strange. This was a town I had driven through many times over the years. Things I didn't notice before now stood out: parks, buildings and people. One of the advantages of being on foot is that you have more time to look at everything around you.

As I approached Main Street, a vehicle stopped and an older woman got out of the car. She crossed the street and looked like she was concealing something in her hand. "Are you running for cancer?" she asked. When I explained myself, she made the quickest U-turn back to her car I'd ever seen. It was like she couldn't get there fast enough. She drove away just as fast and her reaction disappointed me.

Going on from there, I hopped on to Highway 148. Trying to push my stroller through loose gravel and constantly picking stones out of my shoes was frustrating. I didn't think I was ever going to make it to Grenville. However, I did.

Stopping at the Esso gas station, I called Jo. We had pre-planned for me to call her when I got here.

"Hi Jo, I'm in Grenville."

"Hey, congratulations. My friend, Ghislaine, will pick you up. She lives nearby and you can stay with her until we get there. Talk Ottawa is sending over a cameraman and we should both arrive around the same time. He'll start the interview there and then finish at my shelter."

"Great, I'll see you soon."

I had never met Ghislaine before. She arrived promptly and we managed to get everything in her car. While we waited at her home, she kindly made me a sandwich and gave me something to drink. We were sitting outside when Todd the cameraman drove up, with Jo right behind him.

After a brief interview, he filmed me running across the bridge to Hawkesbury. To my surprise, there was another local reporter waiting on the other side. As planned, we completed Talk Ottawa's report at Jo's shelter.

When a community won't take responsibility for animals that suffer, it takes a special kind of person to step up and do something about it. The sacrifices made when such a burden falls on individuals is admirable. Jo's passion and zeal for these creatures was exceptional. However, it made me wonder, if animals are more of a burden to people than a blessing.

That night, I stayed with Jo and enjoyed my visit with her and her many houseguests. Somehow, she managed to take care of both me and all her other demands. Jo was one of the first animal rescuers I had spoken to before I left for St. John's. This was her response to my announcement.

Hello Michelle,

I was more than elated to receive your e-mail and would very much like to chat with you. Yours are words taken right out of my own mouth some 15 years ago as my dream was to of course first win the $40 million and then have a National Rescue for Felines linking every private person who rescues, properly, and they number in the thousands. Anyhow I wanted to have a CAT-MOBILE and gather up all the poor strays. I am quite involved with the educational part of rescue, even though I run this shelter solely myself with not one volunteer and also have been offering a discount spay/neuter service to the public for 10 years in this area.

It is important also for the public to know that people with a good education run many of these rescues. My goal had been to work with the worst serial killers before my accident. Consequently I am doing this work through the animals. As you might be aware, the 3 criteria of these criminals before age 9 are the torture and killing of animals, fire starting and bedwetting.

I have forwarded your e-mail to someone that now has begun a campaign with respect to enlightening the public regarding the huge euthanasia rates in well-funded and known organizations. She and I would very much like to learn more about your plans.

But at this time I am personally worried about continuing the shelter due to huge debts. The public must recognize Private Rescue Groups and as we know the public has little awareness of our existence and no-kill policies and therefore we have little support.

On the other hand the public believes that these large organizations do in fact 'save' all the pets they rescue.

While I was sleeping, Jo had arranged for another local reporter to meet us in the morning. After the interview, she sent me on my way with an envelope for inspiration. On the outside she wrote:

Stay Safe
We need you to win this battle.
With you all the way!

Inside the envelope was a homemade card. It was plastered with many pictures of her cats, including Jazzmine II. The card read:

There are all kinds of thank you's -
All very sincere -
For help or for gifts,
Or for just being near.
There are all kinds of thank you's
For all kinds of things.
But none could mean more
Than the thank you this brings.
Thank you very much on behalf
of all the animals I've met or will meet.
You are our hero.
JazzyJo Havenly Felines (Ching Ching, Jazz, Shabu,
Oro, Munchkin, Doubee and Rambo)

After I read her card, I was reminded of my goal and returning was the vision in my heart. I had a dream no one else could see, a destination, and in a whisper I heard, "Be relentless and run like a giant."

Chapter 4

Eastern Ontario

Home for me has been Ottawa since 1986. The thought of sleeping in my own bed tonight made me want to jump out of my skin. I was so excited. "Let's not get ahead of ourselves," I said and pulled back the reigns. For the moment, a nearby town called Clarence Creek was the object of my attention.

Traffic on Highway 174 was heavy. I passed known landmarks and began shouting repeatedly, "ET go home! ET go home!" All the while, laughing at myself for relating to an alien in a movie.

However, running along this section of the highway offered little encouragement. The vibration from continually pushing my stroller through loose gravel went all the way up my arms causing my teeth to clatter. There was road kill to pass while holding my nose, and I had to fight my way through a swarm of bugs.

Today had plenty for me to think about and I was all over the map. One minute I'm happy to be going home and the next, I'm wondering if I was "chasing the wind". There hadn't been as much interest as I had hoped and I questioned my efforts, "Am I the only Canadian who thinks there is something seriously wrong with killing so many healthy cats and dogs in our country? Does anyone even care?"

Nonetheless, when I reached my target, nothing could wipe the smile off my face, not even a disappointed heart. I was beside myself and did a little happy dance in the middle of the parking lot.

Since no one was looking, I did another one. I hadn't officially run into Ottawa, but it was within my reach.

Sharron didn't make me wait too long before she picked me up. When I saw her car, I started waving and shouting. Seeing her again made my being here feel all the more real. Thankfully, she didn't follow through on her threat to kick my butt all the way down the highway.

Nevertheless, there is at least one person in this world who thinks I should be diagnosed as clinically insane. "You're crazy," she said, but then added, "Your friends are very proud of you. Some of them are worried sick though. Cheryl won't even follow your blog because it worries her so much."

On the ride home, she tried to convince me to come to my senses. "What you've done is more than anyone else would ever do, so if you want you can stop now and no one would think any less of you."

However, I wasn't hearing her. On this bright and sunny day, my heart was still in a fog looking for a place to land. It was as though I was physically present, but my mind didn't know how to find its way home.

Sharron had a house just east of Ottawa in the township of Orleans. I've been renting a room from her for some time now. Initially, it was supposed to be short term but we got along so well that I stayed. As we drove by the neighborhood, I hoped I wasn't going to wake up from a dream.

Walking through the entrance of the house, we were greeted by my two feline friends, Mannie and Kalie. They hadn't forgotten me and showered me with affection. I wasn't getting any further without returning the attention.

Moving past the living room, I climbed the stairs to my bedroom. Once inside, I sat down on my bed and started panning the room. Strangely, it wasn't the joy I was expecting and I was taken back by my emotion. The occupant hadn't lived here in a while and my heart was still bouncing around. There was something out of order in my life.

Oddly enough, I felt like a stranger in a guest room. Going through my stuff was like sifting through someone else's baggage and carefully putting everything back. However, slipping into my favorite jeans reminded me of my reality. Then, I went to my computer where I could be found. To my delight, there were a number of new messages.

I am very much looking forward to following the events and experiences of your journey. Needless to say, I greatly admire your dedication and energy.
Very best wishes,
Mary Ann

Kim said. . . Hey Mich. Let us know when you'll be running through Ottawa. You have lots of fans that would like to cheer you on.

Anonymous said. . .
Hi. We the grade 5 students at Maple Ridge Elementary School have been listening to our teacher, Mrs. Yates, read your blog. Wow, what a journey so far. How are your black fly bites? Please let us know when you will be running through Ottawa. We'd love to meet you in person. Your tentative schedule says that you will be passing through Ottawa tomorrow, but we will still be in class. We think that your cause to save animals is amazing, and after the brief training we did for track and field, we can't imagine running as long as you do each day. Best of luck and take care of yourself. Jodi and 28 superb grade 5 students.

Although I was pleased to receive words of encouragement from the Ottawa group and Dorit, I couldn't help but wonder how much damage had been done.

Hi Michelle,
So glad to see you are safe at home. . .it must feel good. I very much enjoyed your stay and the opportunity to help with your endeavor and the best is yet to come. I thought I would write James to thank him

and you might also wish to contact him in case he has questions etc. I might ask him after the show airs if there is a possibility to have a still of us for a souvenir. My foster home will be able to tape the show (I don't get it here) so I will have that and can make you a copy of course. I hope you have a great celebration Thursday and I'll keep you informed re the other stories here. Hope this media conference will be fruitful on 25th and will hopefully attract more attention from now on. It takes only one person to start the ball rolling and that is YOU! Thanks again, JO

Hello James,
On behalf of Michelle and myself, we would like to just say 'Thanks a lot' for your interest and the opportunity to reach more people through your show for this very important cause. Todd was very nice and easy to work with which made it less stressful for us considering that Michelle was very tired and hungry. I do believe that Michelle can access her e-mail each evening until the 25th if you wish to reach her. I am also available if I can help with any further information regarding this event or in the future should you wish to do a follow-up story regarding Spay/Neuter Programs, pet over-population or the animal/human cruelty link which has been the motivating factor in my work for 12 years.
Regards, Joanne, Jazzy-Jo Havenly Felines

Hi Michelle,
Congratulations on the marathon. We all support your efforts. There are a great deal of animal lovers in Canada and it frustrates me to no end that this doesn't seems to translate into better national legislation, better spaying and neutering and on and on. . .I leave at 7am on Friday and still need to pack and all that. . .sigh. . .so I don't think I can manage to

meet up before then. Keep my email address - and if I can be of some help in the future, just let me know. I'll be sure to follow your progress online. I'll send a note to my colleague who works at CKCU on Thur. to see if they are interested in doing an interview. I'll ask them to contact you by your email address - so perhaps you'll hear from them. Have a safe journey and keep your spirits up – there's really a lot of support out there, though it doesn't always seem that way. . .Heather

Hi Michelle,
Welcome back to Ontario! I hope that you're able to get a bit of rest and relaxation before you head out again. As Jo has explained, it has been an interesting experience in terms of organizing events for this part of your journey. I know I speak for all three of us that we admire your courage and commitment to improve the plight of companion animals across the nation. I have a friend who has a huge media/journalist email list. I didn't realize that he was going to be out of town for a few days; however, he is supposed to be back either late tonight or tomorrow, so I hope the press release will go out on his list tomorrow. I have also sent it out to some individual journalists I know and have urged them to go to your press conference on Monday. I am not sure if it will be possible for the three of us to meet. I believe that Heather is leaving on Friday, and I am catching a flight at 6 am on Sunday morning. I could possibly meet on Friday evening - maybe on a dog walk? My Saturday is going to be pretty busy as I need to clean the house for the person who'll be house-cat-dog sitting for us, get my errands done and then my father will be arriving in the afternoon (he is coming on this trip with me). Take care, Beth

Hi Michelle - glad to see you're back "online". As far as I know, Beth sent the attached to all the national media outlets in Ottawa. We sent them to all the local media in the Windsor area and then sent it to our national shelters mailing list and asked them to forward it to their media outlets. We have no CTV station in our area, and no CTV reporters, so I have no connections with CTV. However, I'm being interviewed by CBC tomorrow - at the station - this is usually a lengthy interview and I will talk to them about using their national connections to get you on one of CBC's shows. SYS, Dorit

Something still lingered in the air. James had asked Jo to sit on the talk show panel with Dorit and myself, and I just assumed she would. However, she had some concerns of her own.

Hi Michelle,
I am forwarding this email from James, Talk Ottawa. I would like to know, considering everything, your opinion re my being there with Dorit (she might still think I'm getting too much attention). I realize you don't need this now however maybe I should just bow out and I can tell him I'd like another show focused on my shelter, etc. It's a tough call because he will probably show the tape of me, but that doesn't matter because I will have said my piece there. I might also ask him if I can conference call during the show if I'm needed (don't know if they like to do that) I can ask a few people to call in but they work so I will try anyhow. Just like to know your opinion and maybe see from James how long the show is. Appreciate it.
Thanks, Jo

Part of me ached with disheartenment after reading her message. Having all three of us on the panel would be good for the show. There wasn't any reason for her not to be there, especially since she had made the arrangements. Somewhere along the way, I had dropped the ball and if I hadn't tripped up, all of this might have been avoided. Now the damage was done and my task got a little bit harder.

That evening, I went to a birthday party. Even though I was happy to see friends I hadn't seen in a while, I felt out of sync with their world. Somehow, everyone had changed, or maybe it was just me.

"How can you run like that every day? Isn't it boring?" someone asked.

"You're like the little energizer bunny that keeps on going and going," everyone laughed.

"Aren't you worried that something bad might happen to you?" another person inquired. "Especially traveling the highways alone. You either have to be crazy or awfully brave to do something like that."

"Have you run into any trouble?"

Where others saw danger and lonely days, I saw an opportunity to make a difference. They didn't really know what to say to me and even though I wasn't expecting them to understand what I was going through, it made me feel different, like a foreigner or an alien. It felt like I was speaking a language only I understood.

Alone in my feelings, I answered their questions as best I could. "Not everyone is out to hurt you. There are still some incredibly kind people in this world," I said.

Then, someone asked me a very good question. "Do you think you are making a difference?"

That was a hard question to answer. "Some days I feel like I am and some days I don't. But how do you measure something like this? If what I'm doing saves just one life, or inspires just one person, it will have made a difference to them. And if not, at least I tried," I responded.

It was at that moment I knew that as long as I could stand on my feet, I would keep on going. My heart's desire was not yet satisfied and I didn't want my journey to end before it was over. Although I didn't know how this was going to turn out, there was still some gas left in my tank and I wanted to run it dry.

In the morning, Sharron drove me back to Clarence Creek. What a joy it was not to push a stroller through gravel. All that I carried was a small backpack, with a few items and some precious water.

Along the way, a reporter heading for Rockland stopped after spotting my flag flapping in the wind. "What are you running for," he asked out of curiosity. His interview was another small victory and it encouraged me that if he took notice maybe others would too. Before he left, he said it was my flag that had caught his eye and prompted him to stop.

As I approached the intersection for Trim Road, Sharron surprised me by driving by honking her horn and taking pictures. Her enthusiasm was contagious and it energized me. "Stop at the Cumberland Veterinary Hospital on Trim Road," she shouted. "The staff there is anxious to meet you so I'll wait for you there," she said and drove off ahead of me.

It didn't take me long to catch up to her and run into the parking lot. To my surprise, another friend from ice hockey, K.P., was waiting there too. She has a couple of dogs of her own and is a huge animal supporter.

I could see the clinic staff waving through the front window and I waved back. This was the clinic where Sharron brought her two cats. After a couple of pictures, we went inside to meet everyone, including an adorable kitten. Their support was appreciated and they wished me luck the rest of the way.

From there, it was a short jog along our neighborhood streets. As I ran up to Sharron's front door, the idea that I had run all the way from St. John's Newfoundland to Ottawa was hard to grasp.. I was so ecstatic I kissed the ground before going inside.

To my disappointment, I learned that Dorit would not be able to join us on Talk Ottawa. She had to catch a flight home immediately following the media conference. This was a huge blow for the show, and me, as everyone would have benefited from her expertise, knowledge, and contribution to the welfare of animals. However, I understood. She went to great lengths just to be in Ottawa and I was grateful that she was still coming.

My fear of being alone on the show didn't last. This email response from Jo was a relief to me.

Okay. Michelle, I will just reply to James to say that I will confirm tomorrow, as I will have to see if I can rearrange my schedule, if I can be there. Am I to write to James or will you confirm who will be there? Beth and I would really like to know if you want to be interviewed BEFORE the 25th by anyone? The reason for contacting CJOH separately was to be doubly sure they would attend on the 25th, then they would air the interview on 25th at 6 p.m. I am PRESUMING that you want everyone to know at the same time on the 25th? Otherwise if you say hold off, we won't ask anyone to contact you now. Thanks, JO

In preparation for the media conference, Dorit felt it would be best to hold off on contacting any media beforehand to encourage their presence on the 25th. I was also delighted to see this email Sharron sent out to some of her contacts.

HELLO EVERYONE,

Some of you know my roommate Michelle (Mich) Jameus and be aware of her courageous ***MARATHON across Canada to raise awareness and support for saving healthy Animals from euthanization.*** *AND some may not know her, but I've sent this along anyway, either for interest sake or in case you see her on the road or hear her story in the news over the next few days and months.*

Mich started her ***"marathon a day"*** *journey at St. John's Harbour, Nfld on April 15th - and has made it to OTTAWA - on schedule. AMAZING, @ 3000 km behind her. She will be here for a few days, getting some much needed rest and then will depart for the rest of her cross Canada Marathon scheduled to end in Vancouver, BC in the fall.*

Attached is a press release for a Media Conference (open to the public) scheduled for next Monday, June 25th - 12:00 noon at the RA Centre – Curling lounge (for those in the Ottawa area that may be interested in attending).

I know Mich would be thrilled to see some friends and would welcome the support - so IF you can make it out, that would be GREAT. The Media session is at noon; those who can stick around or come later should find us in the Fieldhouse Bar and Grill for a late lunch.

If you can't make it out on Monday, but would like to see Mich enroute and sign her flag - she will be running from Orleans to the Ottawa Humane Society THIS Saturday, June 23rd, leaving Orleans at 9 am – her route is outlined on her blog.

For those interested, below is the link to her BLOG - which she updates every chance she gets - check it out - she has met some pretty interesting folks and several angels along the way. Let's hope the angels guide her to the finish line.

http://nokillcanada.blogspot.com/

You can post comments on her blog if you wish to send her a message. Easiest way is to do it as anonymous and just put your name at the end of the text of your message, if you want her to know who it's from.

If you know folks that may not be part of "my email contact list" but who know Mich or are animal lovers and would be interested in this, please feel free to pass this along . . . apologies if you get this or a similar notice more than once. She is involved in so many activities between playing ice hockey, reffing ice hockey, RA Squash member, etc it's quite possible there will be overlap in contact lists. . . .but better to get it twice than not at all.

May our positive thoughts and support pave her path to Vancouver.

Good Luck Mich on the rest of your Journey.
Sharron

Everyone had plans for the weekend. Dorit was attending her granddaughter's graduation and then flying here Sunday. Jo had a rescue shelter to operate. Family and friends had other commitments. I needed to complete my run into Ottawa.

Waking up Saturday morning, I had few expectations except that a longtime friend was joining me on my run. Let me push the pause button for a moment and introduce you to Andree.

I met Andree through work a number of years ago. We got along great but then lost touch for several years. Not that long ago, our paths crossed again while we were both on a dog walk in the same park. It was one of those "don't I know you" moments. As soon as Andree said my name, "Michelle, is that you?" I recognized her voice.

We picked up right where we left off, as if there had never been a gap. Neither one of us had changed much, except that we were both a little older and a lot more scarred by the world.

A couple of weeks back, Andree sent me an email inviting me out for lunch. At the time, she had no idea I was running across Canada. My reply caught her by surprise and I told her I would give her a call while I was in Ottawa.

Meanwhile, she read up on my blog. When I called her, she offered to help any way that she could. Including running with me today for a few kilometers and then following in her car.

When Andree and her nine-year-old dog Max pulled up to the house, the sight of them instantly cheered my heart. "Yes, someone to run with," I rejoiced. Her unexpected support put new enthusiasm into my morning. However, first we had to drop off Andree's car at a pre-determined pickup point. Once the car was taken care of, we went back to the house and put our feet into motion.

Pedestrians were prohibited from running on Highway 417, which meant taking an alternative route into Ottawa. We began at my front door and headed for Innes Road.

After a short distance, we were met by a friend, also named Michele, and her dog Buddy sitting on the grass. I met Michele playing women's hockey. She lived in the area and knew all about marathon's as her husband was also a long distance runner.

"Have you been waiting long?" I asked her after we exchanged a hug.

"Well, I almost left because I saw you drive by in a car and I didn't know what was going on," she said puzzled.

"Oh yeah, we had to drop off Andree's car first so she could run with me. Do you want to join us?"

"No thanks, you guys knock yourselves out. Running isn't for me. I'd rather play hockey."

"Well I'm so glad you stuck around."

Michele's dog enjoyed some attention and wagged his tail. We took pictures and then Michele cheered us on. "Thanks for coming out," I said and waved good-bye.

From there, we ran a few blocks and I asked Andree how she was doing.

"I don't know how you do it. I can't imagine running a marathon, never mind a marathon every day. And you ran all the way from Newfoundland to Ottawa. I can't wrap my head around it," said Andree.

"I know Andree, neither can I," I replied.

"It's too unbelievable," she said in disbelief.

"It's pretty unbelievable to me too. But I think I had some help from above."

"Well, you must have a good connection or something because I don't know how it's possible," she said, baffled.

It didn't take long before we reached Andree's car. She hopped in and was happy to follow behind waving one of my flags through her sunroof. As she beeped her horn, people driving by started beeping back.

Along the way, we were excited by a couple of vehicles that stopped. The first car was another friend from ice hockey, Nathalie. She had her two sons with her, Mathieu and Jonathan. After some pictures, they even followed behind us in their car for a short time. Then, shortly after that a friend named Peggy-Sue, stopped briefly to say a few words of encouragement. Both of their support was appreciated.

We reached Bank Street and then headed for Queen Elizabeth Drive. That was as far as Andree could go. There was a lot of traffic and no time for a lengthy good-bye, so Andree went one way and I went the other.

"Thanks for running with me," I shouted at her as she drove off.

"Call me later. I'll schedule you for a foot massage tomorrow," she yelled back.

"You're the best Andre." I waved till she was out of sight.

It was a beautiful run along the canal. From Dows Lake, I headed for the Ottawa Humane Society (OHS) on Champagne Ave. Standing in front of the building and then walking through the doors was like opening the pages of time.

My first exposure to the OHS was as a student when I took the Veterinary Assistant Program through Algonquin College in 2002. Part of the program training was held at this facility. It was here that I learned about the overpopulation problem.

There is no better way to find out the truth about something than to conduct your own study. When I started questioning euthanizing a healthy cat or dog, I had to find truth outside of my own human understanding because I couldn't live with what I knew. I wasn't comfortable with my reality anymore, so I identified myself with God's interest in all this.

It was in this season I discovered God's Word, the Bible, where a whole wealth of truth exploded in front of me. It was like a manual for animals and my life. Everything that competed with it came up empty.

Sometime after I graduated from the program, I approached the OHS and then CFHS with my desire to raise awareness about the overpopulation problem. However, they both turned me down.

With mixed emotions, I walked around and glanced at pets up for adoption on the bulletin board. It was quiet with only a few people lingering. Off to one side was an office where a woman was sitting at a desk and looking in my direction. I walked up to her and introduced myself with an explanation of what I was doing here. She rolled her eyes and said, "There's no one available."

Without looking at me, she continued ruffling through her papers. I stood there for a few moments hoping she would show some interest, but she didn't. Then, I mentioned a few names of people I knew who worked here.

"There's no one here right now," she blurted out with that tone someone uses when they don't care.

I paused before responding. "Well, thank you for your time. Have a nice day," I said and stepped back into the lobby.

On my way out, I glanced at a few cats in their cages and had that feeling someone was watching me. Before I made my exit, I looked over my shoulder and the woman dropped her head before I could make eye contact. "There is something seriously wrong with this picture," I thought as I left.

Receiving a cold shoulder is never a pleasant experience. It makes you feel like you don't measure up. Her dismissal of me cut to the core of my being, like someone had slapped me in the face. The spoiled moment led me to feeling rejected and my emotional barometer took a nosedive. I tried not to let the sadness invade my soul, but on days when you feel like you're losing more than you're winning, it's easy to be discouraged.

I walked to the busy intersection at Carling and Bronson. All the way, I battled intense feelings of isolation and loneliness. I sat down on the curb just wanting to be lost in a crowd. Watching cars drive by, I felt very much alone and wondered, "What is wrong with people?" After a while, I hopped in a cab and it was a lonely ride home.

Sometime later, I sat in silence in my room and went through another pity party. It was hard being someone going against the flow of everyone else. "Why should I care, no one else does," I protested and the voice in my head wanted me to quit. "No one expects you to continue anyway," I rationalized. "There would be no shame in ending your run here," they said. However, to me, not finishing would mean defeat.

There was nothing stopping me from staying put, except the voice in my heart that wanted to fight.

"Don't let your disappointments cloud the good this event has already done," it petitioned.

"Don't surrender to that voice in your head and leave nothing to doubt," it requested.

"If you quit now, think of how much will be lost," it pleaded.

All of a sudden, my eyes were drawn to the words that were flowing with affection on my flags. My mind picked up speed as I saw how my journey was growing in value with the number of days and miles I had already run. Keeping me poised at the center of all my trials was my convictions and compassion, strong enough to hold me up. Motivating me was that I had taken ownership of the problem and there were people counting on me.

Then the song that gave voice to my heart returned even stronger. Tracing my steps back to the beginning, I found my fighting spirit once again.

"Forget the things that are behind you and reach forward to what's ahead," I proclaimed.

"Leave it all out on the highway," I roared and was determined in my heart to persevere, and see this through to the end no matter what.

Early Sunday morning, I read the last minute email Dorit sent out before she left Windsor.

> *Hi Ladies:*
>
> *As you know, I have to go to London today, so I don't have much time. I've attached a quickly-drawn up follow-up media release which I hope somebody can distribute to the Ottawa media today.*
>
> *Beth, I know you're on your way out of town, but if you could forward the appropriate email addresses or*

fax numbers to Julia, she could send them out - or if one of you in Ottawa could do it, that would be great.

If somebody wants to polish up my quicky media announcement, feel free.

All the best,
Dorit

Later that morning, I was the beneficiary of a complimentary foot massage. Andree was a massage therapist and treated my feet with some care. Our visit generated new excitement as she offered to be my support vehicle while I ran to Arnprior. We also laughed about how much fun it would be if she came on the road with me.

Encouraged by her involvement, this set into motion another relay team and a support system made up of family and friends. Their assistance would help continue my swing west of Ottawa, and give me something to hold onto.

At dinner that evening, the doorbell rang. It was Dorit and having her in my house was a special moment.

"It's so great to see you again," I said as I gave her a hug. "The last time I saw you, I was putting up my tent on the side of the highway and it was freezing out."

"Congratulations on making it to Ottawa," she said.

"Thanks. Come in. I think there are a couple of people you might like to meet."

My sister Angel and Sharron were sitting at the kitchen table. Up until now, everyone had been communicating by phone or email. Considering the circumstances that brought us together, all of us in one room was remarkable.

Sharron took great pleasure in telling Dorit the story of how she dropped me off at the airport and had no idea I was going to do something so crazy.

"Some of her friends can't bear to follow her blog because it makes them sick with worry," said Sharron.

While we delighted in being together and exchanging stories, everyone needed a good night sleep. Dorit was tired from her weekend of traveling, and tomorrow wasn't far off. We cut our evening short and as Dorit left, I let her know that I still had her grandmother's amulet tucked safely away.

Up in my room, there was a TV. Flicking between channels, I found programs that fed my hungry soul. That's when I came across that Godly man again. This time, I wanted to get his name. It was Charles Stanley. He said, "Trust God and leave all the consequences to him."

Other than some people I met a few times at my sister's church, I didn't know anyone who knew God personally. It was obvious this guy did, and I wanted to know God too. I had a few questions I needed to ask Him. Like, how badly had I messed up my life?

Hearing this man speak, I was discovering a spiritual component that was missing from my life. That's when I started listening to what God had to say.

Before I went to sleep, I read this message from Jo. She was still hard at work and inspired me with her own fight.

> *Good Day Mr. Ruttle,*
>
> *I am forwarding this press release on the off chance you did not receive this information.*
>
> *A few years back you had interviewed me at my shelter. By miracles I continue this work, hoping to see the light that may just now be visible through Michelle Jameus' solitary run across Canada to enlighten Canadians regarding our non-chalantness in throwing away our pets like lifeless objects and the massive numbers of healthy pets euthanized each year.*
>
> *My work is twofold; that of rescuing abandoned pets and also offering a low-cost spay/neuter service to my community, completely unfunded, for 10 years resulting in 1,500,000 unborn felines that would have survived without homes.*

Media Conference – June 25

Monday was a big day and I didn't want to miss it. After an early morning by myself, I made my way to the R.A. Centre. Feeling a little exposed and vulnerable, I wondered if I was up for the task.

Sneaking its way back into my mind was that inner fear when you feel like you are a nobody and who is going to listen to a nobody. I found it funny that physically I would do just about anything without fear, but when it came to public speaking the thought of having to say something filled me with all kinds of anxieties. However, I had to step out of my comfort zone and push back those boundaries of restraint. I needed to share what I knew and believed strongly enough that what I had to say was important. This was no time to back down now.

Dorit and I arrived around the same time. We found our way to the conference room and Sharron was already setting up tables and chairs. My sister Angel and her daughter came in shortly afterward. We put my flags on display for people to sign as they came in and waited in anticipation for everyone to come.

I was overjoyed to see so many friends slowly filling the room and even happier with the arrival of two reporters from the *Ottawa Sun*. Sadly, there was no representation from any of the local animal shelters.

Looking more confident than I felt, my stomach was full of knots as things got started. We had some technical difficulties with sound but Dorit was able to begin with an overview of the problem and why it was so critical to solve. It is important to note at this point more about Dorit's credentials.

> *Her educational background is in biological sciences but she is also a graduate of Organizational Administration and Behavior studies. This is in addition to her aviation expertise. It was while traveling to Denver on a work related project that Dorit accidentally encountered a volunteer for the Denver Cat Care Society, a no-kill shelter, and this led to the founding of Jazzpurr Society for Animal Protection*

> *– a Windsor-based volunteer organization, and then Let Live Canada as a division of Jazzpurr in an effort to facilitate the conversion of Canada to a no-kill nation. Her knowledge in this area is quite extensive with her participation in a number of national and international no-kill conferences, including two by Let Live Canada. She is well known for the work she has accomplished to date and a number of organizations in Canada follow Jazzpurr's model. But we still lack national unity and a national program and until then the problem will persist.*

Dorit provided handouts that included her discussion paper on the "Overpopulation of Cats: Complaints, Concerns, Choices" where she wrote, "Submitted with the respectful hope that this problem can be solved permanently and compassionately." Also, inside was a cd of the video "The Humane Solution, Alley Cat Allies."

The tone was set with her narration and she focused our attention on prevention while showing the video. Her presentation explained the humane approach of Trap-Neuter-Return (TNR) to reduce the feral cat population, the cornerstone of the no-kill movement. She provided an insightful look at the problem while building on the TNR model as a step in the right direction to solving the problem once and for all.

Dorit addressed everyone gathered with the implications as she discussed statistics and facts.

> *The overpopulation of cats and dogs cannot be solved by building more shelters or using the "catch and kill" method. The "trap-neuter-return" concept has proven to work in several U.S. communities by decreasing the population through low birthrates. I am convinced you can decrease the population without killing.*

She concluded with evidence that was considerable and pointed out that when we look at statistics the facts are on our side and the success of prevention brings lasting results yet no one in government or mainstream shelters are willing to consider it.

Once again, I was humbled by Dorit's introduction. I told everyone I too believed that prevention was a more ethical solution than euthanizing.

"There are so many people who volunteer and donate their time to helping unwanted animals but it's not enough," I said. "We all have to take some of the responsibility and do our part, speak out and no longer accept killing these healthy animals. The killing has to stop. We have to learn to do the right thing and stop doing the wrong thing." I ended with a vow, "I am not going to stop until I know at the end of the day our healthy pets are still alive."

Today, I didn't have to stand alone and I felt surrounded by people who supported me. My friends sat and listened and I loved them for it. Their presence reinforced to me that public demonstration wasn't as important as the lives we touch.

When the conference came to a close, some people started to leave. I thanked them for being here and they wished me luck. About a dozen friends went upstairs to the Fieldhouse Restaurant for a social gathering and some food.

Before I joined them, I had to say good-bye to Dorit.

"Thank you so much for coming. It meant a lot to me," I said as we exchanged a hug.

"Good luck the rest of the way," she wished me and had to rush off to catch her flight home.

"I'll call you in a few days," I said as she left.

Then, the *Ottawa Sun* took me aside for an interview. It wasn't national news, but it felt like another victory. Everyone's support was helping to build backup my confidence. Before Angel left to drive back to Montreal, she asked me one more time, "Are you sure you want to keep going?"

I responded, "I have to at least try."

Talk Ottawa – June 25

After an eventful day, I spent some downtime at home alone collecting my thoughts. It was then that the fear of appearing on live T.V. set in. The thought of putting myself out there scared me to death.

On my way to Rogers Television, I tried calming my nerves by telling myself it was just another vehicle to engage people and even if it doesn't go well, it couldn't hurt. Anything was better than nothing.

Jo was already at the studio when I arrived and I could tell she was as nervous as I was. We tried to encourage one another by saying we would be fine. All the while, I was wishing Dorit were here. I didn't want to do this without her.

We were ushered into the studio and while we waited I could feel stage fright coming over me. I don't know what it is about being in front of cameras, but it was nerve racking and not a good feeling. In my mind I was thinking, "Where's the bucket?"

My greatest fear was being put on the spot and drawing a blank. Somehow, remembering everything you want to say openly escapes you and you find yourself struggling for words and a place to start. Even Jo, who is usually talkative and emotional about her shelter, had trouble finding her words.

However, once the discussion began I forgot all about the cameras and James, the talk show host, did a terrific job of helping us get through it. There were mixed reactions from listeners who called in. Some for and some against.

In a forum like this, there was always the possibility of compelling a change of attitude in people toward animals. Yet, in this evil world where we love to exterminate, I was starting to wonder whether people even wanted the kind of change we were talking about.

Time went by so fast and before we could cover all the issues, the show was over. I drove home feeling dissatisfied. Before I left St. John's, I was sure people would be on board with this. However, now I had my doubts and woke up to a reality that didn't match my hopes. My vision of a no-kill country was a bit naïve and I had to recognize that I might be clinging to a pretense.

One positive that came out of the show happened as we were leaving the studio. James suggested a follow up panel in the future to include other participants, like Dorit.

Daylong discussions of questions and answers caught up to me, as did the emotional fatigue. My Goliath was growing bigger by the day and what is now obvious to me, but wasn't at the time, is that there is no quick fix to this problem. Not even this event will make it all better any time soon. The most I could hope for was to inspire others.

To me, the clock was ticking. The 197,000 casualties I calculated to date, were now ghosts on the road in front of me. To anyone else this might have appeared foolish, but not to me. If my desire to save every innocent healthy cat and dog looked like foolishness, I was incurable.

Alone in my room just after midnight, I was disappointed to read this message.

> *Hi, Michelle:*
>
> *A mutual acquaintance, Shelley, suggested I get in touch with you. I don't know if you are still in the Ottawa area or have already left for Montreal. But, if you're still around, by all means please give me a call.*
>
> *Best wishes for your continued success on your Let Live Canada run across the country.*
>
> *Thanks,*
> *Steve Carrol*
> *CEO-CFHS*

Like all human beings, I only had a certain amount of fortitude and that capacity was only going to carry me so far. In my heart of hearts, I believed my perseverance would outweigh anything I endured. Nothing could equal the longing I had to make the impossible happen. However, it was sapping every drop of energy I had and every day demanded more. Every challenge repeatedly tested the validity of my run to the edge.

To progress from here, I had to leave the disappointments behind and find the energy and peace I needed to go on. I did that by shifting my mental focus from my circumstances to dwelling on my convictions. In the privacy of my own heart, I was running the race of my life. Whatever the cost, I was convinced this was worth pursuing and I saw my path clearly. I was ready for my dusty road.

Playing competitive sports had taught me to have a winner's attitude, and I would rather win than lose. I was relentless in the pursuit of my goal and my desire to reach new heights was like a seed that grows into a huge tree.

Spurring me on were the words of wisdom from the award-winning film *Chariots of Fire*: "if you don't run you can't win". I understood most people burst out of the starting blocks with incredible energy, but to win the prize of any race you have to have an unwavering determination to go all the way to the finish line. Not only do you have to start well, you have to finish well.

Andree and Max arrived early and they came prepared for an extremely hot and humid day.

"You're a real trooper for doing this Andree," I said gratefully.

"Hey, I didn't have anything planned today anyway so it worked out great. I'm glad I can help. Maybe Max will run a bit with you later before it gets too hot," she hinted.

"I'd like that," I smiled.

After we got all my stuff in her wagon, we stopped at a nearby Tim Horton's for a morning cup of coffee. As we walked in, there was an older gentleman reading *The Ottawa Sun*. He took one look at me and said, "Hey, it's you." Lifting it up, he pointed to the article in the paper. I smiled at him and Andree chuckled, "You're famous."

We took our coffee to go and then stopped to pick up a copy of the *Sun*. On the second page was a large picture and a wonderfully written article. "Surely this would capture the hearts of a few more people," I thought. I didn't know how many copies were circulated, but I figured it was a lot. Every little victory was adding to my sense of purpose and meaning to my journey.

Between the article and Andree's support, I was off to a great start. However, once again restrictions on the main highway forced me to take an alternate route. The majority of it was along Old Carp Road.

Andree brought walkie-talkies so we could chat back and forth while I ran ahead of her. We talked at length about her traveling with me, but it just wasn't possible. Every now and then, she would check in on me.

"How are you doing buddy?" said Andree.

"It's a hot one but so far so good, thanks. How you doing?" I'd ask her.

"Hey, you're the one doing all the work. I've got it easy. I wish I could do some of the running for you but someone's got to drive the car," she laughed.

"How's your car holding out? It won't overheat, will it?"

"I hope not," she replied.

For a short distance, Max ran with me proudly and did a pretty good job for an old dog. Then he took refuge in Andree's air-conditioned car. Once in a while, she disappeared behind me, but it was only to let Max take care of business.

Along our route, we came across Tripp Farm. A good-looking young man named Brent spotted us. He came out to the road and inquired about what we were doing. "Wait just a minute," he said and returned with a Senators mug filled with ice-cold water. "You can keep the cup," he said kindly. We thanked him and then kept on going.

"Too bad he didn't come with the mug," Andree laughed.

She was quite the comedian and probably could have made a career as a standup comic. I was often in stitches and crying with laughter after some of her great impersonations. Then she said, "I don't understand why you're not getting more support or national coverage. What do you have to do, run across the country naked? Maybe if you put on a mini skirt and some pumps, I bet that would get some attention!" I was laughing so hard I could barely breathe.

Although I appreciated her enthusiasm, for my own safety I wasn't trying to be glamorous. "I don't understand why someone hasn't sponsored you," she continued. "I'll try and look into that for you." Regardless, that wasn't the kind of help I was looking for. In my mind, my task wasn't supposed to be easy or sugar coated. Any help I received had to be given freely without asking and out of a heart of compassion.

As the morning progressed, so did the heat and humidity. It was incredible. Later that day, we learned that the humidex had risen above 50 C. "I don't know how you can do it," Andree kept saying.

With so much running, my effort had turned into a habit of perpetual motion. My body was now adept and efficient under most conditions, but these drastic changes in the weather didn't give my system much time to get acclimatized. This humidity was brutal and the air so thick that Andree was concerned for my well-being. I kept reassuring her that I was fine. All the while thinking, I might not have been if she hadn't been with me.

We finally reached the Humane Society in Arnprior, where we met Steph and Jill.

"Wow. I can't believe you ran in this heat," Steph said. "It's pretty remarkable that you ran all the way from Newfoundland to here by yourself. We're so happy to have you visit our shelter."

"Well, I've had some incredible help along the way. Like today, with Andree and Max."

Peter, from the *Arnprior Chronicle*, is a huge supporter of the shelter and met us inside for an interview. After a hot run, the air conditioning was a welcome change. I enjoyed our tour and meeting the animals. We took a few pictures and before we left they said, "The animals thank you for taking on this huge task, and so do we." It was always encouraging when I encountered support.

Andree left me at Tim Horton's where I had pre-arranged to be picked up by another friend who lived in the area.

"I don't know how I can ever thank you for today Andree. I couldn't have made it without you."

"I wish I could go all the way with you."

"Me too."

"Make sure you keep massaging and icing your feet."

"I will. Thanks."

"See you in a couple of days."

I took some comfort in knowing that she was going to meet up with me again in Pembroke, where her mom lives.

Not long after Andree drove away, Lynda arrived. At the sight of her, I smiled and gave her a hug. I hadn't seen her in a while, still, I think I've known her forever. We met in Edmonton Alberta a long time ago and when I first moved to Ottawa, I stayed with her while I was getting my feet on the ground. Now she lives on a hobby farm in Renfrew and we've kept in touch all these years. Our friendship was such that it didn't seem to matter when we got together or under what circumstance, we could pick up right where we left off.

I was thrilled that she could help me for the next couple of days and it gave us a chance to catch up.

"It's good to see you again," I said.

"You crazy girl running across Canada by yourself," Lynda said as she hugged me back. "I heard about it from some friends and I think what you're doing is pretty amazing. I know I could never do something like that."

"Well, it's been an amazing journey so far. How's life on the farm?"

"I think you'll see a big change since the last time you were here. We've cleaned out the old barns and made some renovations to the house. We've got the pool working too so you'll be able to go for a swim to cool off."

As we approached her home, off to the side of the property was a camper trailer. "You'll be able to stay in it and have it all to yourself," Lynda said.

"Great. That'll be an upgrade from my tent."

Lynda too loved animals and she updated me on their barn cats and a newly acquired Sharpe.

Greeting us at the door was Lynda's roommate, Jen. She was a mechanic by trade and within a half hour she had given my running stroller, now named Gidget, an overhaul.

"I've fixed her flat tire but the wheel bearings are wearing out. That's why you hear a squeaking noise. You're probably going to need to replace the wheels at some point," she said.

Gidget was road ready once again, even though she was beginning to show signs of wear and tear. I didn't know how long she was going to last.

That evening, we enjoyed a great meal and reminiscing about our days in Edmonton. We jogged our memory with, "Do you remember when. . ." or, "do you remember 'so and so'?" Times had changed and so did I, but there was a familiarity about Lynda that had remained the same and a friendship I trusted.

I wandered over to the camper and looked forward to getting a good night's rest. That is until I settled in and was comfortable lying down. Then, it started. I was under attack by intruders that had somehow found their way into the camper. Mosquitoes had invaded my space and it baffled me how they got in. Staying under the blankets helped until I needed to breathe. Any attempt to get rid of them was futile, and I lost my battle with the biters.

In the morning, Lynda drove me back to the Tim Horton's in Arnprior and would pick me up again later in Renfrew. Not wanting to complain, I didn't bring up my sleepless night. Gidget had the day off and was "resting" while I ran. All I needed was a few things in my backpack.

Feeling a bit tired from my night of war with mosquitoes, I settled into an easy pace and enjoyed the quiet that came with being by myself. It was another hot day and I was starting to feel the effects of running in back-to-back days of high humidity. Under normal circumstances, I wouldn't even attempt running in this kind of heat.

Lynda surprised me, by driving out to check on me and her timing was perfect.

"How you doing in this heat?" she asked with concern. "I thought you could use a cold drink and something to eat."

"You're the best Lynda, thanks," I said as I took a big mouth full.

"It's really hot out here. Are you sure you're okay?"

"I am but I think a swim is going to feel great later."

"You're sure you're okay?"

"I'm good now. Thanks."

"Okay. I'll be back later."

"See you in Renfrew."

Diving into the swimming pool, clothes and all, was incredibly refreshing. It was a huge in-ground pool with a walkway all around it and a diving board. Unfortunately, I wasn't in the water for long when my calf muscles started to spasm. The pain was so excruciating that I had to pull myself out of the pool before drowning.

I just lay there trying to relax and catching my breath. Once the spasm subsided, I stayed there in the sun listening to the birds singing sweetly in the trees. Then, Lynda called me in for supper.

Bedtime comes early in the country. I never needed persuading to go to sleep. Once again, the trailer was overrun by mosquitoes. From the outside, I imagine the scene must have been quite comical with lights flicking off and on casting a shadow of me swatting at flies. I spent the night trying to fight them off but their presence never ended. They must have had radar, because there was no escaping them.

At breakfast I couldn't resist telling Lynda about my experience with the nasty pests.

"How was your sleep?" Lynda asked.

"It's the camper from hell," I answered.

"Oh no, why? What happened?"

"I had to fight off mosquitos all night. The night before too."

"Poor you. I'm really sorry. You should have come inside."

"I thought about it, but I didn't want to disturb anyone. I could have setup my tent too, but it was dark and I didn't want to risk something else happening. You'll need to plug up the holes though before your next victim," I laughed.

"You're not going to write that on your blog are you?"

"I'm thinking about it," I chuckled. I knew Lynda felt terrible about the whole thing.

That morning, Jen took Gidget and me back to the highway. My next stop was Pembroke, where I would be staying with a cousin.

"I can't thank both of you enough for everything," I said. "You guys are the best."

"Take care of yourself," Jen replied.

"We'll be in touch."

As I watched Jen pull away, I started singing a well-known Beatles tune, "I get by with a little help from my friends. I'm gonna try with a little help from my friends."

Shortly after that, I heard someone honk his or her horn behind me. To my delight, it was Andree and Max. Seeing them again made me smile from ear to ear; it brought me great joy.

"This is a nice surprise," I said happily.

"I decided to take the day off. Check out the goods," Andree gestured with her eyes to the back seat. She had turned her car into a mobile clinic and snack bar.

"Wow. You thought of everything. Things are looking up already."

We put Gidget and all my stuff in the back of her car. Not long after, another vehicle pulled up.

"This is Cecile, a friend of my mother's. She also lives in Pembroke," said Andree.

"Nice to meet you," I greeted her.

"I've been following your blog every day and sometimes I check it three or four times wondering what's happening to you. You are an angel for animals and I think what you are doing for them is amazing," Cecile said excitedly.

"Well, thank you. They need all the help they can get."

I felt at a bit of a disadvantage meeting her. She knew a lot about me, but I didn't know anything about her. However, that quickly changed as Cecile's enthusiastic support and eagerness to help paved the way to a new friendship. I was happy not to be alone and having a small convoy follow gave me an extra boost.

The high temperatures had finally cooled off. I couldn't explain why, but it felt almost effortless to run today, even with sore feet.

"I don't know how you do it. You're a physical marvel," Andree kept saying.

"I don't know about that, but it sure feels good to run," I smiled.

When I felt this good, I believed not even the wind could catch me. My pace may not have qualified for the Boston Marathon, but considering how many miles I had come, I was well pleased with my time. I was even happier to reach the exit for Pembroke.

We stopped just before the hill, and then drove to the marina. It was so much cooler and windier by the water. In the comfort of friends, I waited for my cousin to pick me up. Cecile had bought coffee and even with a fleece pullover on, it took a while for me to stop from shivering.

Then, Andree brought out a bucket of ice and water.

"You're not going to make me put my feet in there, are you?" I asked her with that fear you get when you know something is going to hurt.

"It'll only hurt for a minute, but it will help keep the swelling down," Andree insisted.

"But it's going to really hurt."

"I know, but you need to keep icing and massaging your feet every day or you're not going to make it to Vancouver."

In went my feet. The unbearable pain shot through to my bones like the brain-freeze you get when you eat something cold too quickly, or toes that thaw out from frostbite. Although Andree wasn't my favorite person at that moment, I knew she had my best interests at heart. "It gets easier each time," she reassured me.

Andree's mom, Colette, found us in the parking lot. As we watched her slowly approaching, using a rolling walker, it was apparent that she had some health issues.

"Hello everyone," said Colette.

"Hello Colette," we responded.

"My mom worries about you. She always calls me when you haven't updated your blog to find out if you are okay," Andree said.

"That's so sweet. It's nice to finally meet you in person and thank you for your support," I said.

"It's dangerous for a girl to travel alone. You have to be careful," Colette said, concerned. "What do you do when you get sick?" she asked.

"My mom worries about your health," said Andree.

"Well, so far I've been fortunate to stay healthy. Just my feet are giving me problems."

"I brought you a small bottle of Oreganum Plus, in case you catch a cold or something. It's just a natural herb from oregano oil for treating various ailments and it's good for anything," Colette said kindly. "If you get sick, just take some orally in water or you can even use it externally."

"Thank you. That's thoughtful of you," I said gratefully.

After a brief visit, Andree's Mom had to go back home. I was astonished that she even made the effort to come. She reminded me, for good or bad, we have the ability to influence our own environment. With the right attitude, we can genuinely make things better just by showing up.

My cousin's name was also Andre and it got a bit confusing between the two. He owned his own equipment rental store in Pembroke. However, he and his wife Cathy lived in the country near the village of Chapeau, Quebec.

Cousin Andre is the same age as my older sister Chris and they have remained close friends since their youth. Chris made Andre promise he would take care of me while I was passing through his neck of the woods.

Briefly, we exchanged introductions and then everyone had to be on their way. Cecile lived in the area and was going to check in on me from time to time. Before my friend Andree left she said, "Keep in touch and call me anytime. I can still consult you on any health issues over the phone." It was the last time I would see her and Max. It saddened me to see them go.

The drive to my cousin's place took about fifteen minutes. "Be on the lookout for wild turkeys," he said as he slowly followed the long driveway leading up to his house. "Sometimes you can see them walking along the road." Though, today, they had eluded us.

Andre and his dad had built their home from the ground up and it was surrounded by acres of land. Their family dog was slow to get up and greet us. "She's getting pretty old now and sticks close to the house," Andre said. "I'm afraid that one day the wolves might get her."

Returning to his place brought back fond memories of the last time I was here with my three sisters. We were quite the handful and invaded his home with our loudness and laughter. On our way out the door, Andre jokingly said, "Come back again, just not together!" We still laugh about that today.

Cathy prepared a wonderful dinner and afterward we sat around talking. I mentioned Gidget's squeaky wheel problem and Andre offered to look at her tomorrow. "I can't promise you anything, but I'll see what I can do," he said.

We also called my sister, Chris, and she was relieved to know I was there. As long as I was with someone and not on the highway, she could relax from worry. Before bed, I updated my blog and smiled at this comment from Jo. While I lay awake thinking, I continued to be encouraged by all the help I was receiving.

From Jazzy-Jo Havenly Felines
. . ."Keep Floating on those Cat Angel Paws!"

Once again, the sun came up the following morning. Andre drove me back to the highway before going to work. He left me his cell phone in case of emergency. Not knowing what to expect from the weather, I brought Gidget to carry my load. "See you in Chalk River," I said confidently.

I was just about to get going when Cecile drove up.

"Hi Cecile. This is a nice surprise."

"Well, I worry about you being out here all alone. I have to be somewhere later, but I can follow you for a few hours."

"That's really kind of you. And look at you. You even brought coffee and muffins. Thanks."

I don't know if Cecile realized it or not, but the difference her presence made was huge. Knowing someone was following me was comforting and having support was like moving from the basement to the penthouse. It lifted me up to a whole new level of energy.

My running may have appeared easy at times, but the struggles I faced to push through every day were many. Today, I was trying to run through a slightly pulled groin. This had happened once before, in Newfoundland and I ran through it. I just had to take it easy and not push too hard. "Slow and steady," I coached myself.

With a few miles under my belt, we were stopped by a reporter, Anthony, from the *Pembroke Observer.* Cecile had arranged the interview and I was surprised by how much fun he was. The experience helped me see media people in a different light. They are human after all and have a job to do, just like everyone else.

Cecile stayed with me until we reached the Big Stop and then she had to leave. Inside, I used the facilities and made a few phone calls. Then, back to running. Traffic had increased with everyone going away for the long weekend and I was encouraged periodically when the odd person honked or waved.

A happy moment hit me at the unexpected sight of two friends from ice hockey, Carol and France. As soon as they spotted me running, they pulled over. They were both huge animal supporters.

On occasion, I would cat sit for them. Frosty and Sprite were two of the most adorable felines you could ever meet.

"I don't believe it," I said as I gave them both a hug.

"What are the odds of bumping into you out here?" said Carol.

"I know; it's crazy. Where are you headed?" I asked them.

"We just restored this old canoe and now we're going to test it out on the water. But neither one of us knows how to paddle so it should be interesting," Carol said.

We had a good laugh over that and then got caught up on any hockey news. After a short version about my journey, they had to leave.

"Be careful," they said.

"Have fun canoeing," I shouted and waved good-bye.

Running into them like that gave me a happy boost.

The shoulders along this section of the highway were a lot softer. Pushing Gidget was increasingly getting harder. About ten miles before Chalk River, I was surprised to see Cecil return.

"I was worried about you being out here with a groin problem, so I had to come back and check on you. I called your cousin and told him I would drive you back when you're done," said Cecile. She also brought a couple of cold Mountain Dew soft drinks.

"God bless you for having such a big heart Cecile," I said thankfully.

For the sake of time, we put Gidget in the trunk of her car and I was able to run that much faster. As I ran, I thought how tremendously supportive Cecile has been. It reinforced my belief that most people really do care. After all, half the population of Canada had pets. Still, I had no way of knowing if any information I was willing to communicate would even reach them.

We made it to today's marker, just short of Chalk River. Then, drove back to my cousin's store in Pembroke where another surprise awaited me. Andre's younger brother, Marcel, was visiting with his fourteen-year-old son, Joel.

I hadn't seen him in years and said, "I don't know how many more surprises I can take in one day." Then, gave him a hug.

"So you're running across Canada. Wow. I've done some running myself, but nothing like that. Do you think you can make it all the way?" Marcel asked.

"I'm sure going to try," I responded.

Cecile had to be going and I thanked her for her help. After she left, Andre very proudly gave me a tour of his shop. Business was good and he and his dad built an extension at the front of the store. It was impressive, tidy and organized, and he had a good reputation in town.

Once he locked the doors, we returned to his place for another great meal. I thought it would be my last, until Andre offered to pick me up again after my run tomorrow. His willingness moved me to tears considering how far west I was getting. This wouldn't be a short drive for him.

The next morning, Gidget got another day off. My backpack was light and I kept checking behind me to see if anyone was there, but there wasn't. No one was coming today. I missed Cecile and being able to draw from her energy. There were clouds forming in the sky and thunder that announced a coming storm.

About half way to Deep River, I watched as a car pulled over in the distance. It was too far ahead of me to make out who was waving and calling me by name. I waved back, but it wasn't until I got closer that I realized who it was. "I don't believe it," I uttered as I approached the vehicle.

"Kim, is that really you? What are the odds?" I said.

"Yep. My family is camping near Sturgeon Falls so I'm heading there for the weekend. At first I thought you were just a little kid running and I said, 'Oh that's so cute.' Then I realized, 'Hey that's Mich'. So I had to stop," she laughed.

"Well I've lost a few pounds so I probably look pretty small out here."

"When you told everyone you were taking the summer off from ball hockey, I had no idea it was because you were running across Canada."

"Well, I miss playing. How's the team doing?"

"Great, but it's not the same without you. I can't believe you ran all the way from Newfoundland to here without a support vehicle. That's so amazing."

"I know; it's pretty amazing to me too. It goes against all logic but I think there's another force at work here."

"Where's Gidget?" Kim asked.

"She needed some rest so I gave her the day off," I laughed. "My cousin's picking me up later."

"I'm sorry I don't have any water or anything to give you. Are you all right?"

"Not to worry. I'm good. I have plenty, thanks anyway."

"Well if you want to stop at our campground on your way by, I know my parents would love to see you."

"That would be fun. If I get there in time, I will."

Kim proceeded to give me directions and then signed my flag *"Go Mich! I'm so proud!"* Before she left, we exchanged a hug and then I watched her drive away. Of all the people I ran into, I was glad she was one of them. Not just because she was a friend, but because she has been consistently sending me words of encouragement since I left St. John's. Those words, and the words of others, have carried me a long way.

I didn't quite make it to Deep River when I was interrupted by a storm. By the time I reached the Subway for cover, I was drenched. My tolerance for discomfort was pretty high now and sitting in cold wet clothing didn't seem to bother me much anymore.

While I waited out the heavy rains, I went to Canadian Tire and purchased a yellow rain suit. I also thought it would make me more visible on the road.

As I approached Rolphton, I looked behind me and saw Andre following, like an angel on my shoulder. That put a big smile on my face and I waved at him. When he drove up to me, I asked him how long he had been there.

"Not long," he said.

"Do I have time to run as far as Mackey?"

"Take all the time you need," he said supportively. I threw all my stuff in his truck and then off I went.

Driving behind someone on foot wasn't easy on this highway. In fact, it was pretty slow going and boring for the person behind the wheel. Andre drove ahead of me and then would stop to read the newspaper, until I caught up to him. Then, he would do it again.

At one point, there were three big dogs on my heels. I was relieved when they lost interest and thankful that Andre had my back if they hadn't backed off.

Despite the hills, I finished feeling pretty good and it felt like I had run the last eight kilometers in record time. "All done," I told Andre happily and jumped into his truck.

On our way back, he took a detour through Petawawa. It was located in a beautiful section of the Ottawa Valley, along the river and adjacent to Algonquin Provincial Park. I had never been to the base before and he thought it might be of interest to me. We were just passing through and didn't stop.

When I got out of the truck, I had stiffened up from the ride home. A shower was going to feel great. Before the end of the evening, Andre took me into the garage. "Gidget got a makeover," he said. "I put new tires on her and was able to blow the grit out of the wheel bearings."

Both Andre and his son, Albert, called around looking for replacement wheels, but with no luck. "I don't know how long she'll last, but this should get you a little further," Andre said. I was heart-frozen by their efforts.

Chris called again that night. I could sense the concern in her voice now that I was leaving Andre's care.

"Are you done yet?" she asked.

"Not quite, but I'll be in Thunder Bay soon."

"Can you hurry up before I die of a heart attack?"

I knew she meant that in the kindest way.

While I lay in bed, thinking about every day that led up to this one was overwhelming. The weight of all my yesterdays was increasing and putting them on a shelf was critical to me not buckling under my emotions.

Andre drove a long way to get me back to my starting point. Before he left, he gave me the phone numbers for his two sisters in North Bay and they were expecting me to call. It was comforting to know they were looking out for me. There were no words to express my gratitude for everything he had done. How do you thank someone who gives you his or her heart? Or for the priceless moments, I could never repay.

Standing alone on the side of the highway once again, the distance in front of me felt enormous. Sometimes, it felt like the next town was just too far for me to reach. The road was getting longer the further west I went and the remoteness of northern Ontario was looming in the air. Somehow, my eyes managed to fix themselves on the horizon and not what was in between.

Pushed by the wind, I ran and I ran, and I ran. Each hurdle cleared, was adding to my endurance. Then, something made me look behind and I saw a wonderful sight. The faces of every person who helped get me this far.

They were clapping and cheering. I smiled and waved at them. Seeing them again helped me find a reserve of strength I didn't think I had. Their encouragement made me feel like everything was going to be all right because I desperately needed them to believe the impossible was possible.

Then, I rubbed the tears from my eyes and their faces disappeared – all except one. Cecile was following me in her car. I had to stop to make sure that what I saw was real.

"Cecile?"

"Your cousin was going to accompany you all the way to Deux Rivieres if I hadn't volunteered," Cecile smiled.

It was at that moment I understood why Andre and my sister had stayed friends all these years. He was like an older brother I never had. What could I say about Cecile? She was this big ball of energy I could draw from. "Wow. Both of you are incredible! I can't believe you're really here," I said, a little shocked.

Happy to have an escort, I frequently turned around and waved at Cecile. She followed and was my shadow all the way into Antler's Kingfisher Campground. The campground was located right off the highway and overlooked Sunset Bay on the Upper Ottawa River. It was packed for the July 1st weekend. Fortunately, the owners, Sandy and Doug, had a spot for me. They also didn't charge me in support of my run.

Cecile stayed until she felt confident I was safe inside my tent. It was just starting to rain when we said good-bye for the last time.

"Are you sure you will be all right here for the night?" asked Cecile.

"I'll be fine, and tomorrow I'll be with another cousin," I answered.

"Send me an email and let me know how you are doing."

"I will and I can't thank you enough for everything you've done Cecile. I'll miss you."

"I'll be following your blog too," Cecile said as she reluctantly drove away. Her kindness was a gift in friendship I would never forget.

My tent was protected under some towering pine trees. Once nightfall set in, there were fireworks and celebrations in spite of the rain. It was close to midnight before the campground was quiet again, except for the weather. The rain continued throughout the night and into the next day.

I was hoping for a peaceful sleep, but my tent wasn't as enjoyable as I remembered. Sleeping in a bed for the past couple of weeks had spoiled me. Begrudgingly, I got up in the morning and complained the whole time I packed up. I don't know why I was so grumpy. It wasn't like I hadn't been rained on before. "You better check your attitude at the door on your way out," I nipped at me. "I'm not going to put up with your bad mood today," I continued. "There's no place for negative thinking on this trip."

Gidget got an ear full. I think if I hadn't got over myself quickly, she was going to show me the door. Then I thanked her for letting me vent and looked around to see if anyone was listening. Of course I laughed at myself for having this conversation with a stroller. "You're a good listener, Gidget," I whispered and patted her handle as if it were an arm.

On the highway, it was just me and Gidget again. She wasn't squeaking anymore and we were moving at a fairly good clip. There was an endless stream of traffic from people heading home after the long weekend.

Ottawa was about 160 miles behind me now. Surrounded by unspoiled wilderness helped put me back in the right frame of mind.

I reveled in the rugged beauty etched into the landscape and the serenity of each moment. I was at peace with nature all around me and the great outdoors. The havoc of a city was a dim memory.

On the edge of the forest and lakes, I watched the shorelines for bears, deer, or moose coming to the water's edge for a drink. I listened for the haunting, lonely cry of the loons on the water.

In the heart of an area featured in a number of outdoor magazines, I was pleasantly affected by the presence of wildlife in their natural habitat. There were uninterrupted miles of magnificent forest and it was a unique outdoor experience.

Winding through timber cuts and rolling hills made for some spectacular scenery, but it also felt like a continuous climb. Thankfully, it was a downhill run into Mattawa. However before I descended, I met two young teenage boys, Karl and Joel, as they were walking their bikes up the long hill.

"Hi guys," I said.

"Hello," they both replied.

"That's quite a climb. I'm glad I'm running downhill and not up."

"What are you running for?" asked Joel.

"I'm running solitary across Canada," I told them and they listened intently as I explained why.

"Wow. That's pretty amazing. Our dogs are fixed."

"I'm glad to hear that."

"We shouldn't kill animals though if we don't need to," they both agreed.

"Would you like to sign my flag?"

"Sure. I think I have a dollar I can donate too," Joel said as he searched his trouser pocket.

"Thanks for your support."

"No problem. We hope you make it. Good luck," they encouraged me. They also left an impression on me and blew me away with their maturity. Their genuine concern would put a lot of adults to shame.

Down the hill I went. Keeping Gidget from speeding away from me was a chore. I called my cousin, Blanche-Helene, from the Valois Motel. When I saw her, it wasn't hard to see the family resemblance. She reminded me of my older sister, Chris. My dad often told me I looked like her mom, my Aunt May who lived in North Bay. I was looking forward to visiting with her too.

"You haven't changed much Blanche-Helene," I said.

"Well, I'm a grandmother now and you'll meet my grandson, Dali, when we get to the house. We're babysitting him today. He's with his grandfather right now," she said.

Arriving at their home, I also met her two sons, Anthony and Alexander. They were working on a racecar in the garage – a hobby of theirs. Inside, I met her grandson Dali. They had areas of the house barricaded because he had just started walking and was getting into everything. What a bundle of joy he was.

Blanche-Helene's husband, Noel, came home and prepared an excellent roast beef dinner for us. We all gathered in the dining room for a great meal.

"You must be hungry after all that running today," said Noel.

"That's quite the adventure you're on," Blanche-Helene said.

"It's a challenge for sure and I do get pretty hungry."

"How are your mom and dad doing?" asked Blanche-Helene.

"They're doing well. Florida seems to agree with them and keeps them healthy," I answered.

"Mom would love to see your dad sometime."

"Yes, it would be nice to get them together. I'm looking forward to seeing her and Francine again. I had a great visit with Andre and Cathy."

We chatted for a while and I enjoyed their company, but it was all I could do to stay awake after eating so well. It was never long after a meal that I needed to sleep.

In the morning, Blanche-Helene drove me back to the motel. We delighted in deer sightings along the way. "We get lots of deer out here," she told me.

"They're such beautiful creatures," I said.

Today, there were more hills to climb but I was uplifted by another encounter with some familiar faces. What were the odds that I would run into Kim's parents traveling back to Ottawa? I met Kim's parents when they came out to watch our ball hockey games. They were our biggest fans and some of the nicest people you will ever meet. Everyone loved them.

"Hello," we said while exchanging hugs.

"Kim said she saw you running on the highway and to watch out for you," said Kim's mom.

"I must have missed her on her return trip. How was camping?" I asked.

"We had a great time and wished we could have stayed longer. How are you doing? How are your feet? Can we get you anything?" replied Kim's dad.

"I'm doing okay, thank you. My feet are holding up so far and I'm staying with some cousins who live nearby."

While we were talking on the side of the road, an OPP car pulled up. They did that from time to time.

"Everything okay?" the officer in the passenger seat asked.

"Oh yeah. These are my friends," I answered.

"Where's your running stroller?" he asked.

"I gave Gidget the day off. She needed the rest," I smiled and we all had a good laugh over that.

"Well, have yourselves a nice day," they said and drove off.

"Thanks for stopping," I waved.

Then, I took out my flag and pointed to where Kim signed her name. They signed their names next to hers and then had to leave.

"Thank you so much for stopping," I said and gave them both a hug.

"Be careful and take care of yourself. Good luck the rest of the way," they said.

As they drove off, I thought how glad I was that I hadn't missed them, or the joy of seeing them again.

Sometime later, in the cool and quiet of the afternoon, I stopped at a rest stop. They were always a welcome sight and a great place to meet people. As I paused to take in some of the beauty of my surroundings, I met a wonderful couple from the United States.

"We're very familiar with TNR," they said. "It has been extremely successful in our community and many others. It's good to hear Canada is trying to do something similar."

"I hope you're right," I replied.

Blanche-Helene faithfully picked me up at the Bonfield junction. There was a house full of people when we got back. Her father, my

Uncle Clay, was there but he didn't remember me. In the early years, both our families lived in Elliot Lake and he was a schoolteacher at the high school. My sister Chris was one of his students. Teaching ran in their family. Blanche-Helene, her younger sister Francine, and their mom were all schoolteachers.

Dali's mom was also in the living room. After my Uncle Clay left, we moved outside onto the deck while I iced my feet. I started playing tag with Dali. "I'm going to get you," I kept teasing him. He ran back and forth and around the chairs laughing so hard from his belly that he had the rest of us in stitches. He was so much fun to play with, but then it took a while for him to unwind.

Evening passed and then it was morning. Blanche-Helen took me for breakfast at the junction restaurant. From there, I was looking forward to spending the next few days with her sister, Francine, in North Bay.

Before we left the restaurant, I had a brief encounter with the waitress while Blanche-Helen used the restroom. "I would donate to children before ever making a donation to animals," she said and walked away. Her comment caught me off guard. She was so nice when she served our food.

Certainly, if push comes to shove I would save a child before an animal, but not without trying to rescue the animal too. People who belittle other people's efforts typically like to console themselves by saying their heart is in the right place and thinking they are kind, or that they would never hurt a fly. Yet, they are usually the ones who have never made the slightest sacrifice for a fellow creature.

Standing outside and saying good-bye, I found myself again searching for words of gratitude.

"Thanks for everything Blanche-Helene," I said. Reconnecting with her and meeting her family was a delight I wasn't expecting.

"Enjoy your stay with Francine. I think she's taking you to have dinner with Mom tomorrow," she said.

What great cousins I had. Their support was precious to me and my visits memorable.

Everything was set for today's handoff. This morning, Noel had taken Gidget with him to his store in North Bay. Francine and I would pick her up later. It was exciting to think I would be in North Bay by this afternoon.

On my way there, I ran through some pretty rugged road. Once again, I had another joyful encounter. This time, it was with Sharron's Dad driving east.

"Hello there," I said, surprised to see him.

"Sharron told me about your run across Canada and to keep an eye out for you," he said.

"Sharron's got all kinds of people watching out for me," I chuckled.

"That's quite the feat you've taken on. How are you doing?"

"Today is a good day."

"How far do you think you'll get?"

"All the way I hope."

"Are you getting lots of support?"

"I couldn't have made it this far without the help of so many incredible people. It's been amazing. Right now, I've got relatives in this part of the country and they are taking really good care of me."

"That's great. You sure you're okay?"

"I'm good. Thank you," I assured him.

"Well, take care then and good luck to you."

"Thanks for stopping and say hi to Sharron for me."

Along this stretch of the highway, people were beeping and waving as they drove by. Every honk had that new experience about it, causing me to perk up. I had forgotten what that felt like and appreciated the encouraging reminder.

After running down a hill, I approached the exit for North Bay. To my surprise, there was a reporter from the *North Bay Nugget* waiting for me at the turnoff. He had snapped some pictures long before I knew he was there.

"You're running at a pretty good pace," he said and shook my hand.

"Yeah, I do a lot better when I'm not pushing a stroller," I laughed. He was fun to talk to.

Reaching North Bay was another milestone in my run and a huge confidence builder. It was the gateway to Northern Ontario. As I passed through, my eyes were as big as quarters and I had a happy face on.

Francine found me at the northwest edge of the city.

"Hey cousin, good to see you again. It's been awhile," I said as we exchanged a hug.

"That's quite the adventure you're on," she smiled.

"I know; it's kind of an insane thing to do."

"I don't think so," she said.

Francine was a little older than I was and the last time I saw her was at my parents' fiftieth wedding anniversary. As a schoolteacher, she had the summer off and the timing for her to help me worked out perfectly.

Before going to her home, we stopped at SportChek so I could pick up a new pair of running shoes. Then, to Active Running for some socks. Our last stop was at Noel's photography store to pick up Gidget and my stuff. From there, we went to her house.

After dinner, Francine took me on a tour of North Bay's beautifully constructed waterfront. We strolled along the shores of Lake Nipissing and I was mesmerized by the grandeur of the water and shoreline. "You'll enjoy the scenery from here on," she encouraged me. I did.

The next day, every other bend displayed a splendid view of the lake and I was surrounded by more natural beauty. Often I caught myself saying, "Wow, what a beautiful country I live in."

Then, I came to a long strait stretch of highway leading to Sturgeon Falls. Staring it down was like looking at a large body of water thinking it's not that far to swim across until you've been in it for a while and realize the other side is further than you think.

To my left was a railroad track that ran parallel to the highway. I watched as a small train car headed toward me. It slowed down and one of the two maintenance men shouted at me, "Would you like a bottle of cold water?"

I looked around to make sure he was talking to me and then yelled back, "That would be great." I crossed the road and started down the ditch when he shouted, "Wait there and I'll come to you. The ditch is pretty marshy and if you don't have boots on, you'll get wet."

He jumped off the car and brought me two bottles of iced cold water.

"Thank you so much," I beamed. "That's very kind of you."

"No problem," he said and hopped back on the car.

"Wow," I thought and waved at them. I was astonished that he did that.

Not five minutes later, a woman in a car stopped. Her name was Manon and she lived in Sturgeon Falls.

"I saw you earlier," she said. "I just had to come back and give you something cold to drink. You have to be careful in this heat and get enough fluids in you," she warned me and handed me a bottle of Gatorade and more water.

"Thank you. That's very thoughtful of you," I replied and then she drove away.

"Wow," I said astonished a second time. I wasn't going to be thirsty today.

Before I left Sturgeon Falls, I made one last stop at the information centre. Inside I met two workers, both named Julie.

"You're the woman running across Canada," they said as I brought a pop to the counter.

"Yes, I am," I smiled.

"We read about you in the *Nugget*. It's wonderful to meet you in person."

"It's nice to meet both of you too."

"You're very brave to do something like this for animals. We're both animal lovers and think what you are doing is amazing."

"Thank you. Hopefully, this will help in some way. How much do I owe you for the drink?"

"Nothing, I think you've earned it."

"Well thank you. That's very kind."

"Good luck the rest of the way. We'll be cheering for you."

I continued running past Cache Bay and then Francine picked me up.

"You certainly run a long way," she said.

"Yeah, I'm like the Energizer Bunny, I just keep on going," I laughed.

We headed back to North Bay and Francine surprised me with a special appointment.

"I talked to some people at PhysioTherapy Works and they can give you a foot massage today if you like. They'll take you right away," she said.

I was stunned and excited at the same time. "Really? That's fantastic. Let's go before they change their mind."

When we walked into the clinic, I started to introduce myself but was interrupted midstream.

"We know who you are. We read about you in the paper. Congratulations on making it this far," the person at the front desk said as other staff members came over to greet me and show their support.

"Thank you and thank you for squeezing me in on such short notice."

"Well it's not every day we meet someone running solitary across Canada without a support vehicle, especially a girl. It's amazing that you've been able to run all this way alone."

"I know; it even amazes me."

Then, a young girl stepped forward and said in a soft voice, "Hi, I'm Laura and I'll be your massage therapist."

"It's really nice to meet you," I said.

"Follow me and I'll start you off in the therapeutic tub," said Laura.

"I think my feet are going to enjoy this," I smiled and followed her.

Laura barely looked twenty years old, but she conducted herself professionally. While my feet were soaking in the tub, she asked some questions.

"What sort of problems are you having?" she inquired.

"It feels like my feet are bruised and I'm walking on twigs. Like I have little balls or something growing underneath and I'm standing on marbles. It started shortly after I left St. John's Newfoundland. At first, it was mild but it's been progressively getting worse. More recently, the arches of my feet and ankles are painful."

After a period of time, we moved into a massage room where Laura began explaining the mechanics of the foot and what could be happening. While she massaged my feet, we carried on a wonderful conversation.

"I have a dog and I could never give her up. I think it is terrible what's happening to abandoned animals and how some animals are mistreated," said Laura.

"It's very disturbing," I said.

"There should be stricter laws to protect them."

"Unfortunately, laws only work if they are enforced."

"How long did it take you to train for this?"

"About eighteen months, but in hindsight I really undertrained and the mental challenges have been a lot harder than the physical ones."

"Oh, what do you mean?"

"Besides problems with my feet, I wasn't expecting that the conscious focus over such a long period of time would be so extremely draining. You have to keep working at it and constantly finding ways to persevere. Chances are, you will give up unless your passion is strong enough."

> *"The human heart is stronger than any power on earth."*
>
> *– D. Bonhoeffer*

Anyone who has ever been seriously involved in sports knows that it takes a lot of hard work and discipline to stay fit. Physically, you can train your body to do just about anything. Being physically fit makes you feel like you can accomplish anything, but only as long as you can keep going. Making this kind of effort every day might feel impossible, but with the right stuff, it can be done. Part of it is a belief that you can't fail. That'll carry you most of the time.

The emotional side of my fitness has been occasionally unpredictable. However, over time, I was discovering that the body and the mind are amazing creations and physical strength is something that shouldn't be underestimated.

"What kind of things did you do to prepare yourself?" asked Laura.

"Mostly I ran in all kinds of conditions. I think it helped that I've been active most of my life too. But I also did some cross training."

"What kind of cross training?"

"I played a lot of hockey and squash."

It felt like I had faded in and out of our conversation, but I couldn't be sure. Then Laura said, "Okay, we're done." I apologized for dosing off and Laura kindly responded, "Not a problem. Take your time getting up."

At that moment, a nap sounded pretty good. Instead, I forced myself up and headed back to the front desk.

"How much do I owe you Laura?"

"Your cousin wanted to pay for your massage, but I'd like to donate the fee to your cause," Laura offered.

"Wow. That's really kind of you."

"I think it's a great cause."

"Thank you very much, and my feet thank you too."

"Good luck the rest of the way."

"What a great group of people," I said to Francine as we left the building.

I was having an exceptional day and it continued with an unplanned stop at the Humane Society. When we entered the building, I saw a portrait of a woman hanging on the wall. Her name was Marjorie Wright and she's remembered for her many years of dedication and volunteer work for animal welfare in the North Bay area. She was one of the Humane Society's past presidents and the staff spoke highly of her. Like everyone else, I was inspired by her life story.

One of the animal control officers said to me, "Educating the public about spay and neutering and responsible pet ownership is key to reducing the overpopulation problem. Your raising awareness should help. Good luck to you."

From there, we returned to Francine's house to get ready for dinner with her mom. I was a little short on clothes and we had some fun fitting me into a pair of her jeans and a t-shirt. They were a little long for my limbs, but it felt good to wear something different.

Dinner was at Francine's mom's residency.

"Hi Auntie May, it's good to see you again," I said as we exchanged a hug.

"It's good to see you too. Francine tells me you're running across Canada. That's quite the adventure."

"Yes it is and your kids have been great helping me out."

"You must be hungry."

"I am. Running so much has given me a very big appetite."

"I'm glad you could join us for dinner."

There was a common dining room and when we sat down I met some of her friends. It was interesting to hear their comments. There was something about hurting a helpless creature that didn't sit right with people.

"Pet owners are the ones who should be put down," one woman shouted.

"People shouldn't have pets if they can't take care of them," another one said.

"It's shameful," someone added.

Then, the conversations shifted to other matters.

"How are your parents doing?" asked Auntie May.

"They're doing well and still enjoy being snowbirds. It seems to agree with them. Dad might be a little jealous though when he finds out I had dinner with you."

"Is your dad still playing golf?"

"Yes, he still gets out there once in a while. How about you?"

"No, I'm getting too old for that now," she laughed.

"I hear you're a pretty good pool player."

"Yes. They have a table here. Would you like to play a game?"

"Sure. I'd love to."

After we finished eating, we moved to the game room. Francine didn't play pool, but she sat and watched.

"You must have taken it easy on me Auntie May," I said after I sunk the eight ball.

"You've played before have you?"

"A little when I was in the military. My dad's a good pool player. Have you ever played with him?"

"No. We've never played together."

Once our game ended, we went upstairs to her apartment. It was a small room but large enough for her. The walls were full of family photographs and we took a trip down memory lane. She brought out the family tree she had been working on for years. When we came to my mom and dad's page, I helped her fill in a few blanks.

There was little time left in the day and impossible to squeeze any more in. Leaving the residency, I thought how precious these moments are and you never forget them. I fell asleep satisfied and while I slept, Francine stepped out to pick up a few things she would surprise me with in the morning.

Before she drove me back to the highway, she made sure I had enough to eat and put together a care package to go. It included creams for my sunburned nose, some jellybeans, and a "smiley face". Saying good-bye was my least favorite part.

"Thanks for everything Francine," I said as we exchanged a hug.

"You can do it," she encouraged me.

"I don't know if I'll make it all the way, but I'll give it my best."

"You'll do it," she said more confidently than I felt.

"I'll have to come back again for a visit. Maybe we can go for a hike or something."

"I'll be here."

"Thanks again Francine," I said one last time. "Here I go."

Francine watched from her car until I was out of sight. She had been terrific and did just about everything to help, except run for me. I don't think she realized the impact her support had on me. It helped to renew my challenge to finish. Outwardly, things have the appearance of looking easy, but what is not seen is the inward struggle and the times we wrestle with doubt. I wouldn't be here without her help.

Although the highway to Sudbury was relatively flat, it wasn't as flat on foot as it is when a car powers you. After eighty-three days of long distance running, I could feel every bump in the road and even the little hills felt like mountains.

My next lifeline was in knowing my parents were picking me up later. They had arrived in Sudbury yesterday and staying at my cousin Kim's house, the daughter of my mom's twin sister. My Aunt Jeanie had been hospitalized after a number of strokes and was also visiting for the weekend.

I made two phone calls that day. The first one to CTV News in Sudbury and the second to my parents when I reached the town of Hagar.

"We looked for you yesterday on the highway," my dad said disappointedly.

"Yeah, it's easy to miss me if I'm off the road. I'm glad you're here," I said.

When he picked me up, I told him I spoke with someone from CTV news. "If we stop at the studio today, they'll do an interview." My dad didn't hesitate when he replied, "Sure, no problem." Then we joked about the possibility of him being on T.V.

We arrived at the studio and a reporter met us outside. The interview was done in the parking lot and I considered it another small victory.

"It'll be shown on the six o'clock and eleven o'clock news," they said.

"Thank you very much," I responded and hopped back into my dad's van.

"That was short and sweet," my parents thought.

Going on from there, we pulled into Kim's driveway. There was a house full of people, plus their beautiful dog. Kim and her husband Lorenzo are the kind of people who are well prepared for visitors. "I keep a freezer full of readymade food so all I have to do is thaw and serve," Kim said cheerfully. Nobody ever lacked anything at their place.

They also had a camper trailer parked in the driveway.

"We thought you might enjoy staying in it for the next two nights. Everyone else will be in the house so it should be quiet for you," said Kim.

"Any problems with mosquitoes?" I asked.

"No, not that I know of. It's fairly new. Why?" she asked a little baffled by my question.

"No reason. Just wondering," I smiled. As it turned out, it was the best room in the house.

While I was updating my blog, Kim let me know they were all following my journey.

"My mom checks your blog everyday religiously," she said. "She worries when you haven't updated it for a few days and calls me to see if I've heard anything."

I was also deeply moved by this comment on my blog from someone in the area.

> *July 7, Ginger said. . .*
> *Oh, wow, Michelle–I saw you on Hwy 17 between Mattawa and Bonfield. At the time I had not yet heard of your mission, but when I saw you I had an urge to stop. Due to the road and traffic I didn't stop, but now I wish that I had found a spot and waited for you so that I could meet you and sign your flag. What you are doing for the sake of animals is awe-inspiring.*
>
> *My husband and I are lifelong animal lovers and rescuers. We are poor financially but rich in spirit and love for all living creatures. We have eight cats, two dogs, one pot-bellied pig and many birds that we care for. We have rescued several chickens from a poultry auction and given them a good home where they can roam free in the daytime and be safe at night. All of our cats and dogs either came from an animal shelter or were obviously unwanted strays, including a pregnant female cat who presented us with three beautiful kittens. All of our cats and dogs are spayed or neutered, save for the two female kittens who we hope to have spayed soon. It would be so wonderful to have a spay-neuter clinic or other financial help for those of us with very limited income but very big hearts.*
>
> *Thank you for all you are doing to raise awareness of the plight of dogs, cats and other creatures "thrown away" by thoughtless humans. None of them deserved to be killed.*

Over the next couple of days, my dad drove me back and forth to the highway. He brought me snacks, picked blueberries for me, waited patiently, and I loved him for it. Sharing this time with him was priceless.

On one occasion while I was running, I stopped to change my socks across from a riding stable. As I sat there watching the riders come in, a car pulled up and two women got out. "Hi, my name is Amanda and this is Cathy. We love animals too and it's a shame what's happening to cats and dogs. There's a place somewhere just outside Sudbury that tries to assist people with spay and neutering their pets, but I can't remember the name of it." I appreciated they took the time to stop and say hello.

Shortly after they left, I encountered a reporter from CBC radio. His name was Dan and he just happened to be driving by, when he caught sight of me. "We don't usually conduct interviews this way but a girl running across Canada alone without a support vehicle is a little unusual," he said.

With a recorder on hand, he asked me some fun questions.

"What do you do when you have to go to the bathroom?"

"Well, the great outdoors is a pretty big outhouse," I laughed.

"Do you have any favorite songs you like to sing?"

"I like the old highway songs."

"Are you getting lots of response?"

"People must have watched the news last night because drivers are honking and waving as they pass by."

"Well thanks for talking to us," he said and wished me luck.

The days were swifter than I could run. One afternoon, my dad and Lorenzo left to go fishing while the rest of us went to visit Kim's sister in the hospital. While we were there, Kim received a phone call that Lorenzo had taken my dad to emergency, but we didn't know where or why.

On our way back home, we dropped my Aunt Jeanie off at her residency. "Call me when you have some news," she said with concern. All we knew was that a fishing hook had struck him.

Not long after we arrived at the house, Lorenzo and my dad walked in.

"What happened? Are you all right?" asked Kim.

"A fishing hook got stuck in my finger," my dad answered.

"How bad is it?" I asked.

"He'll be okay after a few beers," Lorenzo laughed.

"How did it happen?" asked Kim.

"I was taking the fishing rods out of the boat and the hook dug into my finger. I must have grabbed it the wrong way," my dad said.

"That's it," my mom responded.

"We thought you got a hook in the eye or something while you were casting," said Kim.

"We didn't even get the boat off the trailer," my dad replied.

"You mean the boat wasn't even in the water?" said Mom.

"No. It was still on the trailer attached to the truck," said my dad.

Well, we all had a good laugh over that one and didn't let him live it down for the rest of the night. All the while we were thankful that it wasn't more serious than it was.

Packing up the next morning was an emotional struggle for me. I could put on a brave face but today I was not looking forward to being dropped off. Once again, we would be parting ways.

"Thanks for everything Kim," I said. "As always, you've been a great hostess."

"We'll be following your blog," she replied.

"I'll try my best to keep it up to date so your mom doesn't worry."

"That would be great. Good luck." They waved good-bye.

In the van, my parents raved about the good time they had. The only downside was me not driving home with them. Then, we stood at the highway junction to Coniston for a few minutes exchanging hugs.

I tried to hide what was going on inside, but extended fatigue, mixed with emotions, is not a good combination. I could tell everyone how great I was doing, but in reality I was wearing down. Every day, slowly sucking the life out of me.

"Well, this is it," I said a little shaky.

"You sure you don't want to come home with us?" my mom asked.

"I'm sure mom. I have to finish this."

"Well, you be careful and phone when you can."

"I will. I'll get to John and Susan's tonight and stay with them for the next few days, so that's good." I managed to get out but I was no longer able to control my emotions and tears welled up in my eyes.

"You sure you're all right?" she asked, sensing something might be wrong.

"I'm okay. Really. I'm just tired. I'll be all right once I start running."

"You want us to wait with you a little longer?" my dad asked.

"No, you better get going before I change my mind," I laughed.

"You sure?"

"I'm sure."

"Well, you take care of yourself," mom said.

"I will and thanks for being here."

"We love you," they repeated as they got back in the van.

"Have a safe trip home," I said as I fought back the tears.

"Bye mom. Bye dad. I love you both," I shouted, but I don't think anything came out. I felt the way being left behind makes you feel.

They hadn't left my sight and I longed for them to turn around. I wanted them to put their arms around me again and tell me everything was going to be okay. Instead, streams of tears rolled down my cheeks. The floodgate opened and my heart poured out on the ground. My sobs were so deep, they hurt.

These emotional reversals, after leaving my safety nets, came quickly and more often now. They were totally unexpected and I found it difficult to snap out of them and pull myself together. "I can't do this anymore," I whimpered. I couldn't see how I was going to get up and do this again tomorrow, or the next day, or the day after that.

However, somehow in my weakest moments, I was able to force myself to put one foot in front of the other. Through those same tears came tears of healing. Above my sobs, I began hearing the sounds of beeping horns again and I acknowledged drivers by waving back. Slowly, I regained my composure and once again my emotions were in check. Finally, I managed to let out a laugh, "Honestly Michelle, you're such a baby. What's with the crying anyways? Seriously." I always felt bad after my little meltdowns.

Pushing Gidget through the freshly, graded gravel was slow going. I was more than happy to get through the construction zone and reach the city center of Sudbury. Before leaving the city limits,

I was uplifted by the support of an older couple. "You're making a difference," they said.

Pedestrians were prohibited on the four-lane highway out of town. I hopped on Highway 55 through to Whitefish. Just before getting back on Highway 17, I had another encounter with a couple from the area. They were driving by and stopped to say hello.

"If you don't have anywhere to stay tonight, we'd be delighted to have you stay with us," they kindly offered.

"Wow, that's really nice of you, but I have relatives who live nearby and they are picking me up. But thank you anyway."

"Okay. Good luck to you and keep it up," they encouraged me.

By the time I reached Blueberry Station, I had run almost thirty miles. John and Susan, were my sister Chris' in-laws and they had a beautiful country home off the highway. They sent their daughter Rose to pick me up and bring me back to their house.

When we arrived, there were hens running around in the yard.

"They're everywhere," I chuckled.

John was outside and said, "The rooster's in the barn, that's why they are out."

Then their two beautiful Bishon dogs came running outside and greeted us.

Inside, I hugged Susan and John proceeded to give me a tour of their home. He explained all about their renovations over the years and the ones they were still working on. His workmanship was excellent. Taking it all in was helping me to forget all about my little breakdown earlier in the day.

The next morning, Rose's husband Mike took me back to Blueberry Station on his way into Sudbury. It was about five miles from where John and Susan lived, and I would have to run right by their property.

To my surprise, they were watching and waiting for me.

"We knew you were coming when we heard the neighbor's dog barking," Susan confessed. After exchanging hugs, they took some pictures and cheered me on.

"See you in a while," I shouted.

Going a little further, I passed by Mike and Rose's house. They had bought an old church and converted it into a home. It was interesting to hear about their plans and I was looking forward to seeing the inside later.

About halfway to Espanola, I ran into another cyclist heading east and we talked at length.

"That's quite the load you're carrying," I said.

"I'm a musician from B.C. and heading for Halifax. My next gig is in Sudbury."

"Are you any good?" I asked him.

"Some people think so," he laughed.

"Too bad my timing's off. I would have enjoyed seeing you play, but Sudbury is behind me now."

"How far are you going?" he asked.

"All the way to Vancouver."

"Wow, makes cycling seem like nothing compared to what you're doing," he marveled. Then he signed my flag and we wished each other safe travels.

When I arrived at the junction for Espanola, I waited at the trading post. Rose was picking me up after work. I had some time to kill and made a few phone calls. Then, I browsed through the store. It was really hot, so I bought an ice cream and sat outside on a picnic table. Across from me was a young family of four eating oranges.

"Would you like one?" the father asked.

"Thank you, I love oranges."

"We're leaving now so if you like you can have the rest," he said as he handed me a bag of freshly cut oranges.

"Thanks. That's very kind of you," and off they went.

After sitting in my own sweat for a few hours, I enjoyed immensely taking a shower and knowing my bed would comfort me soon.

Susan made a wonderful last meal of meat and potatoes. Then, we went to visit Rose and Mike at their house. They showed me before and after pictures from the start of their renovations. On the outside, they wanted to preserve the church's structure and look. However, on the inside, it needed redesigning to include all the amenities of a home. The end result was going to be beautiful.

In the morning, John and Susan drove me back to the turnoff for Espanola. John took Gidget out from the back of his vehicle and we discovered she had a flat tire. Somewhere along the way, she snagged a safety pin. John felt bad but was confident someone at Canadian Tire could fix it quickly, and they did. I was grateful they didn't charge me.

With a repaired tire, Gidget and I reached the top of the hill. Looking back over the junction, John and Susan were behind us now and I would be too far for anyone to pick me up. "Looks like it's just you and me again, Gidget," I sighed.

Before leaving the area, I thought how being relayed through this part of Ontario had carried me a long way. It was helping to keep my dream alive. If not for that, I would have given up a long time ago.

Then, I glared down the highway in the direction of Thunder Bay, where my sisters were still a long way off. "Run in the footsteps of your heart," I heard the whisper of the wind say, "and you'll get through this. Run, and don't look back."

Dorit & Michelle in St. John's NL

Mile One supporters in St. John's NL

Michelle at Mile One, St John's NL

Setting up my tent outside St. John's NL

Michelle, Megan, Matthew & Darryl, Thorburn NS

Meeting Richard Ralph near St. Alexander QC

Cumberland Veterinary Hospital staff in the window, Orleans ON

Michelle & Andree, Orleans ON

Michelle with Nathalie & her two sons, Ottawa, ON

AHS volunteers, Arnprior ON

Michelle & cousin Andre, Pembroke ON

Michelle & Cecile, Pembroke ON

Michelle with Mom & Dad, Sudbury ON

Kelly, Andrea, Michelle, Lorne, Kay & Beth, Bruce Mines, ON

Michelle & Bob Lewis, Neys Provincial Park ON

Michelle & Tylar near Nipigon ON

Running with New Hope Rescue supporters, Thunder Bay ON

At Terry Fox Monument, Thunder Bay ON

A selfie with Gordon Robb near Raith ON

Running with Tracey from Medicine Hat to Suffield AB

Running with Tracey from Medicine Hat to Suffield AB

Running with Tracey from Medicine Hat to Suffield AB

Michelle & Tracey enjoying a pizza, Lethbridge AB

Michelle, Tracey, Barb & Laney, Lethbridge AB

Ethel & Ron of LHS, Lethbridge AB

LHS volunteers, Lethbridge AB

Me with Jennifer's cats, Calgary AB

Jake, Cheryl, Kelly, Deb & Michelle, Calgary AB

Reception cake, Calgary AB

Calgary reception with MEOW Foundation & CHS, AB

Calgary reception at The Cat House, AB

Jim from the Roadrunner running group, Calgary AB

Finishing in Vancouver BC

Lion's Gate Bridge and Stanley Park in background from Ambleside Park

Me putting my hand in the Pacific Ocean at Ambleside Park BC

Homecoming reception at Ottawa Airport, ON

Sharron & me leaving Ottawa Airport, ON

One of my flags with signatures

Chapter 5

Northern Ontario

There was something wonderfully different and fresh about how I felt today. I sprung up like a flower and longed to reach beyond the horizon in front of me. With eyes wide open, I fixed them on what I could not see. Once again, I was filled with the romantic urge to run to Vancouver.

Absorbed by this single-minded thought, it fuelled my all-consuming passion all over again. "This land is my land," I screamed at the top of my lungs. "And this highway is my highway," I claimed to no one except myself. With that, the power of the wind was like the sound of rushing water and a voice calling, "Come and claim your prize if you dare."

Once more, I looked to the east and saw the far side of an ocean. Then again to the west, where the wings of dawn and victory is sure for those who endure. Suddenly, every hill appeared lower, every rough ground level, and every valley rose enticing me to step forward. This was my highway to run.

Three days later, I approached the KOA Campground near Spragge. Under a cloud of rain, I set up my tent and then hung out in the laundry room to dry off. It was always tempting to take up refuge there.

When I made my escape back to my tent, I met two female cyclists taking cover under a tree. The rain came down in buckets. One of them said with excitement and a distinct accent, "We're from Ireland and come to see Canada."

As everyone darted for their tent they shouted, "If this keeps up we'll all be flooded by morning." That was the last I heard of them for the night. While I lay in the warmth of my sleeping bag, I recalled the words of encouragement from my blog.

> *Hey Michelle. I wanted to let you know I saw you on Rogers TV in Ottawa last night. I can't believe what a commitment you are making. You are my hero. This is a courageous task you've taken on. To make it as far as you have is amazing, and you are to be commended. You're doing a wonderful thing. I wish you all the best on your journey. You are making a difference. Take care of yourself. Denise*

> *Watching your progress and praying for you Michelle. Hope you gain publicity as you go. Margaret, Helping Homeless Pets*

> *Remember when you look at the stars at night that all your friends are looking at the same stars, thinking of you and cheering for you. M.C.*

> *Hi Michelle just a few lines to say we are thinking of u and hopefully everything is going good. Everyday when Lorenzo and I get home from work we check to see for your updates and see where u are. It was great having all of yous here and hopefully don't have to wait 20 years to do it again. I bought more 649 tickets with our winnings and won another 10 bucks, hopefully we hit big this time, so if u see us coming up behind u you know we hit it good. Heck we will send a helicopter to pick u up why drive. . .lol. . .man it's sure nice to dream. Well that's about all for now and keep your head up and keep smiling we are all behind you for as far as u make it and I'm sure u will,. . .have full confidence in you. bye for now love and kisses and hugs Kim and Lorenzo YOU GO GIRL*

Michelle,
We had a call this morning from Canadian Pets and Animals magazine. The publisher/owner Jody Calen would like to do a piece about you. She'd like to do three separate issues, tracking your progress and including excerpts from your blog and photos. The magazine is freely distributed from 600 distribution points in east Canada and Ontario at animal related. The last printed was 41,000 copies. Just need an okay to send her photos and that she can use excerpts from your blog. Julia

Later that evening, I was woken on two occasions. Something wild ran through the park and all the dogs started barking at once. It took some time for them to settle down. My tent was located right beside a train track. Trains passed by with a loud rumble and the ground shook so violently it felt like an earthquake.

The following day, heavy rains continued. I put on my rain suit and ran across the highway to Rocky's Restaurant. That's where I met David and his wife, Michelle. They were regulars and started up a conversation.

"Not very good weather for camping," David sympathized.

"I might find my tent under water when I get back," I laughed.

"We live in Elliot Lake and come out here for breakfast every now and then," he said.

"My family lived in Elliot Lake a long time ago, when my dad worked in the mines. I was much younger then," I smiled.

"It's a retirement community now. You should come into town and see how much it has changed."

"I'd like that but it's too far for me to go on foot."

That sparked several questions that led to an invitation.

"We have a camper trailer at a place called South Bay Park. Would you like to stay in it for the night? You'd be out of this downpour and we can drive you back in the morning," they offered.

"Wow. That would be great if you're sure it's no trouble," I responded.

"No trouble at all. We'd be happy to," David said.

I couldn't believe this was happening and soaked in my tour of Elliot Lake. We stopped briefly at their home on the edge of town. "One day a bear came right up to the door while I was in the backyard," Michelle shared with me. "Lucky for me, he wasn't the attacking kind."

Their campground was a picture of geographic beauty and for at least one night, it was paradise to me. Once I was settled in, they left but returned sometime later with a hot meal and some snack foods.

"This is so kind of you. I don't know what else to say except thank you," I said and gratitude filled my heart.

"We wanted to make sure you had something to eat. Is everything okay?" Michelle asked.

"It's perfect. I'm dry. I'm comfortable. I have lots of food. It's better than a five star motel. I can't thank you enough."

"Well, have a good night and we'll see you again in the morning," said David.

Later that evening and just before dark, I went for a short walk. Not a sound could be heard except the rain. No noise from other campers or traffic, not even in the distance. It made me feel isolated and alone.

When night had fallen, the land was deep in total darkness. It was so black and quiet, that I felt secluded and trapped in my small space. Periodically, I peered through the window and imagined things prowling in the hollows of the woods. "Stay away from the glass," I feared and wondered, "Is this what cabin fever feels like? What if David and Michelle don't come back?" Then, I laughed at myself, "You've been spending way too much time alone."

That night, the rain continued and I experienced solitude unlike any other time. The kind of solitude most people cannot bear. I was alone with only my thoughts and a dead silence that opened the stings of my conscience.

Early in the morning, the rain was hushed and the wind reduced to a whisper. Michelle and David returned as promised and the comfort of their presence brought me relief.

"How was your evening?" they asked.

"It's very quiet out here at night."

"Yeah, it takes some getting used to. We love it. Can we interest you in some breakfast before we take you back to the highway?"

"That would be wonderful. Thank you."

We went to one of their favorite places in downtown Elliot Lake, where everyone knew their name. My new friends made me feel special just by being with them. I watched and listened, and thought how some people live their whole lives in the same small town and appear content. While others move away to pursue something else. Most people, like me, never return to the small towns we grew up in except for the odd visit. Being here brought back childhood memories I had forgotten.

As I removed all my things from Dave's hatchback, I thanked them again for their kindness. "I'll never forget it," I said. In such a short time, they had touched me in a way that only kindness can. There were no words to describe how it made me feel.

Rain clouds lingered overhead persuading me to press on. While I ran, it reminded me of the times our family drove up and down this highway to visit with relatives. As an adult, I'd driven this road many times. However, it wasn't until now that I realized what my eyes had missed before: scenic landscapes, hilly terrain and ridges, and all its geographical uniqueness. Being an outdoor enthusiast, I reveled in the beautiful natural surroundings of the lakes and rivers, and mile upon mile of unmolested forests.

This area of Ontario was a hunter's haven and a fisherman's dream. However, the tranquility along some stretches of the road was quite spooky at times. Even creepy, with thick forest that occasionally let out eerie noises from within the shades of the trees. I needed to be on constant guard against wild animals.

When I arrived in Blind River, it occurred to me that it was exactly three months to the day since I ran my first steps out of St. John's Newfoundland. The realization that I was still going put a big smile on my face. "This is cause for celebration Gidget," I told her excitedly.

My celebration included staying at the Old Mill Motel and ordering a large Double Double at Tim Horton's across the street. "Close enough to a drink," I laughed.

Kim said. . .
Mich. . .too funny. . .celebrating with a large DD at Timmy's. Love it. Keep goin' kiddo.

The next morning, I didn't have a hangover, but it was slow going after a night of massaging and icing my feet. I took a deep breath of fresh air and let the warm easterly wind carry me. Forgetting all about my troubles, I recalled them only as waters gone by.

This part of the countryside was spectacular and good weather had returned. "This was God's country created for my enjoyment," I shouted. The warmth from the sun felt great on my face and I appreciated all the rest stops next to water. With so much scenery to adore, I barely noticed the time, or that cars had stopped beeping their horns.

At the Iron Bridge, I paused briefly to admire the Mississagi River and then ventured over to the Del Mar campground for the night. Inside, I met the owners, Marian and her daughter Peggy. They also had a dog named Willow. I ordered a milkshake and while I waited, they listened to my story. Marian only charged me five dollars to camp and Peggy bought my milkshake.

After they made my drink, they closed the office.

"We don't sleep here at night. I live just up the road," said Marian.

"Is there anyone else here?" I asked.

"The campground is empty right now but it's always possible campers might pull in late at night."

"Have you had any problems with any wildlife?"

"We have a black bear that likes to rummage through the garbage bin at night so you may want to keep any food outside your tent. You can leave your stuff in the laundry room if you like."

"Thanks. I'll do that." No wonder they thought I was brave.

I followed the dirt road that led to the laundry room and showers. Scanning the area, I planted myself close to the highway and hoping to be less appealing to bears. While I assembled my tent, I watched as Marian and Peggy drove by. Then it occurred to me, I was all alone.

With that thought, I could feel the fear crawling up the back of my neck. "Maybe I should skip my shower," I paused for a moment but then shook my head. "Nah, you've watched way too many scary movies Michelle. You need a shower." I proceeded to take one of the quickest showers I have ever taken.

By the time I settled into my tent, daylight was disappearing quickly. Evening shadows from the trees were growing long and the woods were getting dark fast. Approximately halfway back toward the office was a public pay phone hanging on a post. I stared at it for a few minutes and thought, "I should have made my call when I first got here."

I looked around for any bears but there was nothing in sight. "What if I make a mad dash for the phone and I can't get back to the laundry room? Maybe I should wait until tomorrow," I debated with myself. "What if something sneaks up behind me while I'm on the phone and decides to have me for dinner?"

With these thoughts, I talked myself out of leaving the safety of my tent. Was I really safe though? The Hollywood thriller "Grizzly" came to mind and when darkness came over the whole area, I spooked myself into abandoning my tent. A night in the laundry room sounded like a better option to me. "My tent can be a decoy," I decided.

On my way there, I had to pass a hard top trailer. I decided to try the door and it opened. Slipping inside, I found the light switch and it worked. The trailer was empty, but there was a bench I could sleep on. "This works for me," I said to myself and ran back to my tent to grab my sleeping bag. No one would ever know.

Sometime during the night, I woke up to flashing lights and loud engine noises. As the sky lit up, it sounded like an invasion. I lifted my head enough to peek out the window to see what was going on. An RV was driving through the campground and I watched him go up the hill. It took him several tries to park and then the campground was quiet again. I was glad someone else was around.

At daybreak, I felt like the neighborhood thief sneaking back into my tent. "You big chicken Michelle," I laughed. So much for bravery. As brave a person as I was, I couldn't always be courageous.

From there, I ran past Marian's house. She was outside with her dog Willow. He started barking and when she looked up she started waving at the sight of me. I think she was relieved to see me alive. "Hope to see you again," she shouted.

Every morning, I wondered what was in store for me and every day brought a new adventure. I came around a bend in the road and saw a deer walking along the shoulder. He just froze in his tracks and stared at me. "Go on, get out of here before you get hit by a car," I shouted but he didn't move. "Didn't your parents teach you not to play on the road?" I yelled and started blowing my whistle. As he ran toward the trees, I shouted one more time, "Stay in the woods where it's safe." I'd like to think it might have saved his life.

Clouds threatened all around, but they either passed to the south or to the north. Everywhere except above me. On my way to Bruce Mines, I crossed paths with more cyclists.

Near Thessalon, I met Mark and Cindy heading east.

"Traveling by bike in pairs is the best way to go. You should get a bike," they said. "That's what everyone keeps telling me," I chuckled.

After that, I waved at two other cyclists heading west, but they didn't stop. Then, I met Wendy and Barry from the States. "We cycle around the Great Lakes every year and we love it. You should try it," they said. Every cyclist I met said the same thing, like a repeating phone call.

Bruce Mines is a small town nestled on a beautiful bay off Lake Huron. I followed the signs to the campground and RV park. When I found it, there was a building, but no one on duty. I approached the only RV campers in sight and drilled them with questions.

"Hello," I shouted.

"Hello," an older man shouted back.

"Do you know where I can find someone who works here?"

"There isn't anyone. It works on the honor system. You just leave your money in the drop box."

"Oh, okay. Thanks. Does it matter where I camp?"

"No. You can pick any spot you like."

As I looked around, there was a lot of forest to choose from. A dirt road led deeper into the woods, but I wasn't going to wonder that far. These people seemed nice enough, so I decided to stay close by.

"Do you know if there have been any problems with bears in the area?" I continued.

"Not that we know of. We've been here a few days and haven't seen any. That's not to say there aren't any around."

"That's good to know. I'm alone with a small tent, would it be okay if I set up next to your camp site?"

"Not at all and you're welcome to join us for dinner later if you'd like."

"Sure. That would be great. Thank you. I'll get settled and come over."

While I was setting up my tent, a young couple walked out of the woods and stopped when they saw me.

"Hi there," a handsome and athletic man said.

"Hello," I replied.

"My name is Kelly and this is Andrea. We were the two cyclists who waved at you on the highway and we wondered if you were going to stop here for the night."

"Oh wow. What are the odds we'd end up at the same campground? It's great to meet you. Where are you headed?"

"Well, we've never done anything like this before but we'll try and make it to B.C. We heard the stretch between Sault Ste. Marie and Wawa has some pretty big hills and not much else so we're thinking of taking the bus through it."

"Yes, I heard that too."

"Well, we just wanted to say hi and wish you luck."

"Thanks and good luck to you too."

After I cleaned up with a hot shower, I walked over to my neighbor's campsite. Kay was setting the table and her husband, Lorne, was barbequing. Ray and Beth came out of their RV to join us and we sat down to a wonderful meal. Immediately, I felt a connection and drank up the moment like water. I was amongst friends and it felt like I had known them all my life.

While we were having tea, Kelly and Andrea stopped by. We were probably the only people in the campground and it wasn't uncommon for campers to join other campers. Our conversation was engaging and it was fun exchanging travel stories.

The night faded quickly as always and so did I. Before I left, Kay kindly offered, "If you see the coffee sign in the window in the morning, you're welcome to join us for a cup before you leave."

Upon hearing this, my eyes lit up. "Thank you. I'll be sure to check." Then, she showed me what it looked like.

With a full belly, I stumbled around in the dark trying to find my way back to my tent. It was comforting to know that friends were nearby. As I lay in my sleeping bag, I thought about all of the simple things I took for granted, like a cup of coffee. I just knew the coffee sign would be there when I got up.

The sun lifted and I felt the agony of my own body after a restless night. What do you do on those mornings when you just can't get out of bed? You have a conversation with yourself that goes something like this.

"Michelle, what are you doing still in bed?"

"I can't get up."

"Yes you can."

"No. I'm pretty sure I can't."

"You can and you will, because you have to."

"Not today."

"If you don't get up, you'll regret it."

"I'm just too tired and I don't feel like it. I want to sleep."

"Okay, but don't cry when everyone says, 'I told you so.'"

"Told me so about what?"

"That you couldn't finish this."

"I still need sleep."

"Can you live with the disappointment?"

"What disappointment?"

"Letting yourself down."

"No."

"Do you want to fail?"

"Of course not."

"Then get up."

"Okay, okay. I've heard enough, now leave me alone."

"If you get up, I'll leave you alone."

"Good because you're really getting on my nerves."

"You just say that because you're tired."

"Maybe, but I would appreciate some quiet time now."

"I just don't want you to give up."

"Don't worry, I won't give up."

"Really?"

"Yes, really."

"Will you keep going then?"

"Yes, I'm not a quitter."

"That's the spirit. Now, I'll leave you alone."

It is amazing how the fear of failing can motivate a person. Everyone wants to succeed at what they do. That pushes us to do our best and there was a little voice inside me working overtime to sustain my fighting spirit. "You can go the rest of the way on heart if you have to," it said, not wanting me to give up.

When I came out of the washroom, I was happy to see the coffee sign in the window. Kay must have been watching for me. It made me forget all about my lack of enthusiasm this morning. To my delight, coffee came with a bowl of cereal and some toast.

We exchanged addresses and Ray printed copies of the photos he took the night before. If the timing was right, I might see them again near Nipigon. I returned to Gidget and found a banana sitting there. Beth must have slipped passed me while I was having coffee. With a thankful heart, I left the campground.

Maximizing my recovery time between runs wasn't working out as well as I had hoped. My body was feeling like a rusty old motor that needed oil to get it cranking again. Every minute of rest was critical.

I was in bear country and constantly on the lookout. Whenever I saw references to bears on signs or posts, I ran a little faster. Reaching Echo Bay was my target and in spite of more hills, I was making pretty good time.

Kelly and Andrea caught up to me near the small community of Desbarats. They decided to hop on a bus when they get to Sault Ste Marie. There were also two walkers heading east. We all converged at the same place and had a brief conversation about our journeys.

The walkers were part of a six-man team and were on a tight schedule. "We have to keep moving," they said and everyone went their separate way. I crossed the highway to the trading post to ice my feet.

Sometime later and along a straight stretch of the highway, I watched as a westbound vehicle slowed down and turned onto the emergency road. I found it odd that it just sat there.

As I got closer, I could see a camera sticking out the window. To my delight, it was John and Susan. Once I realized who they were, I started waving.

"What a nice surprise," I grinned from ear to ear.

"We're on our way to the States to celebrate our forty-eighth wedding anniversary," Susan said.

"Oh wow, that's exciting."

"We spotted you and had to stop," said John.

"I'm so glad you did."

The hugs felt great, but the only problem with hello was saying good-bye.

After gazing at the Big Loonie in Echo Bay, I headed for the beautiful campground of Ojibway Park. It was located along a huge body of water in Lake George and Echo Bay. There were miles of campsites to choose from but I parked myself right beside the showers.

At the park store, I met Penny. She took a huge interest in what I was doing and asked lots of questions.

"The milk and snacks are on me," she generously offered.

"Tomorrow, I'm planning to visit the Humane Society in Sault Ste. Marie," I told her and she gave me directions. She also wanted to sign my flag, but I didn't have it with me.

"I'll stop by your campsite after work," she said.

Between dusk and dawn, it was not the night of rest I was hoping for and sleep did not come easy. The night dragged on and I spent most of it moaning and groaning. In the morning, I got off to another sluggish start.

When I reached the Soo, I called Betty from the Husky gas station. She was a friend of John and Susan's and offered to put me up for the night. I got directions to her house and then headed for the Humane Society.

A reporter from the *Sault Star*, Mike, tracked me down just before I got there. I had phoned them from the campground. "The article should be in tomorrow's paper," he said and then left. "It's better than nothing," I thought.

The staff at the Humane Society was friendly and supportive. They gave me something to drink and signed my flag. "All the best – be safe on your journey," they wrote. I enjoyed my tour of the shelter and our conversation was all too familiar. The problems were the same everywhere I went.

From there, I went to Betty's house. When I arrived, she had lunch waiting for me–soup and a sandwich. After that, she drove me to station mall where I bought a new pair of running shoes. While we drove around, I had a good look at St. Mary's River and facing each other were the Ontario and Michigan twin cities of Sault Ste. Marie. Then, we took a ride up the highway to help me mentally prepare for my run.

In the morning, Betty made a healthy breakfast for us. I enjoyed my time with her and found her easy to talk to. She was understanding and from her own experiences could relate to some of what I was going through. I was deeply grateful for her compassion and kindness. She thoughtfully gave me a water filter bottle in case I needed to take water from the lakes.

I also took with me more encouraging messages from my blog.

> *I'm barely doing anything compared to you, Michelle. I wouldn't walk across town, never mind the whole country. You are simply incredible girlie. Good luck on those nice little 'hills' they have up there. Looking forward to reading your blog updates, but only do it if you're not too tired. Rest is the most important thing. I'm glad you are getting some good press now. This will make difference. . . I'm sure it's already starting to change the way people think about animals. All the best. Julia*

> *Hi Michelle from all of your friends at the PEI Humane Society. We've been staying in touch with your blog every once in a while and are very happy to see you're making such great progress and keeping*

> *your spirits up along the way. Continued safe journies. Keep up the good work and thanks from the animals and everyone interested in their wellbeing.*
>
> *Hi Michelle, I have been following your trip across Canada. It has been tiring for sure and you have faced many challenges but your purpose is keeping you going. I thought I would share a poem written by 3 frustrated rescue workers at the Clarenville Area SPCA in NL. It is posted on the front page of our website. Just thought it might be of interest to you. Keep the Faith and you will finish your journey knowing you are working to save so many innocent animals. Hugs. Jewel Clarenville Area SPCA*

On my way out of town, I stopped and pumped Gidget's tires full of air. "Over-inflated wheels should help conquer some of these hills," I thought and before I knew it, I was closing in on mile twenty.

The region I was running through has inspired the Group of Seven to create some of Canada's most notable landscape art and I could understand why. There were breath-taking views along the water, with tall trees and awesome rock formations. The spectacular beauty was captivating.

Then, unforeseeably, Gidget's front wheel fell off and I couldn't get it back on. I had to run with the front end up and balance her on the two back wheels. Losing my third wheel made it inconvenient at times.

Not far from McAuley's Motel and Restaurant, I met two more cyclists riding around Lake Superior. They forewarned me, "You're coming up to some pretty big hills and a tough stretch ahead. It's a challenge with a bike so, good luck on foot."

Shortly after that, Betty and her friend pulled up beside me. She asked how I was doing.

"What a nice surprise," I smiled as I wasn't expecting to see her again.

"We're on our way to dinner," she replied and that was the last time I saw her.

When I arrived at the motel, I entered the souvenir and gift shop. Inside, I met the owner, Ady.

"Would it be okay if I set up my tent on your grass out back?" I asked him.

"Well, there's a bunkhouse for hitchhikers next to the motel. I can show it to you and if you like, you can stay in it for the night," he said kindly.

Ady unlocked the door for me to peak in. It was big enough for two single beds and a small table and chair. There was no washroom or water, but it was safer than my tent. "I'll take it," I said and thanked him.

Once I settled in, I sat outside icing my feet. There was a dirt road that led to a small community of houses. A woman driving by stopped to say hello.

"I saw you running earlier today. Do you have a place to stay tonight? Loretta asked with some concern for me.

"Ady's letting me stay in the bunkhouse," I replied happily.

Loretta spoke with me for a few minutes and then returned with some homemade jam and banana bread. I was awestruck by her kindness.

A little later, I went to the restaurant for something to eat. There were two women working, Vicki and Laura. One served, while the other cooked and they made a great team. "We've been doing this for a few years," they said proudly.

I enjoyed the food as well as our conversations that covered everything under the sun. We didn't solve any of the problems of the world that day, but I was having fun with my new friends.

"See you for breakfast," I said.

"We'll be here," they replied.

While I was lying down in the bunkhouse resting, Ady came over to tell me I could take a shower in one of the motel rooms. Then, he returned again later to say I could have the room for the night, complimentary of the motel.

"Really?" I said in disbelief.

"Really," he smiled.

As he walked away, I figured his wife must have put him up to it and I was grateful. The bunkhouse would have been fine, but a room with a bathroom and a TV was like winning the lottery.

With the appearance of dawn, I encouraged myself to go for breakfast. It felt like a good idea yesterday but in the morning, sleep always sounded like a better idea. Vicki and Laura bought my meal and then cheered me on, "Good luck the rest of the way and watch out for moose," they said.

Before I left, I went over to the gift shop. While I was there, I had another cup of coffee and chatted for a bit. "Thank you for everything Ady," I said on my way out and his wife gave me some water to take with me. My trek through this part of the north was off to a great start.

It was hot and the further north I went, the more isolated I felt. Along the scenic shoreline to Pancake Bay, there were the occasional steep grades and little traffic. The few people I encountered on the highway that day were a couple of cyclists and an OPP car. "Everything all right?" the officer asked and I appreciated their stopping to check in on me.

The Agawa Crafts and Store was a popular destination. I stopped at the motel to ask for directions to the Pancake Bay Provincial Park. "It's just up the road on your left," the manager said. "You can't miss it." To my delight, he sent me away with a cold pop and some water.

Turning into the park, I met a park ranger named Shannon. He stopped his truck and said, "I saw you running earlier and wondered what you were doing." After I explained myself he added, "I'll meet you at the park office and we'll get you all fixed up."

At the front desk, a young girl named Megan was helpful in finding me a quiet area and a ride to my campsite. Once I was settled, the first place I went for was the shower. However, there was such a long line up I turned around and would try again later.

On my way back to my tent, I strolled through the beachfront sites staring across the stunning blue water of Lake Superior. Somewhere out there was the wreck of the Edmund Fitzgerald that sank in 1975. The *Mighty Fitz* was the "Titanic of the Great Lakes", and its legend lives on.

Surrounded by the finest of Ontario's densely wooded forest, I stepped back onto the highway the next day. It was a morning without clouds. The sky was blue and you could see the heat rising off the pavement. Thankfully, there was a bit of a breeze. Gidget's squeaky wheels grew louder with every mile. I passed more cyclists who warned me about the steep hill at Montreal River–every cyclist's nightmare.

Halfway into my run, my feet were on fire. I stopped to dip them into the cold water of Lake Superior and found some relief. After twenty-five miles, I reached the NorthGate Restaurant. The sign on the top of the hill read, "Last service station till Wawa 105 km." I stood there, staring at it thinking, "How bad could it be? Was it really too far for me to run alone?"

While inside the restaurant, I was happy to learn of a campground about a mile and a half up the road. The Twilight Campground was located near the bridge that crosses the Montreal River.

When I arrived, I parked my tent along a ridge overlooking Lake Superior. It was an excellent view and there were other campers around. That night, dark clouds rolled in and with them a storm. It rained heavily through the next day.

July 24, 2007 - Coldwater River, Ontario

In a land home to moose and bears, this was the stretch of highway my family feared the most. With over a hundred kilometers of wilderness and wildlife, there was always the possibility of me falling prey to a predator.

For me, facing this dangerous and difficult section was an opportunity to be true to my mission. Although I didn't know how this was going to turn out, I believed I would come out on the other end. Nevertheless, I wanted to hurry and get the next couple of days out of the way.

Kim said. . .
Keep going Mich. . .you have so many supporters.
We're all behind you.

The scenic shoreline along Lake Superior was spectacular at times, but oh the hills. What goes up must come down. My run began with a long climb up the steep hill of Montreal River and when I reached the top I started my descent. Cyclists going in the opposite direction took a double take when they saw me, but couldn't stop or lose their momentum.

Today, I wished I didn't have Gidget to push. It was hot and it felt like her weight had tripled. Her squeaky wheels were progressively getting worse and the noise was making it easy for anything to hear me coming.

Sometime later, I came up to a building in the middle of nowhere. "Welcome to the Agawa Info Centre" the sign read. Unsurprisingly, the parking lot was empty. However, there was someone inside and I was informed about some bear problems a little further up the shoreline in the backcountry. On hearing this, my heart shook like the trees of the forest in the wind.

The presence of any wild animal was reason enough to proceed cautiously. Listening to the rustling of the woods, I kept an eye out for bears, moose, wolves, or even a cougar. I'm not sure what I would have done if I came face to face with one, but I didn't want to find out and decided not to wander too far off the highway. The only wildlife I saw was a deer crossing the road and birds that flew above me.

Going on from there, I stayed my course and reached my target: Coldwater River that flowed into Lake Superior. As I walked along the water's edge, I decided to jump in for a swim. After running in the hot sun most of the day, it was refreshing. However, the water was so cold I didn't stay in long.

While sitting on the shore, I felt dwarfed by the expanse of open water in front of me. It was a picture of the size and complexity of my life and my inability to manage it on my own. I recognized my own smallness and it led me to embrace God's greatness.

"O God, Thy sea is so great, and my boat is so small."
-Winfred Ernest Garrison

After some travelers left, I hung my food up high and nestled into the trees. It was early evening and I took refuge in my tent to escape the mosquitoes. Through the screen door, the view of the lake and sky were framed by surrounding branches. In peaceful surrender, I listened to nature's songs and the crashing of the waves pounding on the rocks.

> *"He makes me lie down in green pastures, he leads me beside quiet waters, he restores my soul."*
>
> *-Psalm 23:2,3 (NIV)*

In the absence of any outside world, I was in one of the remotest parts of Ontario. It was a place where my former self could not follow me. Being alone with God drew me away from everything that entangled my mind. In solitude and silence, I was separated from everyone–except myself.

When night fell, the winds hushed and the waters stilled. Hidden in its deepest shadows, I peered through the evening darkness and looked up into the mystery of the universe. The greatness of God was on full display and the star-studded sky was like watching a movie screen.

> *"The heavens declare the glory of God; the skies proclaim the work of his hands."*
>
> *-Psalm 19:1 (NIV)*

Dazzled by the variety of stars shining brightly, I gazed at the sight beyond my reach. Under its vastness, I stared in breathtaking wonder at a gallery of pictures flung across the inky blackness of space, as if God had autographed the sky. The grandeur and beauty of the unending northern twilight held me spellbound for hours.

Nothing gives you a greater sense of remoteness and distance like seeing millions of stars high in the sky and light years away. "There's a whole lot going on above the world," I thought. How could anyone say there is no God? When you see the splendor of creation, you know there is something behind it. His fingerprints are all over it.

Once in a while, there was crackling in the trees or noise from the highway. As long as I was looking up at heaven, I wasn't afraid. However, when I closed my eyes, I did a lot of thinking about fear. Deep in this remote area, I repeated the same prayer over and over again, until finally I fell asleep.

> *"When I am afraid, I will trust in you. In God, whose word I praise, in God I trust, I will not be afraid."*
> *-Psalm 56:3-4 (NIV)*

Sometime during the coolness of the night, I saw something that changed my life forever. It captured me, gripped me, and I would never be the same.

The dark corners of my tent lit up like rays of sunshine. The walls were as bright as a flash of lightning and suddenly, I was surrounded by an incomprehensible brilliant white light.

Then, radiant hands that shone as the sun covered me with a white blanket like a warm embrace. It was as if heaven's love reached down to comfort me. Instantly, a sense of peace and security flooded my being.

I wished the moment had forever frozen in time, but when I opened my eyes, He was gone and so was the blanket. I closed my eyes again hoping He would come back, but I saw no one.

Once again, I was wrapped in thick darkness. Amazingly, His peace did not leave me. Peace that chased away my fear and dispelled my loneliness. In the strength of that security, I fell deep into a sound sleep and a quiet confidence that my tent was secure.

> *"I will lie down and sleep in peace, for you alone, O LORD, make me dwell in safety."*
> *-Psalm 4:8 (NIV)*

In my place of dreams, Jesus came and touched me personally. While I was sleeping, He put His light in my heart and a light in my darkness. My supernatural encounter was unmatched by anything I had ever experienced before.

Early the next morning, I woke up with an enlarged view of my God, the keeper of the stars. He gave me a new image that will be forever etched in my memory, replacing the old one that haunted me for so long.

Overwhelmed with awe by something beyond explanation, I could hardly believe He was here, or that I was the reason He came. Could I have been the object of His special affection? From that moment on, I stopped looking for heaven on earth. Instead, I kept my eyes on things above.

While soaking my feet in the lake, I leaned on the wings of dawn and watched as the horizon broke into a new and glorious morning. Clouds sailed in the breeze across the blue sky as the day turned bright and beautiful. The sun was warm to my skin and it was already hot by the time I hit the highway.

Energized by eternal encouragement, I ran and ascended the heights of the hills. There were the occasional steep grades and it felt like I was on a constant climb. People don't usually last long at such a constant emotional level; they wear out. However, with fresh motivation, I found with certainty what enabled me to transcend my circumstances.

Leaving the wild shoreline, I entered the rugged backcountry of Lake Superior Park – another Canadian treasure. I stayed the night in safety at the Rabbit Blanket Lake campground.

After a refreshing swim, I sat on my picnic table icing my feet. That's where I met Dennis. He was walking by and saw me munching on ice cubes.

"Have you ever experienced some trail magic?" he stopped and asked me.

"What's that?" I replied.

"It's when someone leaves you a bottle of water on a rock."

I thought about it for a moment and then answered him, "I get it. Like leaving someone a banana on a stroller." However, I called them angels–God's agents in my time of need.

Dennis invited me to join him for dinner and not only did I enjoy a great meal, I enjoyed his company. "My wife is at home and so are the kids and grandchildren," he said with love and affection for his family. "I retired early and started a wood carving business called

Chipping Away. But I love to get away camping whenever I can," he shared.

I didn't know it at the time, but Dennis was somewhat of a celebrity. His "Father and Son" team is loved across North America and "Chipping Away" is the producer of "Carving Magical Tree Houses", starring Rick Jensen.

When the sun came up, I made my way back to the highway. I left that place filled with appreciation for every beautiful sunrise and sunset.

On my way to Wawa, I came across Michipicoten River. When I saw the water, I longed to jump in. It had been so hot and my body was burning up, soaked in sweat. I followed the road that led under the bridge.

The river was shallow and the current swift. I floated on my back and let the current take me downstream a ways. Then, I stood up and did it all over again, several times. I laughed and played in the river like a little child.

After two people in a canoe waved at me, I left there feeling refreshed. I crossed the bridge and advertising signs began appearing. Wawa was about ten miles ahead of me now and I ran a little faster. Service stations popped up and at the sight of them, I ran even faster. My heart started pounding with excitement.

When I saw the Big Goose, I jumped up and down for joy, "I can't believe I made it." It felt almost too good to be true. Like losing something valuable and then it turns up after hours of searching. Finally, I was here and I let out a sigh of relief. To say I was happy was an understatement.

It was raining in Wawa. I celebrated my surviving an almost impossibility with a room for the night. Feeling exhausted and slipping into a mild depression, all I did was crash.

Upon leaving Wawa, I was stopped by an OPP cruiser near the Big Goose.

"We've been looking for you," he said.

"Really, why?"

"Do you know Marie Parsons?"

"Yes, she's my sister."

"She asked us to look for you. Your family thought something might have happened to you because they hadn't heard from you in a couple of days."

Immediately, I felt awful for not calling her last night. I knew our communication breakdown was my fault. Once we straightened things out, he drove away and I called Marie from the information centre. She had jumped the gun, but I should have called.

From the top of the hill, I looked with a blank stare at the land and highway that disappeared into the distance. Somewhere out there was Nipigon and my two sisters. Emotionally, I hadn't prepared myself for this next stage. For some reason, I thought these long stretches of isolation would be over with once I reached Wawa. Or maybe that was the only way I could make it here.

It was ninety-eight kilometers from here to White River and nothing again but wilderness in between. According to the police officer, there was a fishing lodge about half way and I made it my target. "Here we go again Gidget," I sighed and down the hill we went. I tried not to be disheartened with my new challenge. Climbing this mountain every day continued to wear me down.

Up and down the hills I ran. When I arrived at the Halfway Lodge, I couldn't be happier. It was more of a supply store and the owner had no problem with me setting up my tent nearby. Then, he warned me about bears. "Two nights ago, a bear was struck by a car crossing the highway right out here," he pointed. "You can store your food in my truck overnight."

Morning came quickly and I had to coax myself to get up and climb that mountain again today. However, I was more than happy to leave that place. The bugs were extremely bad and even though it hadn't rained, everything was wet.

Today, no matter how hard I tried I could not keep myself from feeling isolated and anxious. Minutes felt like hours and my frustration increased with the lack of signs. Around each corner was nothing and there was no end in sight.

Then, I was encouraged by a conversation I had with a cyclist. "There's no campground in White River but the information centre will let you put up your tent. There are a lot of places to eat and you can probably take a shower at the Husky Truck Stop."

White River was a popular destination for highway travelers. Feeling relieved to have finally made it, I slowed down to a walk as I rolled into town.

In this heartland of Northwestern Ontario, I claimed my spot on a piece of grass outside the information centre. There were lots of people around and I met my new neighbors, Jesse and Josette. "Nice bikes," I said. "That's what I need to get me across this country, a motorcycle," I laughed. They kindly invited me to join them for something to eat.

When the sun went down, everyone settled in for the night. My belly was full, my laundry done, and it felt good to be clean again.

Just before midnight, I heard someone nearby shout, "Bear!" The commotion didn't last long and I lie there thinking, I never knew what to expect at any given moment. In any event, where fear fades, tranquility of heart and mind takes its place.

Early in the morning, I sat eating breakfast at a nearby restaurant and watched as a large group of colorful cyclists pass through town in spectacular fashion. They were heading east and some of them stopped for a bite, but they weren't the talking kind. Before I left, I topped up my supplies.

Going on from that place, I spent a night camped at Dunc Lake Lodge. Then, the following night at the Travelodge in Marathon. That night, I spoke to both of my sisters.

"Hi Marie, I'm at the exit for Marathon."

"Congratulations. It's too far for me to pick you up, but when you get to Terrace Bay I can come."

"That's great; I can hardly wait. I'll stay at the provincial campground tomorrow night and should be there the following day."

"A friend of mine from work, Diane, wants to come and meet you. Is that okay? She lives in Marathon."

"Sure, send her over. The people here have been really supportive. They even gave me a discount on my room."

Speaking with Marie gave me a huge boost. Then, I received a double boost from talking to Chris. After bringing her up to speed, I asked her an important question.

"Do you think your church would baptize me while I'm in Nipigon?"

"I'm sure they would if the timing works out. I'll look into it for you," she replied.

It was now clear to me that my infant baptism did not satisfy this command by God and I didn't want to delay any longer. I had decided to follow Jesus and there was no turning back.

When I woke up the next morning, I called the local radio station, CFNO. They did a terrific interview and played it throughout the morning. Before I left the Travelodge, the staff and others signed my flag. Then, they cheered me on.

On a hot summer's day, I got off to a good start. I was one sleep away from being picked up by my sister. Inspired by how close I was, I ran through hills, black flies, high temperatures and humidity, complaining feet, and an upset stomach.

At Neys Provincial Park, the staff took really good care of me. They drove both Gidget and I to our campsite and I fell asleep with the comfort of knowing someone was watching over me. Tomorrow night, I would be with family once again.

On my way out of the park, I met Bob Lewis. He was a sixty-year old Vancouver resident walking from Peace Park in Vancouver all the way to the United Nations building in New York City. "I call it the Walk for Family Peace," he said. "To raise public awareness of the need to create healthy and nurturing families." His wife, Leah Anne, was with him driving the support vehicle.

I joined them for breakfast and enjoyed our conversations. "I walk forty kilometers a day for three days at a time and then take a day off," Bob explained. "I'll stop and talk to anyone who will listen," he said.

While I ran that day, Bob and his story inspired me. His son struggled with drug addiction and it was through that rehabilitation process that Bob decided to dedicate his life to give people the tools they needed to harmonize their families. It was something he felt passionate about and was hoping to make his walk an annual event.

On this first day of August, after running thirty miles, a car pulled up behind me. I could hardly believe my eyes at the sight of my sister and her son, Tylar. My heart started pounding and I thought to myself, "Is it really them?" There was joy and relief wrapped together as I embraced them both. "Take me home," I said happily.

When we turned into their driveway, the family dog met us. Tylar grabbed Gidget and started working on her wheels. He quickly had his tools out and shared his ideas to re-enforce her frame and put bigger tires on. I loved him for it.

After I took a shower, Marie and I sat in her kitchen drinking tea. "You crazy sister," she said. We talked into the night and being with her, comforted me in a way that only a sister can. Filled with more gratitude, I lay in the security and safety of my sister's home.

In the morning, Marie drove me back to Terrace Bay about three miles east of the town. "I'll pick you up later in Rossport," she said and then drove herself back home for work. I was so thankful for her help.

Along one of Canada's most spectacular drives, the scenic route of the North Shore of Lake Superior, was helping to renew my running enthusiasm. Without Gidget to push, I was off to a fast start. In spite of blisters developing on top of blisters, nothing could derail me today.

I met a couple more cyclists and they warned me about their encounter with a bear the night before, this side of Nipigon. "Be careful at the rest stops," they said. However, I didn't run into anything.

The natural beauty approaching the village of Rossport was breathtaking. It was nestled in a harbor overlooking some islands. I stopped at the Rossport Beach, where I waited to be picked up.

Walking along the sandbar, I watched from a distance people swimming and playing in the protected waters of this conservation area. This place had to be the best-kept secret in northern Ontario. Sitting on a picnic table, I basked in the unparalleled peacefulness and serenity of this dream location. It was truly a nature lover's paradise.

When Marie arrived, I beamed with happiness. On the way home, she told me Tylar wanted to bike with me tomorrow and my heart swelled with joy. "I also made a doctor's appointment for you. You should have someone look at your feet and get a checkup," she insisted.

That night, I called Chris in Thunder Bay and she was coming to Nipigon on the weekend. She also gave me the good news that my water baptism was confirmed for Sunday and I was thrilled.

On Friday August 3, it was the first of four days my nephew would bike with me. Tylar's presence not only helped to pass the time, but it made it fun again. We laughed and talked about many things. "We should bike across Canada together some day," we dreamed. The enthusiasm and understanding he demonstrated was beyond his young years. I enjoyed his company immensely.

He also shared his desire to join the military. "You won't regret it," I said. "Some of the best times of my life happened while I was in the Canadian Armed Forces." Things you don't get to experience as a civilian.

Marie arranged for the Nipigon Gazette to interview us when we got back and I was excited about sharing this rare moment with Tylar. It would also help raise awareness throughout the area.

Sometime that evening, Chris showed me an article about a group called "New Hope Rescue" in Thunder Bay. The next day, I called them and sent a follow up email.

> *Aug 4*
> *Hi Valerie,*
> *It was great talking to you and I look forward to meeting you. If the weather stays clear this week, I should reach the Terry Fox Lookout Thursday Aug 9 tentatively at 2pm. Would it be possible to meet me there? I'm going to try to see if someone from the Chronicle/media would be there as well. You mentioned some others could possibly be there as well. . .would anyone be interested in running a bit with me or is there anything else you might suggest? Would it be OK for me to call you Monday evening after 9pm to firm things up?*
> *Michelle*

> *Aug 5*
> *HI Michelle:*
> *Great talking to you too. I will book off Thursday afternoon from work and come to the Terry Fox Lookout. I am trying to gather as many as our rescue*

volunteers to come and cheer you on. Maybe my little niece (12 years old) and I could run with you. I'm sure, I can get others to run as well. Would you like a bunch of runners? I'll work on it as soon as I talk to you on Monday evening.
Cheers,
Val

I completed my run through Nipigon and passed the sleepy town of Red Rock to Marie's front door. After a couple of rest days, my focus would shift to Thunder Bay.

On Sunday August 5, I stepped into the waters of baptism. Someone once said, *"the measure of love is what one is willing to give up for it.*" There is no greater love than to lay down one's life for another.

"For God so loved the world that he gave his one and only Son, that whoever believes in him shall not perish but have eternal life."

-John 3:16 (NIV)

God saw the depths of my heart and still he loved me. Overwhelmed with such a love, I was different because of it and I chose to move in God's direction. Together, with my family and friends from the Nipigon Baptist Church, we walked down to the river behind David and Wendy's home. It was there that God poured his love into my mortally ill heart.

The River (song)
To the river I am going bringing sins I cannot bear
Come and cleanse me come forgive me
Lord I need to meet you there
Precious Jesus I am ready to surrender every care
Take my hand now lead me closer
Lord I need to meet you there
In these waters healing mercy
Flows with freedom from despair

I am going to that river
Lord I need to meet you there
Precious Jesus I am ready to surrender every care
Take my hand now lead me closer
Lord I need to meet you there
-Brian Doerksen

When I got out of the water, Chris wrapped a towel around me. There was plenty of food for everyone as we enjoyed a time of celebration.

"Earth has no sorrow that heaven cannot heal."
-Thomas Moore

I came to understand no one falls beyond the reach of God's love and forgiveness. Forgiveness liberates the soul and removes fear, that`s why it is so powerful. I gained hope in forgiveness; hope that was born from my grief and sorrow. Hope that never disappoints. Christ Jesus my hope, made known to me the path of life and I let Him be at home in my heart. With a fresh supply of grace, I went on from there just a little bit stronger.

There were also more encouraging messages from my blog;

Kim said. . .
Hey Mich
Happy to see you're doing well and getting an opportunity to rest, while spending time with family. Please congratulate Tylar for me. What a champ for biking along side of you. Enjoy the next few days. Take a breather and put your feet up. You deserve it. PS. The Rebels won the league. . .wasn't the same without you Kiddo.

Anonymous said. . .
Way to go Mich. Having driven that way many times, I remember all those little towns. After Thunder Bay, it is pretty much a flat, smooth run. You will get a

few little hills around Dryden. If you haven't past Winnipeg by the 18th, I hope to see you as I'll be driving out to Mom's.
Way to go girl.
Jackie and Elton

The next day, I went to the Nipigon Hospital for my doctor's appointment. X-rays of my feet revealed stress fractures and the doctor suggested I see a foot care specialist when I get to Thunder Bay. The rest of me was in good shape.

After that, Marie brought me to work with her. When I walked into her office, there were pictures and articles from my run posted all over the walls. "I'll turn them into a scrap book for you when you're done," she said.

I met some of her co-workers and one lady, Rose, had a baby bird in her office. It had been rescued and she didn't know if it would survive. Another person, John, was helpful in finding campgrounds along my route. They were all supportive.

The following day, I ran to the town of Pearl. Tylar biked part way until his dad picked him up. He wanted to finish working on Gidget and needed to find some parts. Before leaving the area, I contacted media and touched base with the group from New Hope Rescue. It was an early night in anticipation of reaching another milestone.

August 9, 2007 – Terry Fox Lookout

I looked over at Tylar on his bike and I couldn't be more proud of him than I was at that moment. He had grown up like a tender shoot and it was delightful getting to know him and his heart. I was glad he was with me.

Last night, my sister let me read the school paper he wrote in June of this year. It moved me to tears.

"The person most inspiring to me is my Aunt Michelle Jameus. Michelle is a little known person trying to make a huge difference in the lives of

certain animals and people across Canada, but has already made a big difference in my life. Her current goal is to save the lives of stray animals in Canada by introducing new solutions to over-population instead of killing the animals. Michelle is a loving and religious person with a huge heart for the animals. She is very determined to make a stand in Canada and her ultimate goal is to convert Canada to a "No Kill" country.

On Sunday April 15, 2007 Michelle Jameus started a cross country run known as the "No Kill Canada" marathon in cooperation with Let Live Canada and Jazzpurr, to make an effort to stop the killing of stray animals in Canada. For a long time Michelle has been planning her run across Canada and setting up public and private meetings all in an effort to raise awareness for her campaign. My family and I have been keeping up with her as much as possible and no matter how much we worry for her she insists on moving forward across the country. Her determination and near stubbornness makes me proud of her and how much she wants to change the way we think for cats and dogs of Canada. While she is running Michelle is bound to find many obstacles, but says, "My conscience drives me and I will stop at nothing." I know that she will do more than the best she can and despite horrible weather, rough roads and her 25 pound survival pack Michelle will never quit.

All the years I have known my Aunt Michelle I have never seen her let anyone down or not try to help someone and she always brightens the day with a good joke, fun game or by just being more than happy to have fun with people in any way. I only wish I could be half as good of a person as she is. This quality of hers will be a huge advantage throughout her marathon as she will need to talk to many people to gain their support, their trust, their encouragement and to get them to agree with her ideas about the humanity rights of dogs and cats. I am moved by the way she is devoted to the animals she is fighting for, and the way she adores the people fighting with her. Michelle is very fond of the people who are also trying to save these animals and has written, "People who work in animal shelters are my heroes. They are such caring people and sacrifice so much. They do amazing things for animals." Although she is running alone, Michelle does have people to help her along the way. Her main partner is Dorit Girash of Let Live Canada and Jazzpurr, who has been very supportive. Michelle says she is grateful for the tremendous support and encouragement already shown, and I am sure that, if they could talk, there would be hundreds of cats and dogs across Canada telling Michelle how much they love her for her help, love and care.

The ultimate goal of Michelle Jameus' marathon is to reach out to people from St. John's to Vancouver and make them realize that what we are doing to healthy and treatable stray cats and dogs is morally and ethically wrong. The current solution to the overpopulating stray cats and dogs is to have them destroyed by euthanizing them. Michelle plans to introduce new programs that solve the problem without killing the animals. Michelle says that the problem and "sad reality is some peoples' eyes and hearts see killing as the only solution to the overpopulation problem and have justified it in their own minds so that they are comfortable with it." I am proud to say that my Aunt is the first to really make a big move to stop society from killing our pet companions when it is not at all necessary. I hope that her campaign goes well and she can convert Canada to a No Kill country. Michelle and her partners of Let Live Canada and Jazzpurr really do care about the lives of animals and really want to change the way we treat them.

Michelle Jameus is currently (as of June 17, 2007) in Montreal, Quebec and expects to be in Ottawa, Ontario by next week. She continues to run miles a day and is gaining more and more support for her efforts. Her planned arrival in Vancouver, BC, the end of her journey, is October 10, 2007. She will be in Nipigon, Ontario on July 24, 2007. Michelle really is fighting for a good cause in Canada and has inspired many people, including me. Her goal of converting Canada to a No Kill country will save many animals' lives so I hope it will be reached. Michelle Jameus is truly a great person - with nothing but good, loving thoughts in her mind.

Written by Tylar Parsons (June 18, 2007)

Our rendezvous with New Hope Rescue was at the LakeView Lodge off of LakeShore Drive. From there, we would run together to the Terry Fox Lookout at the northeast entrance to the city of Thunder Bay.

Tylar and I arrived first. When we saw Valerie, Cindy, and Susan, they wowed us with their enthusiasm. They had made a banner that read "New Hope Rescue Supports No Kill Canada" and it stretched out about five feet.

Valerie and Susan carried the banner and were accompanied by Cone, a beautiful husky dog. Cindy drove the truck and another dog, Lillie, was with her. Not far from there, Janie and her dog, Sam, joined us. It wasn't long before she kicked off her high heels.

When we reached the highway, Cone and Sam jumped in the truck. A short hop from there, we climbed the rock cliff overlooking

Lake Superior. Together, we ran through the intimate park setting to the massive nine-foot bronze Terry Fox Monument where Kristi from *TB News* was waiting for us.

It was truly a surreal moment and I wished everyone who helped get me here could have joined us. We snapped some pictures and then marveled at the panoramic view of the water and islands. Off in the distance was the iconic Sleeping Giant and the forested shoreline was spectacular.

After Kristi left, we went to Valerie's sister's place in Thunder Bay for pizza and drinks. Tylar was a trooper and stuck with all us women. There was lots of laughter and my new friends treated us well. Filled with joy, I left there wondering how anything was ever going to top this. Susan kindly drove us to Chris' house.

It had been an exceptional day and it ended on a high. The 6:00 P.M. and 11:00 P.M. evening news carried the story and it raised more awareness. I was also encouraged with these messages.

> *Anonymous said. . .*
> *Keep it up Mich, we are still with you here in Ottawa*

> *Hi Michelle.*
> *Congrats on your efforts and your run, you truly are to be commended, a job very well done. I read your blog with much interest after learning about it from a dear friend of mine. I truly believe in "trail magic" and also what you call 'angels'. Life is truly an incredible journey and also it is what we make it. I have been blessed to have many positive and inspiring role models and live each day to the fullest. The life lessons we learn from those older than us are invaluable and we must pay attention to each 'lesson.'*
> *I am writing this to you, first to congratulate you on your efforts and secondly to say "Thank you", for being someone special that spent some time with my Dad. Yes Dennis is certainly a great man with many lessons to teach all–I wish you the best of luck in your journey, I wish you many sitings/visits of "trail*

magic" and I look forward to reading your continued blogs. Cheers and Congratulations.
Sincerely, Traci Moor
Bon courage. . . que le vent soit toujours au dos et que le soleil brille en chemin. . . Siobhan

Marie came to pick up Tylar and I stayed with Chris in Thunder Bay. I missed him already. We had us a time together and I loved him for sharing in my passion, and taking care of Gidget.

While I was in Thunder Bay, I did some visiting. My first stop was BioPed for a foot assessment. Mark examined my feet and with some minor adjustments, he felt we could reduce some of the pain I was experiencing. He suggested I switch to a wider shoe, like Etonics, and place a gel pad in each shoe at the stress points. "Let's do it," I agreed.

Then, there was a trip to the Tamarack House to see my mom's younger sister, Chris's work place, dinner with her mother-in-law, and a visit with animal services that went well. Meeting some of the shelter animals was inspiring and I was happy to see Valerie again.

Running through some stiffness to the town of Sunshine, it seemed anti-climactic compared to my run to the Terry Fox Lookout. However, my feet were doing much better in my new shoes.

Along the way to Raith, I stopped at the turnoff to Atikokan. This was the town where I was born. It was my birthplace, but I had grown up somewhere else. Although I felt drawn to my hometown, it was too far for me to make a detour.

There was a restaurant and I decided to grab a bite to eat. I met another cyclist going east and he was fun to talk to. I was happy to hear from him later. This is his letter to me.

Hey Michelle,

I don't know if you remember me, but we met in a coffee shop restaurant thingy about 60km outside of Thunder Bay. You were heading west of course and i was heading east on my bike. I'm that cyclist raising money for the Lymphoma foundation of Canada. You wrote about in your blog on day 122 entitled "Raith".

It's so finally good to be done, I arrived in Halifax on the 16th and took a train back home yesterday. I managed to go from coast to coast in about 2 months, 7 days. I know i should have tried to do Newfoundland but i was getting pretty exhausted and riding my bike was by that time losing its touch.

Anyway I can't believe how good you're doing. I'm so impressed. Reading your blog puts a smile to my face after every post. I keep saying to myself "I've been there" and "i hope she stays where i stayed, there's a really good campsite here" etc. Keep up the good work, you're going to be done so soon. After meeting you i ran into a Swedish fellow walking across Canada and then back on down and across the states. He was pulling a cart attached to his chest and had two wooden walking sticks with him. I couldn't help but think of you. You really tuff'ned me up that day we met, i was feeling bad about how much distance i was covering but when i met you, i realized how much harder it could have been. Good on ya for tackling such a remarkable task, you're an inspiration for us all.

Anywho i don't know if you remember but we got a picture together and i snuck one of you as you ran away down the road. See attached and tell me what you think. I'm so glad to have met you. I'll be paying attention to your site and might blast you a couple of emails as your coming into cities I've been to. Hopefully I'll remember some of the places i've camped and maybe they can help you out as the majority did for me. Hope you don't mind

Adios my friend, and take care of yourself

Sincerely
Gordon Robb

Then, I called my younger sister, Angel, and found out that one of my mom's sisters passed away. It was a sad phone call home and a difficult time for my mom. She had another sister battling cancer and a brother recovering from heart surgery. A reminder of how precious life is.

August 15, 2007 – Upsula

The day had to come when I would have to leave the safety net of my sisters. Having these moments was something I struggled to shake. I found it incredibly difficult at times to separate the overflow between my loneliness and happiness.

It was in these moments I hung on by a thread and battled the intensity of my emotions. My journey had become such that my happiness was only happiness when it was being shared with others. I was able to keep going, but only as long as they kept me going. The thought of gearing up again to go it alone was almost enough to take me out.

Chris waited quietly while I loaded up Gidget and then she had to go to work. She honked her horn and as she drove away, I waved until she was out of sight. That's when the tears came. I stood there alone on the side of the highway, sobbing and wishing she would come back. "What am I doing out here," I whimpered.

With no one around, the distance in front of me seemed enormous again with no end in sight. Just as a mountain erodes and crumbles, my moving finish line was wearing me down. This journey was a fight and a lonely road. However, like so many times before, I pushed back the emotion. When your heart is on the line, you'll rise up.

The skies of Northern Ontario were gloomy and rain was coming. "We better get going Gidget," I said. There were dark clouds ahead and our target was thirty miles away. I was glad to have my running buddy and the "extras" I took from my sisters. Like remembering the night they gave me a haircut, or sitting outside the barn watching the horses. It all made me smile once again.

About ten miles down the road, it started to rain and continued to Upsula. At the motel, I met a cyclist going east and we both decided to stay indoors. His knowledge of the western roads was helpful. "You'll need to decide which route to take before you get to Alberta," he said. For now, I could only do one day at a time. I never knew from one day to the next, if tomorrow would be mine.

Hi Michelle,
We met in Upsala, ON. I am the fellow who was riding his bike from Victoria to St. John's in support of Cops for Cancer. I thought of you often as I continued my ride east. I remember you had hoped to finish your trek by October. Were you successful? The remainder of my ride went great and I got home on September 19th.
Hope all is well with you.
Best regards,
Francis Graf

It rained overnight and into the cold morning. Seeing the sun come out was always a comfort. My exposure to storms and adversities had helped to build up my stamina. In the face of another strong head wind, I began a new count.

Mile one and two - warm up
Mile five - halfway to ten
Mile ten - one third done
Mile fifteen - halfway
Mile twenty - two thirds done
Mile twenty-five - only five more miles to go
Mile twenty-nine - closing in on mile thirty

On my way to English River, I was encouraged when a truck driver stopped to chat with me. "I've seen you so many times, I had to stop and find out what you were doing," he said. Then he shook my hand and wished me luck.

English River was an interesting place. There was only a restaurant and hunting lodge, full of bear hunters. Construction workers bought out the motel for their use and all together, there were plenty of men around. Other than the barmaid, I didn't see any other women.

I walked inside wearing my "No Kill" t-shirt and got the strangest looks. "Dogs and cats," I clarified. They allowed me to pitch my tent around back under some trees. While I was setting up I thought, "At least I don't have to worry about bears with all these hunters around. Or maybe, I should worry more about the hunters."

When I returned for something to eat, some men were talking about someone struck and killed by a truck while crossing the highway. It happened in front of the lodge early this morning and it was sure to make the news. I called my sister right away to let her know it wasn't me.

That night, it rained off and on. It was cold and windy. As I lie in wait for another day, I listened to the faint sound of construction workers partying across the water and hunters getting in late. Whatever circumstance I found myself in, my survival was strengthening my trust in God's protection.

More encouraging messages:

> *Charlene said. . .*
> *Hey Michelle,*
> *Want you to know that I am thinking about you and that I look forward to reading your notes. Hang in there Michie, it will get better.*
> *Lots of love*
> *Charlene*
> *P.S. I look forward to playing hockey with you again.*

> *Pamela of Ignace said. . .*
> *Hey, it is an amazing thing you are doing. I live in Ignace, Ontario. I wish you the best of luck on the remaining months of your journey and I truly hope that your trek to Dryden is tolerable. It is a fairly*

long stretch without towns (well, when you are on foot anyways) so all the best to you.
Sincerely, Pamela.

Kim said...
Keep it up Mich. Sending you vibes from Ottawa.

In the morning it took some convincing, but the need for a washroom forced me out of the warmth of my sleeping bag. It was cold and damp, and would be one of the hardest days for me to get through.

The next town was thirty-five miles away. These stretches of isolated highway were long and lonely places. I don't know why I thought it wouldn't be like this passed Thunder Bay. Probably because I couldn't think past each town. Singing to Gidget helped for a little while.

"Wheels on Gidget go round and round, round and round, round and round. Wheels on Gidget go round and round so early in the morning."

For the first time, I felt the misery of my monotonous run. The distance was overwhelming and my loneliness spread out like a desert. I plunged into the depths of discouragement and at times, I felt panicked about being in this situation. I was moments away from quitting. "What is the matter with me," I wondered.

What do you do when you fall down? The question I was challenged with, was did I want to quit? At that moment I did. "I have had enough," I grumbled. "What's the point of all this anyway?" There was another 110-kilometer stretch of isolation to Dryden after this one, and I felt like I couldn't do it anymore.

It shouldn't have been possible for me to pick myself up again, but I did. Somehow, I found a way to fight through the mental challenges and ran thirty-five miles to Ignace. Even though I made it, I knew I couldn't continue this way. "You need a mental health day to figure out what is going on in your head," I decided.

From the highway, I followed the road to the Davy Lake Campground. It had all the amenities I needed and it was peaceful. That night, I rested and didn't leave my tent. It sounded funny to say, but I needed some time alone to think. Somewhere between Thunder Bay and here, I had lost my step and I needed to get it back.

Mostly, I spent the time searching the deepness of my heart for answers. After some reflection, I realized the spoils of comfort had weakened my drive. There was nothing wrong with me, I just needed to be reminded why I was out here. Adding to the problem was a shift in my thinking. My why was being challenged. Lose your why, and you'll lose your drive.

I still felt as strong about what I was doing as I did the day I left Ottawa. There is a lot of power in a can-do attitude if combined with passion and determination. In the beginning, I said I could make it if I didn't give up. I couldn't fail if I did what was right no matter what I faced.

However, to get the prize, I had to finish the race. "Take it one step at a time Michelle," I said and believed that the next step I took could be the step that makes a difference. If I stop now, I might never know what that is. There had to be something good that was going to come out of this.

What a difference a day can make. Everything started looking better again. I wanted to get up tomorrow and run, to finish strong and leave no regrets. It mattered to me how I finished.

I went to the office and talked to the owner of the campground, Bob. He showed me on a map what was between here and Dryden. Basically, nothing except a hunting and fishing lodge about halfway. It was a couple of kilometers off the highway, but a possible place for me to camp overnight.

In the morning, I had a new attitude and I got my mojo back. That was the word printed on the t-shirt given to me by my cousin Francine in North Bay. A mental health day was just what I needed to raise my drooping spirit and I was determined to reach my new target.

Once again, my feet were running in step with my heart. "Take my hand Lord," I said and ran my little heart out to Cobblestone Lodge. Mostly because it was the only way to keep the bugs off my back.

When I saw the dirt road that led to the lodge, I hesitated for a moment about leaving the safety of the highway. "What if something happens?" I feared. I looked around and I was in the middle of nowhere, all alone. Regardless, I didn't have a whole lot of options. "If I stay on the road I should be okay," I assured myself.

Moving cautiously forward, a bit of fear tried to sneak in as I took "a walk in the dark" for a few kilometers. "Anything could happen," I thought. "What if I get shot by a hunter or attacked by an animal? This is just crazy!"

Finally, beyond the overgrowth of brush I saw the water and was relieved. As I came around the corner, I ran into four hunters with rifles resting on their shoulders. They were all decked out in hunting gear and waiting for their ride. I think I startled them, more than they startled me. I wasn't what you would expect to bump into in this wild country.

They read my t-shirt and gave me the oddest looks. We cleared that up quickly and they were helpful. "Most of the fishermen and hunters will be back later tonight," they said and then pointed me in the direction of the office.

The lodge itself was located on a quiet bay overlooking Raleigh Lake and well known for black bear and moose hunting, and fishing. I went inside the lodge to register. "Are there any rooms available?" I asked, but the hunters had booked them all up.

Standing all by myself at the designated camping area, not far from the lodge, I chose the best spot high up on a hill. "This way I could see anything coming," I thought and felt like a watchman guarding my fort.

Just before dark, I observed an RV pull into the camp. They were an older couple with a dog that entertained me for a time as he had the run of the lot. Then, I went down to talk with them briefly but the mosquitoes were so bad I had to retreat to my tent.

After dark, there was a stream of vehicles coming and going. As I lay on the earth's foundation, I thought it wasn't good to be alone or live in isolation. How awful it is that we cage animals and the fear they must feel when the door closes or the lights go out. A shelter is no home and they must feel frightened most of the time. I couldn't imagine living in fear all the time.

As the sun lifted, the light of morning appeared and I was anxious to leave that place. Me and Gidget and all the horse flies in the countryside ran thirty-eight and a half miles to Wabigoon Lake Park to the tune of:

Good morning mornin', hello sunshine
Wake up sleepy head
Why'd you move that bojangle clock
So far away from the bed?

Just one more minute that's why we moved it
One more hug or two
Do you love wakin' up next to me
As much as I love wakin' up next to you?

You make the coffee, I'll make the bed
I'll fix your lunch, and you'll fix mine!
Now tell me the truth do these old shoes look funny?
Honey, it's almost nine.

Now you be careful, got to go
I love you, have a beautiful day!
And kiss the happiest girl in the whole U.S.A.

Now shine on me sunshine. Walk with me world, it's
a skippidy doo da day.
I'm the happiest girl in the whole U.S.A.
-Donna Fargo

That night in the park, I listened to the constant beeping sound of a truck backing up somewhere far off. The driver was working overtime. All through the night, I could hear the low whistle and steady rumble of approaching trains as they passed by. If that wasn't enough to keep me up, it thundered and there was a mighty downpour. Needless to say, I didn't get much sleep.

August 21, 2007 – Dryden

On my way out of the campground, the owner kindly gave me some tomatoes and a cucumber from her garden. Then, I stopped at the Can Op restaurant where I met a family of five having breakfast. They were on vacation and camping in a tent.

"Everything is soaking wet," they laughed. "Including us, but we are having the time of our lives." Their joy was contagious.

The thunder roared and there was scattered lightning. Ominous darkness took over the land and clouds poured down their moisture. Not even the rain could discourage me today. The thought of being in Dryden was exciting, considering three days ago I was about to throw in the towel. Now, I was within days of the Manitoba border and through with the majestic land of northern Ontario. Talk about encouragement. This was the tipping point for me.

With the wind in my lungs, I reached my destination. "I can't believe I'm here," I said repeatedly. It was a frequent thought I was having and saying I was relieved to be in Dryden was another understatement.

Inside the city limits, I stopped at Tim Horton's and enjoyed a cup of coffee. Then, I went to a motel for a good night's rest. The bright lights of the city enchanted me, but home was a long way from here.

Another encouraging message from my blog:

Anonymous said. . .
Michelle loves Animals
and
They love Michelle.
GO MICHELLE GO!

When I woke up, I spoke with Josh from the Dryden Observer. Then, I went to the license bureau to renew my driver's license that had expired, which was odd because my birthday is in January.

Feeling less isolated, I started to run. I breathed in fresh clean air and let the sunshine embrace me. On the way to Vermilion Bay, I stopped at Egli's Sheep Farm and Animal Park where they manufacture sheepskin products. "I may never get the opportunity again," I thought.

As I approached Vermilion Bay, an OPP heading east sounded his siren as he passed me by. It made me smile and wave. However, at the village corner store, a man shook his head and walked away without even speaking. "That's okay," I told myself. Whatever he was thinking, I didn't take it personally. After I bought a few things, I went to the Northside Motel and RV Park for the night.

There were more encouraging messages.

> *Hi Michelle:*
> *I have been trying to find out where you are. When I came back home from Sudbury I thought I might see you along the way, but, due to a fatal accident near Ignace on August 16th the bus was detoured down through Atikokan. Perhaps you were in that area then too. I have not heard if you have come through Kenora yet either. Hope I haven't missed you and I hope that if I haven't that I will get to meet you and perhaps offer you some home comforts for as long as you need them.*
> *Take care and the best of luck.*
> *Carol (Susan and John's friend)*

> *Darn, I was convinced that you are Superwoman and you go and say you have ups and downs and it makes you human again. Take good care of yourself out there. Take breaks, put your feet up and buy a large size coffee.*
> *Julia*

There were more hills passed Vermilion Bay and something was wrong with Gidget. Pushing her felt like moving a heavy boulder and her resistance was like dragging a piano. The new tires were rubbing against her frame and she finally succumbed to the weight. Her wheels didn't go 'round and 'round anymore and it was the end of the road for my Gidget.

No one would stop to help us, so I put everything in my backpack and dragged her several miles to a Can Op restaurant at Stuart Lake. Inside, I met Lawrence. He offered to take me to The Hardware Company bike store in Kenora. This is his letter to me the day after we met.

August 24, 2007
Dear Michelle,
Yes it's kind of funny I write to you now, why, so that I can write to you while my memory is at it's best, but I also realize you will not read my letter till much later. I do hope it is not forgotten by you of our short experience together, it to me was enjoyable and I thought about you all night, thinking you were okay. I know you are a big and brave girl, but in today's life, life can be cut short and you are aware of that so I want you to be careful if not for yourself then do it for me. I do hope that you can carry out your mission to only as far that you can health and physically do it.
I will be thinking about you on your journey to that west, but in one manner you have left God's country when you left Kenora, the last stand of forest and lakes till you have reached some where in B.C.
Personally there is only my-self and Ed and I will think of you each day on your journey, but I told you if you need help call me to the rescue and I will be there for you. I felt that I have known you for some time and yes it sounds unusual but it is a fact. I like you very much as a person trying to achieve their goals as long as your new cart from my country holds out for you. I had idea's of going today to see if you would make it to Falcon Lake and meet with you again. That is how I feel about you, no matter how you feel about me. Not knowing your real circumstances or motives back in Ottawa I do feel you should move up here in God's country, either in Thunder Bay, Dryden, Kenora or Fort Frances you

would be here and I'm positive your self employment would work for you from here, and in that view we would see each other very often.
It is very reasonable to live here compared to Ottawa or ALTA or even B.C. you know what's here lakes and sun-sets and open lands for canoeing, camping to enjoy the Great Outdoors like you have not experienced.
I do not know how you will return from where ever you end up, I do not know for certain if we will meet again, but I will do anything no matter where you are to meet you and be with you for more time then we spent. But I do hope that you make the move out of Ottawa as I can help you in that regard with info etc. etc.
So you have met with the SPCA in Kenora, you have a new Cart but I just cannot understand no sponsorship or support for your endeavor.
I demand that you write back telling me of your last portion of your trip no matter where it takes you or where you must end it, but you must take care and be rational quitting in your circumstances would not mean a failure from where you had started, winning is not a issue it is the mere endeavor and your spirit that took you there.
So yes please consider to move to N.W.Ont and do get back to me with your story and future plans, at least in Thunder Bay you have a part of your family there.
So I will end and hope we will meet again in this century of life, but I do hope it is ASAP in practical terms, so yes I do send my love to you, that you can interpret as you wish but I do miss you no matter how you feel or think.

So take care.
Love Lawrence

At the bike store, they said, "We could try to bend the axles back and switch the wheels around and hope that the same problem doesn't reoccur. Or, you could get a new Gidget. We only have one running stroller left in the store."

When I saw "The Chariot" I knew instantly she was the one to bring me the rest of the way. The store gave me a discount and I had Gidget #2. However, I was saddened to leave Gidget #1 behind. "Bye my friend," I said, "Thanks for getting me this far." I didn't think I could get attached to a stroller, but I did. We covered a lot of ground together and I felt guilty for abandoning her.

That night, I stayed at the LakeVu Motel. The next day, I got in touch with Carol, a friend of the family. My visit with her and her dog Katie was comforting. I felt like I had known Carol all my life. I met her two daughters and granddaughter and she took me around town. Then, I visited briefly with the Kenora Humane Society and spoke with some volunteers before leaving.

More encouraging messages:

> *Julia said. . . Awww Michelle. I didn't know about Gidget– I feel almost sad that I put some pictures of her on the Let Live Canada site this week. But on the other hand, she served you so well. May your new "chariot" last the rest of your journey and safely home.*
>
> *Anonymous said. . .Michelle + Running = Animal Hero*
>
> *Anonymous said. . .Hey my Mom just told me about this, way to go Aun. . .ty, hope to see u on ur way back. Gods speed and hope u keep safe.*
> *From Mark Kilborn*
>
> *Anonymous said. . .My 3 little kitties say "Thank you Mich"*

On the north shore of the Lake of the Woods, the alluring beauty of Kenora was irresistible with the harbor and all the hills. I was charmed by the connection I made with the land and the people. The attraction and comfort of this place made it tempting to stay. "But, oh, the power of purpose!"

Carol and Katie brought me back to the highway. It was always hard to leave the company of others, but I was all fired up to get on with my task. Holding my own in the face of adversity through Northern Ontario, I had gained a heightened sense of confidence that pulled me in and kept me from getting bogged down with myself.

Once I was in motion, nothing but God could stop me now. I was excited to leave the province of Ontario that felt like forever to cross. "Smaller provinces here we come," I said with gladness.

After thirty miles of running on one of the worst stretches of highway in the country, welcome signs came into view. Me and Gidget #2 did a happy dance on the side of the road singing "na na na na, na na na na, hey hey hey, good-bye." It's amazing how silly you can get when you spend too much time with yourself. If only Gidget could talk.

On the 134th day of my run, I left Ontario and entered the province of Manitoba. "Wow, have I really been out here that long?" It felt like many lifetimes ago since I left Newfoundland. At the sight of the welcome centre, my tears flowed freely. Each tear was replaced by relief.

With every step I took, every mile I ran, every province I overcame, and with every passing day, I was wearing down every doubter who said, "It's impossible. She'll never make it."

Chapter 6

Manitoba and Saskatchewan

August 25, 2007 - West Hawk Lake

In the welcome centre parking lot, I felt honored and humbled to meet a Canadian WW2 Veteran in uniform. He was eighty-seven years old and on his way to Timmins. Two young boys riding their bicycles stopped and listened in on our conversation. "I was an Anti-Aircraft Gunner," he said proudly.

Like many war vets, he was reluctant to share stories of his time in the war because the memories were too painful. However, what he did say of the battles and his contribution captivated us. Any successes I might have had paled in comparison to his lifetime achievements. I shook his hand and thanked him for his service. Then, everyone went his or her separate ways.

In West Hawk Lake, the campground was full and crowded. The first spot they put me in didn't work out so well. There were three guys to the left of me and three girls to the right and here I was stuck in the middle. When they got together, it was party time. I had to ask to be moved but they could still be heard from anywhere. "I might as well sit back and enjoy the music," I thought. "It's going to be a long night."

Going on from there, the scenery changed drastically after Falcon Lake. Leaving the boreal forest, I was running on flatter ground. In Prawda, I stopped at the Pine Tree Campground and looked forward to a quieter night. At least, that's what I was hoping for.

Receiving some disturbing news from home, I listened with horror about the death of my nephew's cat and the nature in which it died. Some kids had bashed its head in and it crawled home but didn't live. As well, my niece was battling with her neighbors over leaving their dog on the balcony for hours under the blazing summer sun. If you are like me, you would find these incidents disturbing.

That night, a massive thunderstorm broke free across the sky above me. There were no seconds to count between the flash of lightening and the thunderclap. As the storm's intensity built, the rain was hammering my tent and the sound was nearly deafening. Thunder continued to roar and the bolts of lightning unleashed all around me like a beautiful light show.

The strong wind gusts and the brute power of nature had me laughing almost hysterically thinking, "A tent was not the place to be right now. It might be scooped up with me in it. Who knows where we would land," I laughed.

I went over the design of the tent in my mind and didn't think I had to worry about getting struck by lightning. There wasn't any material that would conduct electricity and I wasn't near any trees. However, if it blows apart, I didn't know what I would do. The visual of my shelter getting whisked away and leaving me exposed made me laugh that much harder.

The storm lasted about an hour before the air was calm again. Thankfully, everything was still intact and dry inside. It was a pretty impressive storm and I don't think it would be an exaggeration to say it was a torrential downpour. The ground was saturated with pools of water all over the park. We survived the night, but packing up the next morning was a little wet.

It was no surprise that the weather was a big topic for discussion at the camp restaurant. That's where I met Jim and Karen from the States. They stopped there for breakfast and were huge animal supporters. Listening to them was like playing a recorder from every person and shelter I've talked to across our country.

They left before me and when I went to pay for my breakfast, it was taken care of. I ran outside to try and catch them, but they were gone. I didn't get a chance to thank them. Two days later, I approached Winnipeg.

August 28-29, 2007 - Winnipeg

From a long way off, I could see the tops of buildings popping up. They faded in and out until boom–there it was at the bottom of the Red River Valley. "Wow, would you look at that Gidget? The Gateway to the west," I said with excitement and gazed at a skyline of domes, curves and angles in downtown Winnipeg. A smile burst out onto my face and I began waving at all the cars passing by, even though no one waved back. My being ecstatic to be here was another understatement.

As I entered the city limits, a truck pulled over in front of me. It was Boris, from the *Winnipeg Free Press*. I had been in touch with them earlier in the day and after he took some pictures, he kindly dropped me off at the downtown hostel. The article would be in the next morning's paper. All of these little victories were adding up.

I met Tanner at the front desk of the hostel. She registered me for two nights. One, at the member rate and the second, she paid for in support of my run. She was very helpful in finding directions to the Humane Society, the shoe stores, the library, and laundry facilities.

That night, I took care of the usual things and made plans for my day in Winnipeg before going to bed.

First thing in the morning I called Aileen, the Manager of Public Relations for the Winnipeg Humane Society (WHS). I was encouraged by our conversation.

"I can stop by around noon if that works," I said and was excited with her response.

"SHAW TV will be here covering a story on adoptions at the same time, so come on down."

When I arrived, everyone welcomed me and there was excitement in the air. Buster, a mix German Shepherd and Husky dog, was up for adoption and being interviewed by SHAW TV along with Vickie, his caregiver. He was playful and had everyone laughing, especially when he knocked Joanne, the reporter, off her feet. It was so much fun being a part of that.

Afterward, Aileen introduced me to Bill, the Assistant Director, and he took me for a tour of the building. There were so many abandoned pets and I admired the staff's passion for them all.

Then, Bill said, "We won't be in this building for much longer." He brought out some sketches of their new building. "After eight years of planning and fundraising, a new state-of-the-art facility is scheduled to open at the end of October this year to accommodate thousands of animals annually. It's been a long haul and we're all very excited about it."

He also spoke about the cat overpopulation problem in Winnipeg and how they try to deal with it. "Shelters can't do it alone," he said. "The problem is much too big. We need the help of our community too. Pets must be spayed or neutered, whether they are owned, strays, or feral. We have staff that make spay or neutering available to people who can't get to clinics. Subsidized costs are needed for those who can't afford it as well. However, animals need to be spayed or neutered before they leave our building too," he concluded.

The Winnipeg Humane Society was doing everything they could to help our companion friends and make a difference in their city. "I'll have to come back sometime to see the new shelter," I said.

Before I left and to my surprise, they handed me a gift: a fleece sweater for those cold nights and a collection they took up to help pay for my next pair of running shoes. I was deeply touched by their kindness and support.

> *Michelle. . .for your continuing journey – Good Luck and Be Safe!*
> *Managers and Staff of The Winnipeg Humane Society*

From there, Aileen drove me to the Canadian Footwear store.

"Thank you again, for everything," I said gratefully.

"I'll get in touch with shelters ahead of you to let them know you're coming," she said before driving away. We waved good-bye and I thought how encouraging and memorable my visit with them had turned out. It was more than I was expecting.

> *Julia said. . .*
> *I'm so glad you are doing well, Michelle. It's good to hear the smiles in your blogs again. And I'm sorry I missed your call the other day, I would have loved to*

chat with you. (Sometimes it hard with only one phone line to catch every call that comes in) Hugs Girlie!

After I picked up my shoes, I went back to the hostel and met my new roommates, Dunja from Switzerland and Angela from the States. It was interesting to hear about their travel adventures. "We're off to experience Winnipeg's night life," they said happily. "You're welcome to join us if you like." Although I appreciated the invitation, I declined graciously, wanting to remain focused on my task.

My trip to the laundromat was an interesting experience. Somehow, I got my directions crossed and ended up lost. Eventually I found one, but I don't think it was the one recommended to me.

There were lots of people coming and going. The store cashier spoke openly about being robbed several times and as recent, as the night before. "Just lovely," I thought and wanted to hurry up and get out of there. However, it was a busy place and I waited a long time for the machines.

As time past, the number of rough-looking characters hanging around outside increased. I must have stood out from the regulars because I was followed when I left. It was dark and when I finally arrived at the hostel, I hung around the lobby with other people until I felt safe. Then, I went off to my room to bed.

Early in the morning, I packed up quietly not wanting to wake my roommates who had crawled in sometime during the night. However, they were both awake when I returned from breakfast. "Good luck," they said and we exchanged hugs.

On my way out of Winnipeg, I stopped at Darcy's A.R.C. The acronym stood for Animal Rescue Centre. I loved the name and saying, "The animals get sent to the A.R.C." Darcy wasn't there but I met Darlene, Karen, and Brenda. "Pets are for life," they said. "We're committed to giving animals in our care shelter until a home can be found and every animal is spayed or neutered. We have saved over 5,000 abandoned animals in our short existence," they added proudly. The A.R.C. was truly a success story and I was happy to learn they work closely with the Winnipeg Humane Society.

Going a little farther, I entered Manitoba's first registered no-kill animal shelter. The Winnipeg Pet Rescue Shelter was committed to provide a euthanasia-free environment for unwanted animals. The founder and director, Carla, wasn't available but I spoke with a volunteer named Kim. "Educating the public is so important," she said. "We try to find a forever home for all the animals."

What an encouraging start to my day and it would end even better. Just west of Winnipeg, I stopped at a little town called Elie. The gas station attendant pointed me in the direction of L'Auberge Clemence B&B and Tea House. It was a historical building.

I knocked on the door and a lady named Linda answered. After I told her my story, I asked if I could camp on a piece of their grass. She kindly invited me in and led me to a sitting room.

Linda's husband, Jean, joined us and they listened to more of my story. They both loved animals and Linda told me Jean even helped a rat cross the street one time. However, one of the most incredible stories they shared was about their cat and dog.

When their cat was a kitten, a tomcat attacked it and her back legs were paralyzed. She was a mess and they didn't expect her to live more than a few days. To their complete amazement, their dog, Naddy, began nursing the kitten and nudging her to get up and walk. This went on for about a month. The kitten was still alive and began to walk. They named her Wobbles because she wobbles when she walks. Both cat and dog have been sleeping together ever since.

Then, I was fascinated by how they converted their home into a bed and breakfast.

"This place used to be a convent for nuns," Linda said.

"After four years of trying, they finally sold it to us. Shortly after we took ownership and started renovating, a nun who lived here before came to visit us. She asked if we had experienced anything unusual and we did. Things like doors opening on their own, perfume smells, and the doorbell going off. We couldn't explain any of it," Jean added.

Inside this jewel of a place was the original chapel, a gift shop, and the walls displayed a gallery of art from a local artist named Estelle Regnier. Outside on the beautiful park-like grounds were flower gardens, a large pond and a waterfall to sit by. It was a sanctuary for both birds and guests.

Jean and Linda continued to astonish me with their stories. "We don't think it's a haunted house though. None of these things are scary. In fact, we think this place is blessed because whenever we need something, it mysteriously happens. Like the art on the walls and statues. And miraculously, this building didn't get hit by the F5 tornado that went through here in June. It came right up to the edge of the grounds and then just turned around."

After some hearty conversation, they floored me when they invited me to stay in one of the rooms for the night. "If you hear anything, don't worry, our ghosts are harmless," Linda assured me.

Linda and Jean fed me and gave me a bed to sleep in. They didn't even ask for a penny. "Stay an extra day if you need to," they offered kindly. I was flabbergasted by their generosity and compassion. No wonder God blessed them. They also had a successful business called "Country Signs".

That evening, I didn't experience anything unusual, just peace and comfort. Although it was tempting to stay, I was on a mission. I left in the morning thinking Linda and Jean are two of the most remarkable people I have ever met.

Every day now to me was a gift. Running across the Canadian Prairies, the roads were mostly flat and there were farms that stretched all the way to the horizon, filled with golden fields of grain.

Five days later, I reached Oak Lake. During that time, I ran through hot and muggy weather, learned about a death in the family and a service I wasn't able to attend, my niece moved in with me without me being there, Labor Day weekend passed, there were dead raccoons, deer, and horses in the field that watched me pass by, a little red car parked with someone in it I thought was dead, and a couple with a flat tire and no spare.

In the small village of Oak Lake, I watched some young guys speed test an old car up and down Main Street. Then, I headed for the campground and I laughed when I saw it. There was just a patch of trees that everyone gathered around. "You've got to be kidding me," I sighed.

I walked by a trailer of construction workers and they said, "Just pick a spot. Don't worry about us, we won't bother you." My only other option was to keep going, but I had already run thirty-two miles and a prairie storm was coming.

While I was lying in my tent and just about to fall asleep, I heard a man's voice say, "Are you sleeping?" I wasn't sure how to respond to that. When I got out of my tent, a native man named William was standing there. "I'm part of the construction crew and I was just curious about what you are doing here," he asked. "There's supposed to be bad weather tonight," he added.

I told him my story and he said he hadn't been home in a while himself and missed his family too. After a brief conversation, I returned to my tent because the mosquitoes were biting me so bad.

All through the night, I could hear the guys playing poker and laughing. The same car raced up and down the side road several times, and the train went by every hour. Thunder and rain came and daybreak couldn't come fast enough. I was usually pretty careful about keeping bugs out of my tent, but this night I missed a spider and my midsection was covered with itchy bites.

Before I left, William stopped by again. He asked a lot of questions about my equipment and where I was headed. I told him I was never sure where I would end up. He told me he was anxious to get home soon himself.

The sky was grey and it was drizzling rain. I hadn't had much to eat in the past few days and I was hungry. Running through a strong headwind, I was encouraged briefly when an RCMP "pulled me over". He was concerned for my safety.

"How are you doing?" he asked.

"I'm okay. Thank you. I'm going as far as Virden and I'll stop there for the night," I replied.

"Okay. Be careful," he said and then drove off.

When I arrived in Virden, I stopped at the first restaurant I saw for something to eat. Then, I went to the Virden Motel where I met Robin. She loved animals and talked about her cat and the animals she fostered once in a while. "My son wants a dog to run with," she said. To show her support, she didn't charge me for my room.

Sometime during the night, I broke out in a burning, itchy rash. "Oh God no, this can't be happening," I cried. "This will break me!" Between the spider bites and poison oak, the itching turned minutes to hours and this was not happiness. "How could this have happened?" I grimaced.

It was in the middle of the night and everyone was sleeping. And I had no idea where to find an all-night pharmacy. Then, I remembered the oregano oil Andree's mom gave me in Pembroke. Rubbing it on gave me some temporary relief and at that moment, I thanked God for her thoughtfulness. It would do until the stores opened.

However, time was the only way to get rid of the nasty rash, which I didn't have, and it caused me to spend an extra day in Virden. To try to reduce the pain and itching, I took several cold baths. It felt like I was being tortured and my frustration increased. "I should have been more careful," I said, upset with myself. "Especially where I stopped for washroom breaks."

With calamine lotion in hand and an antihistamine to prevent spreading, I pressed on. Running and wearing the same clothing didn't help my problem. I kept reminding myself with these timeless words, "Nothing I suffered could equal the mistake I made." If you care enough, you will inconvenience and stretch yourself in ways you never thought possible. I couldn't wait to get my clothes off when I reached Elkhorn.

September 8, 2007 - Saskatchewan

When I saw the sign "Welcome to Saskatchewan", I was in too much discomfort to enjoy the moment. At Moosomin, I headed straight for the pharmacy and loaded up on anything that would help ease the itching. After taking Benadryl and talking to Chris, I slept through the night.

> *Kim said. . .*
> *Hang in there Mich. Saskatchewan already. You're my idol. Keep'er going Kiddo.*

The next day, I discovered that getting caught in the middle of a thunderstorm on the prairies is not good. When I started running toward Whitewood in the morning, there were sculpted clouds to the north and south, but it wasn't until halfway that a storm developed.

Enormous black clouds came together and the whole area was covered in darkness. I stared transfixed by the changing skies and it reminded me of the movie *Twister*. Dark clouds lowered and the thunder roared unbelievably loud. It suddenly occurred to me that I was in the middle of nowhere and about to get poured on. There was nowhere to go and I prayed there wouldn't be any hailstones.

Well, I didn't out run the rain but it was over quick. In a dramatic way, the clouds retreated and opened up holes for sunlight to streak through. However, more storm clouds formed and there was no escaping the rain a few more times before I reached Whitewood. Then, a second heavy rainfall struck the town.

> *Tracey said. . .*
> *Hi Michelle, its Tracey from Lethbridge, you are doing awesome we are following you progress all the time. I can't believe how far you have run, it's amazing. I am sorry I missed your call and when I called back you were gone. I hope that this message finds you well. I see that you may be coming through Brooks. . .we thought we may be able to meet up with you there.*
> *Our thoughts are with you*
> *Tracey and crew*
> *Lethbridge and District Humane Society*

From Tracey in February before I left Ottawa:

> *I will look forward to your call. I have also had some interest from a couple of our volunteers, who are also runners, who thought they might like to show their support for you and the animals whom they care so much about by possibly join you for a few miles of your run the day that you are heading into Calgary. It was a thought that they came up with when we passed the information around the shelter. I know that everyone is very excited and want to show their support in any way that they can. I look forward to*

hearing from you and meeting you, it is always nice to meet someone who shares the same feelings about the innocent animals in the world. All the best of luck on your way

In Broadview, I stopped at the Sweet Dreams Motel. It sounded like a good place to rest. The owner, Perry, ran a few steps with me the next day on my way to Wolseley. He was returning from Regina with his son and stopped when he saw me.

At the diner in front of the Wolseley Motel, I met the owner whose name was also Perry. However, this owner was a musician and the name of his band was Backroad Cowboys. Their country sound is pretty good. Check them out.

On my way to Indian Head, an RV stopped on the other side of the highway shouting my name. It was Richard Ralph's mom and dad. What were the odds of running into them again?

"Richard finished last Saturday," they shouted. "There was a big reception for him. We're on our way home finally. How are you doing? We were wondering if you were still running."

Then, I shouted back, "I'm still going, but I have a ways to go. Tell Richard I said congratulations." When they drove away, I felt really home sick again.

The rain was wet and cold and the nights were much cooler now. There was frost in the mornings and I could see my breath in the air. With the smell of winter coming, I needed warmer clothes.

September 14-15, 2007 - Regina

Since catching poison oak, I hadn't been sleeping well. I constantly covered myself with cream and took Benadryl. Then, at long last, after several days of being tormented, it was settling down and clearing up. When I arrived in Regina, to say I was relieved was another huge understatement.

Gail, the Promotions Coordinator for the Regina Humane Society (RHS), picked me up and my reception was pleasing. At the shelter, she arranged an interview with the *Regina Leader-Post* and

CTV sent a cameraman over. The interview would be included with an article on adoptions with PetSmart.

However, I left there heartbroken to see so many abandoned animals. It was difficult to walk away because my heart toward them was full of love and compassion. From what I know, I could almost understand what made people more compassionate toward animals than people. "They have wronged no one," I thought. I also knew this problem wasn't going to magically disappear.

> *Hi. . .You, Michelle Jameus, are an inspiration. What an amazing feat you have done. Regina. Wow. By the time you read this, you will have gone a lot further. I often think of you. Colette, Andrée's mom, and I always pray together for you. We pray that soon, someone will wake up and see the wonderful thing you are doing. Andrée, her mom, and I often speak about you. Andrée is really trying to organize something but it's not been easy. She has a wonderful presentation. We will continue to pray for you and for some kind heart and kindred spirit to wake up and soon. Take care. . . Keep going, We are all behind you in prayers. I only wish I could do more. . .Bisous Hugs. . .Cécile*

> *Kim said. . . Regina? Mich - you're a machine. Keep going Kiddo.*

> *Stephanie Olsen said. . . We're all cheering you on from St. John's, Newfoundland, Michelle. You're in our hearts and thoughts.*

September 17, 2007 – Moose Jaw

On my way to Moose Jaw, there wasn't much to look at except road-kill and trains that wound their way through this immense land. I discovered that the prairie winds are much stronger than I am. At times, it felt like I was running on the spot and my voice was lost several times from breathing in the blowing dirt.

I also began debating with myself if it was really necessary for me to go all the way to Vancouver. I felt Calgary would be far enough and was considering making it the end of the line.

The gradual uphill climb to Moose Jaw was demanding and oh, the prairie winds. When I reached the information centre, I called the Moose Jaw Humane Society and spoke with a man named Ray. He gave me directions and on my way there, a reporter stopped me. Unknown to me, Ray had made the call.

At the shelter, I met Ray and some of the staff. He told me they believe that the lives of animals have value and they deserve humane and compassionate treatment. However, the reality is there are a percentage of animals that are euthanized, especially cats. "It's difficult getting the message across to people that cats should be spayed or neutered," he said.

The reality of this truth gripped my heart and I was troubled by the deaths behind the statistics. Why? Because their only crime is homelessness. They are allowed to be killed silently, invisibly, and without an advocate. I may have been under an illusion that this mission would fix everything, but it's only because I believed change is possible.

> *"Twenty years from now you will be more disappointed by the things that you didn't do, then by the ones you did do."*
>
> *–Mark Twain*

While talking to Ray, I learned that he was retiring soon and would concentrate on his bread and breakfast for cats. He and his wife Karen called it "The Cat's Country Cottage", a vacation for your cat while you're away. Ray was a kind man and invited me to stay at his place for the night.

Karen and Ray had a beautiful country home off the highway. Inside, I met Karen and was greeted by their rescued dog, Simon, along with some of their house cats. Besides running their cat and grooming business, Karen was an artist and showed me some of her work. "I belong to the Moose Jaw Art Guild," she said, where they encourage originality.

Over dinner, our conversation just naturally gravitated toward solving the overpopulation problems. We all wanted the same things and I was greatly encouraged by their support. "Do you want to see the environment we are building for boarding cats?" Karen asked.

She took me downstairs and I was in awe of the built-in rooms, the playroom, and the outdoor runs. They also offered grooming and clipping and it almost made me want to be a cat on vacation.

Then, Karen led me outside to the barn to see their two horses, Willy and Brisk. They were beautiful creatures and she loved riding. It would have been fun to go for a ride with them.

When we went back inside, we continued our conversation from dinner. They shared their struggles over the past seven years to advance the humane society to where it is today. It was a story of perseverance and success. "If I had a million dollars, I would put it toward spaying and neutering," Karen said and we laughed about ways to come up with the money. It was here in these moments I cherished the connections I had made.

> *Sept 29, from Dorit – arrangements for Vancouver*
> *The City of Vancouver's labour force is on strike. There are some other choices:*
> *- You could go just north of Stanley Park to Ambleside Park in North Vancouver.*
> *I'm going to email Vancouver Tourism and see what they recommend.*

Early in the morning, Ray drove me back to the information centre. Karen sent me away with a lunch bag, washed and dried clothes, and a full belly. They were good people and their kindness was the kind that makes winners of everyone.

I went as far as the Husky in Caronport and pulled out the sandwich Karen made for me. To my surprise, she had stuck a note inside with some well wishes. Not only did it cheer me up, but it picked me up. I can't explain how meaningful that was.

In between Moose Jaw and the Alberta border, I ran the rolling hills for nine days. Occasionally, dogs chased me out of town and I tried to tell them, "I'm on your side." It was good Gidget was doing well, because sometimes I think she kept me going. The gusts of wind rarely let up and I was losing steam.

> *Anonymous said. . .*
> *Michelle, I can't believe you are almost to Alberta already. Are you sure that you are not hiding some roller blades inside Gidget2?*
> *You are AMAZING*

Besides Gidget, trains became a source of companionship for me. The tracks followed close to the highway and they passed by almost every hour. Some of the trains were extremely long and I would imagine myself grabbing on to the caboose and hitching a ride. When they were close enough, I tried to keep up with them and then watched them disappear. I didn't think trains could sneak up on you, but they can. It happened three times where they came up beside me and startled me with their horn.

While I ran, I wondered if it was possible to run out of things to think about. Other than counting fence posts, I reconstructed every day of my run, tried to imagine what everyone back home was doing, and what I would be doing if I were home. I was ready to go home.

Encouragement came in different forms. Once near Chaplin, a huge transport truck pulled over to the side of the road in front of me. This was unusual, until I realized who it was. It was Jim and Helene, my sister Chris's in-laws from Thunder Bay. They had passed me earlier and hoped they would see me again on their way back.

We sat in the cab talking and they gave me something to drink and a deliciously fresh cinnamon bun. We had a chuckle over how much ground they covered compared to me. They had enough time to drive through the states and across the Rockies, when I would run into them again near Gull Lake.

Along the way, I watched antelopes running gracefully through the fields like birds soaring through the air. Horses and llamas rushed to the fences and ran with me – even cows. One time, there was a herd of pintos I thought was the cavalry when the sound of their hoofs galloped toward me. I stood by the fence and marvelled at the power of these animals as they gallantly ran around with their mane flowing and hoofs pounding.

One day, I came up to a coyote and he looked like he was going to cross the highway. He didn't see me right away and I got pretty close. However, once he caught wind of me, he started running for the hills, all the while keeping his eye on me until he disappeared. I'd like to think I saved him from getting hit by a car.

There were so many dead animals on the road and one time I came across a hitchhiker lying down in the ditch. "Oh my God, he's dead," I thought. When I said hello, he answered and I was relieved.

At one point, I had to jump out of the way of a vehicle to avoid getting hit. "The driver must have fallen asleep at the wheel," I gasped. Whenever I passed a cross installed by people whose loved ones died from an accident, chills went up and down my spine.

On one occasion, I met a lone cyclist on his way to Winnipeg from Calgary. It reminded me of all the cyclists I met throughout the summer and that they have long since been at home.

It was the end of September and the days blended together now. One minute I'm kicking myself to get up, and the next thing I know I've covered 375 kilometers and wondering how I got here. The nights set in with a chill and the days were cooler. Watching geese fly south warned me there wasn't much time before winter.

September 27, 2007 – Alberta

Leaving Maple Creek, I kept telling myself, "Hold on for one more day, one more town; just one more time. Hold on to the hope that you have."

Ten miles in to my run, I came up to an overpass for trains. Warning signs read "Wind Gusts." I thought, "It's already really windy. How much worse can it be?"

Thankfully, I had Gidget to hold on to. She kept my feet grounded; otherwise I might have been blown around like the tumbleweeds. At times, I had to hold onto the wire railing when traffic went by.

The wind gusts were incredible and I don't know how we made it through, but we did.

On the 167th day of my marathon, I ran the highway past the Saskatchewan signs and rest area. I started singing the song "*Hold On Tight To Your Dreams*" by ELO. I couldn't believe I was still going or that I had come this far. When I saw "Welcome to Alberta", my heart started dancing. I was a little happy. Me and Gidget, we did us a dance.

Going on from there, I stopped in Walsh. There were eight provinces behind me and only two more to go. When I said it like that, it didn't sound so bad. However, this marathon had progressively worn me out and I was seriously thinking of ending my run in Calgary. There was little left to gain by my running. Any recognition was nice, but I was seeking a different kind of approval. One that would qualify my heart's desire.

Chapter 7

Alberta and British Columbia

In Medicine Hat, I stayed at the Satellite Motel. The SPCA was close by and I had a pleasant visit with them. I met Sheri and Val, and a reporter from the local newspaper. They said, "Our primary concern is to prevent cruelty to animals and to provide care. A lot of effort goes into finding people to adopt pets." After a brief tour, they wished me luck.

That night, I could barely sleep I was so excited. Someone from the Lethbridge Humane Society wanted to run a full marathon with me. Before I left Ottawa, I received this email.

> *Hello, my name is Tracey and I am a volunteer with the Lethbridge and District Humane Society. I just want to start by saying that I think what you are doing is absolutely wonderful, and I know that I can speak for all of the volunteers at the Humane Society when I say that we support you one hundred percent. We are a no kill society and try our best to help spread the word about how precious each and every animal's life is. I understand that you will be traveling along the Trans Canada highway and since we are off the highway we would like the opportunity to come to you and show our support. We are fairly close to Calgary and hope that we may be able to meet you at one of your stops and have the opportunity to tell*

you a bit about our Humane Society and also learn more about the society that you are involved with, and most importantly help support you and spread the word about "The No Kill Canada Marathon".

Tracey
Lethbridge Humane Society, AB

When I got off the phone with Tracey, I was thrilled that she would run with me from Medicine Hat to Suffield. Her mom, Barb, along with a friend, Laney, wanted to drive the support vehicle for us. If that wasn't exciting enough, they invited me back to Lethbridge for the night and would take me back to Suffield the following morning. I was floored and couldn't believe it.

September 29, 2007 – Suffield

Early the next morning, I got up and went for a good breakfast at the nearby Husky Restaurant. It was still dark and raining. Back at my room, I had just finished packing when I heard a knock at the door. They were here. I flung open the door and saw Tracey and Laney standing there. Barb was in the background walking Molson, a dog she was taking care of.

From the moment they arrived, I knew it was going to be an exceptional day and any ill feelings I had quickly disappeared. Tracey was dressed in her running gear and ready to go. They even brought their own cameraman, Moses, from CTV Lethbridge. After he did his interview, he filmed us running on the highway and then left. Everything happened so fast.

It had been quite a while since I had company on the road and I was taking it all in stride. We ran passed miles of short-grass fields adorned with hay bales while getting to know each other. I enjoyed hearing about her history with the humane society and I also learned that she had run an ultra-marathon. It was fun exchanging stories and it felt good to laugh.

Our steps were in sync and so was our conversation. Besides sharing my love for running and animals, she talked about her wedding plans.

"After my wedding day, I'm running in the Vegas marathon," she said, and her fiancé was her biggest fan.

"That is so cool," I responded.

Meanwhile, Barb and Laney drove up and down the highway, checking in on us and supplying us with food and drinks. Somehow, time escaped us and before we knew it, we had reached Suffield. Just like that, we were done. After a high five and a "good run" cheer, we hopped into the car.

The ride from there was lively and full of conversation. At one point I asked them, "How far is it to Lethbridge?"

"It's about 170 kilometers one way from Lethbridge to Medicine Hat," Barb replied.

Then it hit me just how far out of the way they went to be with me today. Including their return trip, they will have covered over seven hundred kilometers. This was remarkable to me. I couldn't believe it.

In Lethbridge, I stayed at Laney's place. Barb and Tracey dropped us off and would return later with a pizza. Laney made me feel right at home while we waited for them. I met her husband, Byron, and their cats. Then, I took a shower and washed my clothes. Laney also very thoughtfully gave me knitted slippers to keep me warm in the mountains.

Not long after, Tracey and Barb came back with a super jumbo-sized pizza. It was the biggest pizza I had ever seen. When I saw it, my eyes were like quarters. "Wow," I smiled. Tracey and I were so hungry we could eat the whole thing by ourselves.

Coming in behind them were two board-of-directors from the Humane Society, Ron and his wife, Ethel. Ron had just celebrated his eightieth birthday. They dropped in briefly to say hello and then had to go. It was a privilege meeting them.

While we ate our pizza, I delighted in hearing the story behind Tracey running with me. "She was so excited when you called," Barb said. "That's all we heard about. She was so determined to run with you."

Hearing something like that touches you in a way only a sincere heart can. When your journey is like taking a walk in the dark, bright lights stand out. Tracey was a shining star and her support filled me with lasting gratitude. She was the one inspiring me.

After we finished eating, we drove to their animal shelter. There, I met Jo and Heather. "It took four years of fundraising to raise the money to build this shelter," Jo said. "It's run mainly by volunteers and limited resources, and has been a no-kill shelter since its inception. We don't euthanize animals to create space. Educating the public about responsible pet ownership and the benefits of spaying and neutering is so important. Your raising awareness will help."

Humbled by their endearing hearts, I admired them for the difference they were making in the lives of companion animals and their community. We took some pictures and I was moved by their gifts. They did everything flawlessly to make this a special day. "What an incredible group of people," I thought. They are my heroes.

The evening came to an end and it couldn't be avoided. Tracey wouldn't be making the drive back with us in the morning because she was running another marathon - the Run for Cure. We both needed our sleep. "Maybe you'll come to Ottawa for the National Capital Marathon one year. You'll always have a place to stay," I said and then we wished each other well.

Morning came quickly. Barb arrived early and we stopped at Tim Horton's for breakfast. I enjoyed Barb and Laney's company. They were a lot of fun to be with. It was a long drive and when we arrived in Suffield, it was difficult to say good-bye. "You have a terrific daughter," I told Barb. "All of you have been terrific. I can't thank you enough for such a memorable day. I'll never forget it."

They made sure I was okay and as I watched them drive away, it saddened me. I would miss them. My run between Suffield and Tilley was quiet and lonely. As I reflected on the past twenty-four hours, I wondered how Tracey was doing. She was one of the most authentic people I'd ever met. I wore the buff and socks she gave me and it made me smile.

Five days later, I reached the city limits of Calgary. It was Friday, October 5 and the temperature was chilly. At the A&W, I just stood there and stared into space, not looking at anything. I was a bit numb and just let out a big sigh. Then I closed my eyes, thanking God that I was here.

After a few frozen moments, I went inside where I waited for Jen. She had picked me up the first time in the small town of Gleichen. I called her from Bassano and she kindly offered to be my host while I was in the city.

> *Hi there. . .I learned about your marathon through a link from a local rescue website here in Calgary. I think what you are doing is wonderful. I made a small donation to No-Kill Canada, but I was wondering if there is anything that we can do for you when you come to Calgary. Both my husband and I are huge animal lovers and we own 4 cats. (We had 2 cats until recently and then I had a weak moment and we adopted 2 kittens from a farm that was overpopulated with cats.) Hope to hear from you. . Jennifer*

I also spoke with Kelly, the President of the MEOW Foundation. It was a foundation for the adoption of abandoned cats. Jen had been in touch with her and they wanted to plan an event on Sunday. I was thrilled when she told me about it.

Before going back to Jen's house, she drove me to the Chariot head office in Calgary to have Gidget checked over. I wanted to make sure she was in good shape for the finish. They were fantastic and did more than I expected. Gidget was given a warranty overhaul. New tires, bearings, and they even threw in a front wheel. Gidget was in better condition than I was.

My Calgary hosts were terrific. I had my own room. The names of their cats were Tigger, Lucas, Liam, and Lexi. They were so much fun to play with. Jen and her husband Allen took me out for dinner and made me feel right at home. She did everything she could to help me and their support was such an encouragement. We were looking forward to Sunday.

October 7, 2007 – The Cat House

Nestled within the city of Calgary is a specialty store for cat lovers called "The Cat House". The owner, Joanne, was a great supporter of the MEOW Foundation. They worked together with Cheryl, the Manager of Communications for the Calgary Humane Society (CHS), to organize today's event.

Jen and Kelly joined me for the short run up to The Cat House. When we came into sight, everyone started cheering. Be that as it may, behind these public events were my private thoughts. I've never been comfortable with being the central figure of anything, or having this kind of attention. I was more comfortable letting my actions speak for themselves. However, everyone's kindness helped put me at ease.

There was a tent erected in the parking lot with supporters gathered to greet us. My heart started pounding as reporters from Shaw TV and City TV began their interviews. It was another surreal moment.

> *"I think it was one of the most inspiring things I've ever seen," Kelly, MEOW's President said of Jameus' marathon. "I don't know of anyone else who has ever taken the time to do something that takes such a personal commitment – and to do this on behalf of our four-legged friends is even more inspiring."*

> *"We agree with Michelle that this is the only way that we – or any other city for that matter – will ever be able to live in a place where no-kill is possible. People must spay and neuter their animals," she said.*

After some mingling, the staff and volunteers from both MEOW and CHS presented me with some thoughtful gifts and a magnificent celebration cake for all to enjoy. It was beautifully decorated with a picture of a cat on top and the words "Let Live Canada, Welcome Michelle". It was delicious.

Then, we entered The Cat House to browse the store and chat with the owner. "I recently lost three cats in a very short span," Joanne said. I understood her grief and there are no words to ease the pain.

Going on from there, I was taken on a tour of the Calgary Humane Society. Cheryl showed us around their newly constructed facility. It was huge. "More room was needed and it has made an improvement in the way we can care for so many more animals," Cheryl said. "It is an impressive building," I responded and appreciated the time she took to take us through it.

Leaving that place, we went to MEOW's cageless shelter. It was a modest house with a no-kill mandate. There, I met the foundation's Operation's Director, Debbie. As she walked me through, her passion and love for the cats was remarkable and the cats returned the love. "We have rescued over 3,200 cats since the beginning," she said. "We are passionate about providing the best care for every cat and finding forever homes for them."

Someone once asked me, "What can one person do?" Well, that's how MEOW got started and they had a story of success. And that's how I ended up here. Debbie was the one person responsible for my being in this place. She read my marathon announcement on Jazzpurr's website and brought it to the attention of the MEOW board. Their support was unanimous.

What an inspiring day I was having. When you find yourself in a place you never expected to be, that's when you discover what you really believe. To dream is powerful. I was driven by my purpose and dream. However, my big dream to run solitary across Canada had that feel of stepping across a canyon – impossible. That's what makes it so unbelievable. The same is true for a no-kill country.

Having that dream is what keeps me fighting. I had the fire of optimism that all things are possible if you believe. I fought through the first 6419 kilometers and I wanted to keep riding the wave of possibilities through the next 939 kilometers. My heart's desire was to continue and fulfill my dream. It was time to empty the tank. The only question left was, "Did I still believe I had enough left to finish?"

Kim said. . .
Calgary? Holy smokes. That's crazy. Keep'er going Mich.

Before I left the city, I contacted Jim of the Roadrunner running group to find out if anyone would be interested in running with me out of Calgary. It was Thanksgiving weekend and Monday was a holiday. He surprised me when he suggested I meet him at 9:00 A.M. near the Valley Ridge turnoff west of Stoney Trail. I was glad I picked up some mitts and a hand-warmer to ward off the early morning chills.

When he arrived, there was an older woman named Barb with him. "I don't run as far as I use to," she confessed, "but I can run a few miles with you." After a short run, Jim picked her up and I appreciated her coming out. They left and then Jim returned with some contact numbers a short time later. He was a long distance runner himself and I could tell he was both intrigued with what I was doing and concerned for my safety. I would see him a few more times.

Alberta's scenery was as diverse as its topography. From the prairies to the peaks, I was headed for high mountains fringed along the western edge. Today the mountains seemed to grow right before my eyes and they were already snow covered. The closer I got, the more spectacular the scenery became and I was delighted to see trees again.

There was a lot of traffic from weekenders going home. After running through the flat prairies, the calves of my legs were sore from running up and down these hills. I was glad Gidget had a third wheel again.

At the Morley turnoff, I went inside the restaurant and changed my clothes before Jen and Allen picked me up. It was the last night I would stay with them.

"I've never met anyone like you and probably will never meet anyone like you again."

-Jennifer

Early the next morning, Jen drove me back. She was a trooper and ran a short distance with me. Before she left I said, "I'll call you in a few days to let you know how I'm doing." All the while thinking to myself, "I don't know how many more of these good-byes I can take." I was going to miss her.

From there, everywhere I looked the view was spectacular. It was natural, beautiful, and wild. I was captivated by the perfection all around me. On one hand it was breathtaking, but on the other hand, it was terrifying being out here alone. The quiet was almost deafening.

As I crossed into Bow Valley, signs read "Attention Elk Crossing next 2 km". Then a little further, there were more signs that said "Caution Wildlife on Highway". I was on high alert, but didn't see anything.

Out of nowhere, a car pulled up and stopped in front of me. To my surprise, it was Jim from the Roadrunner group. He was concerned because I didn't have any bear spray with me and brought me a can. "This is active grizzly country and people from around here know better than to run without it," he said kindly. I thanked him and before he left he added, "I'll catch up with you again in Canmore."

After that, I started looking over my shoulder and prayed I wouldn't have to use the spray. All the same, I was enthralled by my surroundings. I steered Gidget off the road a couple of times because I wasn't paying attention to what I was doing. The views were tremendous.

Canmore is a mountain resort and a gateway to the majestic Canadian Rockies. As I entered the town, I saw a trio of peaks known as The Three Sisters Mountain. Originally called The Three Nuns, the famous rock formation has been an inspiration to many artists and photographers, and a tourist attraction. Individually they are known as Big Sister (Faith), Middle Sister (Charity), and Little Sister (Hope).

Jim gave me the phone number of a runner friend, Magi. I called her from the gas station and she came to pick me up. Unfortunately, Gidget didn't fit in her car. I was about to follow her directions when Jim pulled up. He just missed her. After we looked at some maps together, he gave me a ride to Magi's place. I was so grateful for his help.

That night, Magi brought me to the heart of Canmore's social scene, The Grizzly Paw. Canadian-owned, its unique atmosphere of wooded interior, fireplaces, and mountain views was the delight of many thirsty beer drinkers. It was the first brewpub in Canada and a fixture of Canmore's nightlife.

Magi and I shared a huge plate of nachos and I ordered the salad she recommended. We laughed at how much food two hungry runners could eat. There was probably enough food to feed six people. Although I enjoyed myself, I was dog-tired. My feet were like twigs and I was feeling pretty beat up. It was all I could do to stay awake.

Magi, on the other hand, was young and full of energy. I envied her youth. My spirit was willing, but my body was getting weaker by the day and I was already pushing my limits every time I ran. I was more than happy to call it an early night.

The next morning, Magi went for her daily run. If circumstances were different, I would have enjoyed running the trails with her. She disappeared into the woods and I headed for the Bow Valley SPCA. Located in town, I was glad I didn't have to go far to find it.

As I walked up to the building I thought, "Oh wow. This is no ordinary place." It was surrounded by panoramic mountain views and wooded walking trails. I was greeted at the front door by the adoption centre manager, Sonya, a volunteer, Jennifer, and a photographer friend, Jacques.

Inside, they gave me a guided tour of the facility. "The design is based on our no-kill philosophy," Sonya said. "It's the first no-kill, no-cage adoption centre in Canada. Our program is unique: cats on one side and dogs on the other. We've replaced cages with rooms based on a no-cage model. We rehabilitate, train, and care for the animals until they can be re-homed. We don't give up on them. Our biggest challenge is operating in a sustainable manner over the long-term."

With indoor and outdoor play areas, the environment was people and animal friendly. I was amused by the playfulness of the puppies Jennifer brought into the playroom. "I've always had a deep love for animals," Sonya said.

After a short time of play, everyone needed to get on with his or her day. I left there glad to have met them and thinking, it was a little place overflowing with great big hearts.

Breathing in and filling my lungs with pure, fresh mountain air was heavenly. The cool crispness put roses on my cheeks. I drank in the views of the awe-inspiring scenery around me and wished I had a swivel head so that I wouldn't miss a thing.

Arriving in Banff, I took the Tunnel Mountain exit to enjoy the scenic route to the hostel. There were wonderful viewing points overlooking the valley floor and the Bow River glistening in the distance. The haunting beauty of the landscape was encompassed by lofty peaks and a forest preparing for the onset of winter, and a forest full of changing colors. It was mind-blowing.

Before I reached the hostel, I encountered some Rocky Mountain wildlife: three white-tailed deer grazing on the side of the road. I was within touching distance and they didn't even move. Their eyes of beauty stared right into my soul. It was another one of those moments I wished I could have bottled.

> *Anonymous said. . .*
> *Michelle*
> *I'm thinking of you so much lately and I keep missing your phone calls. You are passed Calgary, I can't believe it. You are doing so great and I wish I was there with you. You know who I am and you know how proud I am of you. You go girl, you're the girl and we know you can do it. I'm thinking of you. Lots of hugs your way*
> *Love you xoxoxoxo*

That night, encircled by the soaring Rockies, I was alone in the dorm resting for my fifty-six kilometers run to Lake Louise in the morning. I tried to keep my mind from running forward to the end before I got there, but it wasn't easy.

With the coming of dawn, I made my way out of the mountain community of Banff. My timing was perfect as I watched a herd of elk grazing along the highway in their natural habitat. Sometimes, not even wildlife watchers can find them out here and it made seeing them all the more incredible.

However, it caused me to be on constant guard for other wild animals, like wolves or cougars, looking for a meal. I felt a little safer knowing there were fences to deter animals from the road. Today was a lonely run to Lake Louise. Not even the scenery or changing colors of autumn could fill that spot. The last ten kilometers of highway construction was a small comfort as I made my way through.

In town, I checked into the hostel and then followed the smell of coffee and breakfast to the restaurant. There, I sat by a window and devoured my food. I watched buses and tourists come and go. At one point, I thought I saw Santa Claus filling up with gas. The driver wore a red cap and a red jacket. Underneath was an elderly man with long white hair and a white beard. He sure looked like old Saint Nick.

I also met two marathon runners who strongly suggested I rest a few days in Field before running to Golden. "It's a brutal fifty-three kilometer run up and down hills," they warned me. Even though I considered what they had to say, rest wasn't something I could afford. I was concerned that my body would seize up if I stopped for too long and winter was in the air, so was the coming of snow. Rest would have to wait until I got home.

> *Wow. Good job Mich. You are like the freakin' energizer bunny. . .you just keep going and going. You're on our home turf now. I hope the natives treat you well. Stay warm and healthy. You can finish these last few miles. A couple little bumps in the road up ahead but keep your eyes on the peaks and they won't seem so bad. Glad to hear Gidget has been reborn a stockier type. You need a reliable travelling companion. Hope you make BC by the 31st as it always snows Oct 31 in the mountains . . . and August 31 as well, oh well good luck see you on the return trip..Jen*

Anonymous said. . .
I stumbled on your link through the MEOW website, what a journey you are undertaking. I rescued my two cats from MEOW, and am proud I did. Keep up the good work, Godspeed.

October 12, 2007 – Field, British Columbia

On a chilly October morning, I ran through the Great Divide where unspoiled wilderness waited in its purest form and nature reigns supreme. The glorious scenery across the western mountains continued and the beautiful vistas from the tops were stunning.

At the summit of Kicking Horse Pass, I paused to take in the awe-inspiring view. Wapta Lake was a glacier-fed reservoir and behind it, a backdrop of the gorgeous Rocky Mountains. The reflection on the crystal-clear water was almost a perfect mirror image of mountain peaks crested with white snow and rock formations hinged against a deep blue sky, and even the browns and mossy greens from the trees. It was breathtaking.

Enthralled by the matchless beauty, I wished it were a hot summer's day. There was a rich peacefulness about the flat calm lake and I would have enjoyed jumping in for a leisurely swim. If the lodge overlooking the lake had been open, I might have stayed for a visit.

Filled with mountain-fresh clean air, I left that place and started my descent down the "Big Hill" toward the town of Field. It's called the Big Hill because of its steep grade over a short distance. The narrow valleys and high mountains limited the space where trains could stretch out and they had trouble descending or climbing. It was the most difficult piece of railway track on the original Canadian Pacific Railway's route until it was replaced by the construction of the "Spiral Tunnels".

Cut deep into the valley walls, these spectacularly engineered upper and lower tunnels doubled the length of the track to reduce some of the hazard. Today, if a train is long enough, you can see three of its parts at once as it loops its way through. It's fascinating to see the first engine emerge out the other end while the tail end is still entering the tunnel at the same time.

Although I was excited about entering the province of British Columbia, the quick transition into steep downhill running caused my over stretched thigh muscles and achy feet to scream at me. At the foot of the mountain, I was thankful that the road flattened. However, the quiet was almost haunting as I passed a sign that read, "End of Avalanche Area". It gave me goose bumps.

When I reached the town site of Field, I saw the info centre and rushed toward it. I asked for directions to the hostel and it took me about five minutes to find it. At the same time, I toured the village. The area and people had that small-town charm you can't help but be attracted to. I found it easy to connect to their way of life.

Up until now, most of the hostels I've stayed at were dorm-like. However, this one was a chalet and had comfortable beds. It was exactly the comfort I needed before another very long run.

Hi - My name is Brooke Lowes. I'm in 6th grade in Vancouver, BC. I am doing a project called Greatest Canadian and I picked you to do my project on because of what you are doing for animals. Hope to hear from you soon. Best wishes on your cross-Canada run.

I am forwarding an e-mail that my granddaughter sent to Michelle Jameus yesterday, Tuesday, October 9th. While we realize that Michelle is really busy with her marathon at the moment (we've been on the web site to look at all the pictures taken along the way), we would really like to receive a reply, if at all possible, so Brooke can complete her project. Thanks, Trudy Lowes

Hi Michelle, my daughter has chosen to do her 6th grade project on you. She was to write about a Canadian Hero, someone who does something that helps everyone. There were the usual David Suzuki types but I encouraged her to find someone (a woman in particular) that isn't as "well known", that is making a difference. She chose someone who helps animals as that is her love. We put our heads together and fingers to keyboards and found you. I know she has e-mailed you once requesting some information, and naturally I know you are quite busy with running a million miles a day right now, but, I'm hoping that you can get back to her when you have a few seconds. I thought my e-mail might help validate her request as I know there are many scammers out there. Her name is Brooke Lowes, she is in grade 6 at Hastings Community Elementary School in Vancouver, she is in French immersion and she's an awesome kid. Thanks Michelle and continued good luck in your journey.

Hi Michelle – I just wanted to thank you so much for all the information you emailed to Brooke on Thursday. She was just ecstatic when she left here that evening on her way home to fill in all the blanks on her project. Thanks again, and please keep us posted as to your whereabouts, especially as you get closer to Vancouver. Happy running. Trudy

At sunrise and the first appearance of light, I was still sleepy and resisted getting out of a warm bed. It looked cold outside my window and it took some convincing to get me moving. With little get up and go, I bundled up for winter and headed for Golden.

Since leaving Lake Louise, I have enjoyed some of the most incredible scenery to be found in Canada. Scenery that constantly changed with the seasons and weather conditions. Surrounded by snow-topped mountain peaks, valleys, rock walls, and the roaring rivers, the dramatic landscape continued through the canyon.

In the deep silent forest of Yoho National Park, the colors and smells of fall were everywhere and there was an abundance of wildlife. Along the side of the road were bear and elk tracks. When I saw the warning sign on a post, "bear in the area", it inspired me to run faster through the park and to make a lot of noise. Especially when I had to make a pit stop.

Winding through a beautiful broad valley, the highway paralleled the Kicking Horse River. The run downhill was exhilarating, but it needed more concentration. Some stretches of the road had little shoulder room and sometimes there was none.

Just east of Golden, the curvy two-lane highway was narrow. There was a steep rock face on one side and a sheer drop to the river below on the other. It was a risky run along the "Ten Mile Hill" section of the road. Plans for a major upgrade to improve safety were in the works, but not until a future date.

Warning signs lined the highway with "sharp curves, obey all signs" and "truckers check your breaks". It didn't give me a warm fuzzy feeling and I was anxious to get out of the danger zone. The road continued to follow the curves of the mountain and the sudden bends and narrow turns had barely enough room for two vehicles. Three was a crowd with Gidget and me.

It was at the bend of a sharp ninety-degree curve when my life flashed before my eyes and I thought I was going to meet my maker. An eighteen-wheeler needed both sides of the road to make the turn and as I watched him come around the corner I thought, "Oh my God, there's not enough room for both of us and I'm going to die."

In a matter of seconds, I was caught between him and the cement railing. "Oh God, I don't want to die," I cringed and hugged the railing as tight as I could. I can't explain what happened next, but somehow the rear end of the transport missed me. It was as if it passed right through me. I didn't stick around to figure it out and made a run for it as soon as the way was clear.

A short distance from there, I came up to another sharp curve with no shoulders. I couldn't see passed the rock cut and when I made the decision to go, I came face to face with a car racing around the bend. At the last second, he swerved to avoid me. Paralyzed with fear, I froze and my heart stopped momentarily. Thankfully, he had quick reflexes.

Not long after that, two transports going in opposite directions passed me at precisely the same time. There was nowhere for me to go and they nearly blew me over the side. "This is insanity," I thought. "I have to get off this road."

When I finally reached Golden, I was relieved beyond belief, but also a little shaken. The realization that I had narrowly escaped being hit three times caused me to break into a sweat. "How in the world am I still alive?" I said, astonished.

Anonymous said. . .
Mich,
BE CAREFUL
Tabarouette.
We miss you out here.
Thinking of you.
Steph
October 15, 2007 7:59 AM

Kim said. . .
Keep'er going Mich. You can do this. . .watch out for those transports. . .love reading your progress. I can't wait to see you when you come back. . .we'll have a Rebels' reunion. . .hang in there kiddo.
October 15, 2007 9:16 AM

Anonymous said. . .
Well Michelle I will be home tonight in at 8:00pm my time 5:00 your time, call me anytime after that.
You know who misses your calls. xo
October 15, 2007 10:22 AM

Anonymous said. . .
Keep it going Mich. Stay safe.
All the Best,
Jess
October 15, 2007 9:01 PM

Anonymous said. . .
I'm shaking just thinking about you being out there alone.
God is watching out for you, the "Animal Angel".
October 16, 2007 10:47 PM

Trail Magic Dennis said. . .
Michelle: You would be surprised how many are 'with you' every step of your journey . . .keeping you safe.

Waking up in Golden, there was a heavy fog over the area. While I was having breakfast at the Husky Restaurant, I thought about my near-death experiences and how close I came to being a statistic. Before I left on this journey, I didn't care if I lived or died. However, today, I was thankful for God's mercy.

A truck driver sitting across from me said, "The highest rates of accidents are along Rogers Pass and Golden. The poorly engineered highway is to blame." Looking into the fog, I had that feeling I shouldn't leave here.

When I walked outside, my eyes were drawn to the Greyhound bus depot and I just stared at it. It made me wonder if someone was trying to tell me something. Maybe it was time for me to stop tempting fate. "Listen to your heart," is what I heard. My heart was telling me I should take the bus over the pass.

As the bus pulled out of Golden, I wondered if I had made the right decision. My gut feeling assured me that I did. If I had a support vehicle, I might have chanced it, but I didn't want to push my luck.

We crossed over narrow bridges and passed through several concrete snow sheds that protect the highway from avalanches. When I saw how little room there was for two vehicles getting through, never mind a pedestrian, it was confirmation to me about my decision. When we drove by a serious car accident where the cement divider had been taken out, it removed any doubts I might have had.

In this hostile weather territory, there was a layer of fresh snow. From the summit, the views were amazing and it looked like you could kiss the sky from the snowy peaks. The road through the rugged mountain wilderness was narrow until it opened up again like a door just passed the little resort town of Sicamous.

Vancouver was still more than 600 kilometers away and over the next four days, I struggled to run to Kamloops. Every mile felt like ten. Inching my way through the towns, there were few moments of encouragement.

Outside Tappen, I was drenched from the rain and the waitress at the Esso Restaurant kindly bought me breakfast. In Sorrento, I encountered a cat named Canada. When she jumped out the window, the owner called her "Air Canada" and I thought that was hilarious.

However, from Sorrento to Chase, I leaned heavily on Gidget to support me. My legs were faltering and they didn't want to work anymore. As I clung to Gidget, my hands tightened their grip and I used her as a crutch to carry me all the way into Chase.

On October 18, after 6958 kilometers of relentless striving, I never thought I would say it, but I had reached my physical limit. I was physically exhausted, worn out, and running on empty. My feet were killing me and any stamina I had was gone. Despite my determined efforts, I wasn't a machine and there was nothing left in the tank. I gave it everything I had and I thought I was done.

> *Oct 18*
> *Hi - I got you a route through Vancouver.*
> *Actually, if you arrive the day before, I can pick you up on the outskirts of the city and then bring you back there on the 29th for the official run - then we can "case out" the route – whatever you like. The Municipal strike is over, so Stanley Park should be OK - but I haven't heard back from the Parks Dept. yet. Got us a hotel room too. SYS Dorit*
>
> *Oct 20*
> *I'm having nothing but trouble with the Vancouver Parks people. They now want us to apply for two types of permits and pay a fee. On the other hand, West Vancouver (Ambleside Park - just north of Stanley Park) emailed me back saying the following:*

Hi Dorit
Kevin passed your message on to me as I deal with Special Events on District land. As long as it is a small group as you say and you are not setting anything up you do not need a permit but thank you very much for letting us know.
They also suggested this:
If Michelle would like a nicer run, she could come into West Van under the Lions Gate and into Ambleside from the Capilano River.

Anonymous said. . .
Hang in there Mich. . .take my strength. . . .I will be with you. . . .I am so proud of you. . .L:)xo
October 19, 2007 6:49 AM

Anonymous said. . .
Mich - don't listen to those legs of yours. . .they're just playing games on you! They know you're almost there and they know how strong you are. Keep going. Find the strength you didn't even know you had. . .(even though we all know it) Hang in there. Sending you some vibes. . .Kim
October 19, 2007 6:38 PM

Anonymous said. . .
Hey Mich, You can do it girl. . .keep going, like the "Little Engine" that could. . .use that beautiful western scenery to kick start those legs. . .I know you can. KYHU
October 20, 2007 9:19 AM

Anonymous said. . .
Mich, May you run like a horse who smells the barn. Bon courage! No.8
Hi Michelle, I just checked your blog again. So glad to see you are still on course and in BC. Keep strong.

We are on schedule and on track. Think of you often. Take care of yourself. Let us know when you will be back in Ottawa. Luck and Health, Leah Anne and Bob

It takes determination to push limits. When I began this journey, I didn't think I could ever exhaust my determination. When I came to the end of my limits, I would always be able to fight the temptation to quit. However, today, my expectations were more than I could live up to and there are limits we simply cannot exceed on our own.

Vancouver was still over 400 kilometers away and all that remained was for me to finish. At a time when I struggled to revive myself and my situation looked bleak, I needed more than inner strength. I turned to the only one who could help me. "Take my hand Lord," I said in desperation, "I can't finish this on my own. Please give me the strength and energy I need."

There is also great power in the entwining gifts of words of encouragement and love from others. Everyone's words were helping me believe I could push the envelope just one more time.

Standing on the edge of the road, my circumstances didn't change, but I hung on to the hope that was mine and took a step forward. Then another one and another one, until my body was in full motion once again. My willingness gave hope to my legs and there was still a little fight left in me. "Be relentless, be strong," I encouraged myself.

On my way to Kamloops, I was reminded of the words from "Footsteps in the Sand" when the Lord replied, "During your times of trial and suffering, when you see only one set of footprints in the sand, it was then that I carried you." I believed there were footsteps I couldn't see.

In the high interior of British Columbia, I ran a highway at war with the weather. The snow of October was already here and when bad weather is forecast, you give it a lot of respect. Out here, the highways have nicknames: "The Highway of Tears" and "The Killer Highway". Crosses planted along the side of the road were a reminder of the dangers.

Reaching Kamloops, I was thrilled to spend some time with relatives from my dad's side of the family: my Uncle Bert, his wife Darlene, their children, and grandchildren. I hadn't seen them in years and it was a joy to connect with them again, even though it was a short visit.

After hearing about a major accident between Kamloops and Hope from snowy conditions, once again I was faced with making another decision. Without a support vehicle, my race with time and winter had expired. I thought it was appropriate to finish my run from a place called Hope to Vancouver. It turned out to be a wise decision.

While looking at a map outside the info centre in Hope, I heard a man's voice say, "There's lots of gold in these areas." At first, I couldn't figure out where it was coming from. Looking all around, I finally spotted a man dressed like a gold digger and peering down at me from the museum. "Sweetheart," he said. "I could take you gold digging." I politely declined but when he persisted, I made my exit.

Running from Hope to Bridal Falls, I was bothered by the traffic but happy to have lots of shoulder room. I shared stretches of the road with a scruffy old man on a custom motorized bicycle. He was pulling a small trailer and picking up empty cans along the side of the highway.

I would get ahead of him, then he would get ahead of me and that went on for quite a while. It became somewhat of a game between us. Finally, I waved at him and when he flashed me a smile, he didn't have any front teeth. It was as if he was trying to shock me. I smiled back and he disappeared. After that, I didn't see him anymore.

Barb, Tracey and Leny said...
Hey Michelle, we have been watching your progress since you left us. We were missing you 5 minutes after you headed out. You are doing great, stay strong and be careful.
October 21, 2007 6:33 PM

Anonymous said. . .
Hope the video we showed you of the pitbulls, gave you some inspiration. It was nice meeting you.
Wayne and Paula

Hey Bud, Hang in there. Thinking of ya. . .it definitely will be a trip to remember. After you have returned and have had a chance to recover. . .you'll remember all the good times, fond memories and you'll be itching to do it again (ok, maybe by car or bike next time). We have a beautiful country, so much to see and so many different roads to travel. . .wait, you'll see. You took on an enormous challenge and succeeded in talking for those that can't. . .you're our Hero . . .the animal's hero, your friends and believers in your program hero. God Bless you. May your internal strength help you as you complete your journey. Your friend always, Heidi-Ho that's Heidi #1 Strack
p.s. . . .I'm sure the animals wish they could talk to thank you too.

At Chilliwack, I was no longer allowed on the TransCanada Highway. I stopped at the welcome centre and a helpful man named Robert mapped out an alternate route for me. It would take me passed the small communities and through the back door into the city of Vancouver.

Dear Michelle. . .haven't heard from you for a while and we know that you were feeling pretty low. . .hope all is well. . .especially with the end so near. All of us are still cheering for you and keeping you in prayer. . .You have made us all so proud. . .love you and take care. . .John and Susan and of course the 2 bichons, Annie and Lucky

Anonymous said. . .
Michie,
Thank-you for doing this. It means a lot to us. My boys Chicken, Teddy, Brutus and Alonzo thank-you. My only girl Tammy thanks you too. Lots of love and all my energy.
Char xoxo
October 26, 2007 3:19 PM

Anonymous said. . .
Mich. . . You have run across Canada it's OK to say. . . "I never thought I would say it but I think I've reached my physical limit." (Mich's comment from Oct 18) You're doing an amazing job. . .Karen

The increased traffic and noise reminded me of how crowded and busy city living is. I missed the tranquility of the wilderness and the peace I found in silence. My roundabout detour to Abbotsford was quieter, but I was also on guard for dogs.

One time, a heavy-duty truck drove by and I had to jump out of the way into the driveway of a home. To my surprise, a big dog off leash came out of nowhere and it looked like he was going to attack me. I was about to pull out my bear spray, when he stopped dead in his tracks, right in front of me. It was so abrupt that it made me wonder if there was an invisible fence. Whatever the reason, I didn't hang around to find out.

Then, a funny thing happened when I came across an interesting horse. He was really close to the fence and looked like he had just rolled in the mud. His head was covered with thistles and I took pity on him. I stopped briefly to pat him but when I stuck out my arm, the wire zapped me. The horse shook his head up and down and it sounded like he was laughing at me. I looked at him puzzled and if I didn't know any better, I would think he purposely lured me to the fence. It made me smile, but I didn't make any more stops after that.

Getting through the intersections in Abbotsford was stressful. They were confusing to me and the ruckus and noise from vehicles hurt my ears. It drove me to the point where I just wanted to get this over with. I was anxious to be off the roads and out of harm's way once and for all. That night, I had sweet dreams of going home.

The following day, I reached the city limits of Vancouver. I should have been more excited than I was but when you've focused on a goal for so long, reaching it just feels like relief and momentary satisfaction.

Standing on Boundary Rd. with Burnaby on one side of me and Vancouver on the other, it wasn't as exciting as I thought it would be. I knew how I should feel; I just wasn't feeling it. I was numb and emotionally unresponsive to the reality of my being here.

When I called Dorit, she had just landed in Vancouver. She was there for my first mile and it felt only right that she should be here for my last. I was glad she made the trip. "Maybe I'll feel differently when I see her," I thought.

While I waited for her at Starbucks, my mind could barely believe that I ran across Canada. It felt like a dream and I wondered if it really happened. Nothing felt real to me, not even the coffee I was drinking. Surviving a solitary run across Canada was just crazy insane. I couldn't make any sense of it, nor could I process it.

At the sight of Dorit, it did make it feel more exciting, but no less surreal. Giving Dorit back her grandmother's amulet pleased me, because it meant I did what I said I would do and I had kept a promise. Sounds like a formula for success, right? After all, it would be great to find out that my effort worked, but I can't brighten up the ending.

After some food, conversation, and a bit of sightseeing, it was an early night in anticipation of tomorrow's reception. A press release went out to all the media and animal shelters in Vancouver.

October 29, 2007 – Ambleside Park, West Vancouver

Getting up the next morning, a new day had dawned. Dorit and I started this marathon together and we would finish it together. We shared a compassion for animals and a desire for change. She poured her heart into Jazzpurr and Let Live Canada and I poured out my soul into this run. However, my need to do something for the lives of companion friends paralleled a greater need I had for freedom. It was there that I found lasting change.

Before Dorit dropped me off I said to her, "No matter what happens, I'm glad you're here." While she drove away, I recalled that first day at "Mile One" in St. John's Newfoundland and my first night on the highway. I can still see the look on Dorit's face when she left me there. It felt like such a long time ago and I'm not sure if she believed back then we would be here today.

Watching her disappear in traffic, reality was already sinking in. The pounding of my heart was getting louder in my ears as I left Stanley Park to cross the south end of Lions Gate Bridge. This was it! This was the moment I had been waiting for.

On the other side of the bridge was my elusive target. Only this time, it wasn't moving. There were only two miles between the finish line and me. My final destination was Ambleside Park in West Vancouver and the end of a long road.

The bridge appeared massive to me. There was a pair of concrete lions on either side and vehicles slithered through three lanes. Once I passed the statues, I followed the pedestrian and bicycle lane to get across.

Surprisingly, I wasn't in any hurry to get to the other side. I wanted to take in as much of my surroundings as possible. The views toward the coastline were pleasing to my seeing eyes and I was captivated by the perfection of Vancouver's natural beauty. Subconsciously, I don't think I wanted this marathon to end. After running in the footsteps of my heart for six and a half months, I couldn't see how I was going to separate myself from it.

For a moment I had a smile on my face, until someone walking a dog caught my attention. It shot straight into the center of my pain and caused me to hang my head in shame, reminding me of the horrible regret I sheltered in the depth of my soul. My thoughts going back several years to a dreadful night of images I can never erase from my head. They were as fresh in my mind as if it had happened only yesterday. A time when I made a terrible mistake.

I stopped briefly to stare out over the water. When I finally let my heart show up, the flood of memories was too much for me to handle. I started gasping for air and struggled to breathe, and the tears from the pit of my stomach fell freely.

Behind the sadness of my heart was my poor decision to euthanize two healthy dogs and my soul was overwhelmed. Struggling with the regret, I remorsefully said, "I wished I could take it back." I couldn't. The deed was done and it couldn't be undone. There was no reversing it. The error of my heart wasn't easy to live with and I couldn't forgive myself. How could I have done such a thing?

My morally ill heart was desperate to find a remedy to right my wrong. The passion of my heart was driven by a deep sorrow and nothing I suffered could equal the costly mistake I made. My search to help myself prompted me to want to do something for cats and dogs that had never been done before. Motivated by a promise I couldn't break or fail, I was compelled to make something happen as if my life depended on it.

During a program I took to teach me something about caring for an animal, I learned about the overpopulation problem. I was greatly disturbed by the number of healthy pets euthanized every year and I could not live with that knowledge or that I had been a part of the problem. It made me feel personally responsible. That's when I saw a way to make up for my wrong and I was convinced it was the right thing to do.

However, no matter how far I ran, or for how long, it was no remedy for the ache in my heart. I could not escape the guilt I felt for ending the lives of the two dogs I loved. My self-redemptive plan could not win the secret war of my heart and this marathon could not set me free. Missing was forgiveness from my guilt. The only way to make things right is to admit when you've been wrong. From the top of Lion's Gate Bridge I cried, "I am so sorry! Please forgive me."

Mysteriously, the light rain was comforting. It was as though God's tears were falling with mine and replacing each one with a deep sense of relief. Crying out to God was the strongest moment of my life. He heard the true expression of my heart and the voice of my Savior tenderly whispered "you are forgiven" and the forgiven have the freedom to walk in His grace.

God loved me and had freely given me forgiveness. Not because of anything I did or could do, but because of what Jesus did for me.

He took my guilt and bore my shame on the cross. He understood my sorrow and showed me the way forward. God's grace and mercy reached farther than my wrong could ever go.

My target was Vancouver, but God's target was my heart. I was free to let go and put my soul in His hand. I didn't have to hold myself in judgment or recrimination any longer. In the gentle whisper of the rain I heard, "Come and claim your victory."

Today was a glorious day like no other and I was able to smile above my tears and know what victory feels like. I felt at peace with myself for the first time and I didn't have to be ashamed of my tears anymore.

Listening to the crashing of waves and the rhythm of my feet were soothing to my ears. There was a quiet calmness about how I felt and I was running in the restful peace that comes with knowing God loves me. Finally, the journey of my heart could rest.

On the 198th day of my marathon, I ran my last mile. Once I got to the other side of the bridge, I passed through a parking lot and onto a trail lined with trees leading to the park. To my listening ears, all of nature was singing. When I think of all the wonders of God's creation, the mighty tree especially awes me. It starts out so small and grows to be so big and tall and strong. All the trees sounded like they were clapping for me as I ran my victory mile. "Thank you," I responded appreciatively and bowed to my friends.

Reaching the shoreline and having the spectacular view of the bridge, Stanley Park, and downtown Vancouver in sight was spine tingling. There were times when I thought I would never see this day, when I couldn't imagine being here. Times when it felt impossible. Looking out into the Pacific Ocean, I could see clearly passed all the obstacles that had been in my way.

Running along the sandy beach, I watched some birds in flight and soaring through the air. It was as if they were my escort to the finish line. When Dorit came into view, she was the only one standing there. I would be lying if I said I wasn't disappointed or that it didn't hurt a little to see no one else with her for the completion of my run.

In the few seconds it took me to reach her, several thoughts ran through my head. "What happened? Did we get the time mixed up? Is this the right place? Are animals really not that important? Was my effort for nothing? Does anyone care?" These were questions without answers.

Nevertheless, my journey of adversity had taught me to deal positively with the sting of disappointment. My inspiration to run used to be in front of me with any success from this marathon that was going to fix everything. Today, the source of my inspiration comes from behind me. My destination all along has been the journey and the prize, the victory of my heart. I won the one war that had to be won–the war of my heart.

In my place of victory, I looked up and victoriously raised my arms shouting, "We did it!" It was the victory shout of my soul. "Thank you Jesus!" Then, it was an exciting moment to put my hand into the cold water of the Pacific Ocean. Touchdown!

My dream had been realized and I completed my heart's desire. I did something for animals that had never been done before. My solitary run from the Atlantic to the Pacific Ocean was my gift to companion friends, with love.

I am only one,
But still I am one.
I cannot do everything,
But still I can do something;
And because I cannot do everything
I will not refuse to do the something that I can do.
- Edward Everett Hale

It was extremely surreal and hard to describe how it feels to do such a thing. You almost have to experience it for yourself to uncover the hidden treasure that comes with it, and without a doubt, I emerged a stronger person for not giving up. I didn't know that I could endure such a journey until my journey taught me that I could.

"Give me one moment in time when I'm more than I thought I could be."
– Whitney Houston

However, it was a sobering conclusion and a bittersweet victory. Dorit and I left there in disbelief at the lack of public support and interest. Although this was a personal victory, it was a hollow one nationally and my heart was marked with silence rather than joy over the continued use of euthanasia for animal control.

In spite of the disappointment, I held my head high. This was a once in a lifetime achievement. I had to overcome tremendous obstacles to reach a seemingly impossible goal and I experienced the thrill of victory that only a battle hard fought can bring. How could I not be happy?

Maybe I wasn't a trained Olympian, but I couldn't have done any better or tried any harder. I did my best and left it all out on the highway. My heart matched my words and even my smallest effort was big enough. I can go home feeling good about that. Nonetheless, this isn't the end of the story. There is more.

Thank you very much for your inquiry (animal advocates (Vancouver)) about the ceremony marking the completion of Michelle Jameus' solo trek across our country on behalf of animals. Yes, it was in Ambleside Park in West Vancouver this morning at 10:00 am. It was foggy and misty, but quite historic. It's unfortunate that you missed it.
Perhaps you could tell us more about your organization?
Thank you,
Dorit Girash
Let Live Canada

Anonymous said. . .
Congratulations Michelle. I knew you could do it. It was so nice meeting you in Clarenville, NL. I have been following your trip and know it must be a big relief to be finished. Way to Go!

Anonymous said. . .
Hey Mich. Congrats girl, you did an amazing thing. Thank-you for doing what you did.
Char and family

Barb, Tracey andLeny said. . .
You are fantastic Michelle. We wished that we could have been at the finish with you. Shame on the Vancouver media for not responding. . .but we all know how hard the fight is. Take a well-deserved rest and we will look forward to a book.

Julia said. . .
I'm so disappointed about your lack of reception in BC, but I'm so incredibly proud of your accomplishment. Way to go M

Ginger said. . .
My husband and I have been with you in spirit all the way, eagerly awaiting each update to your blog, and are thrilled that you completed your mission safely. We were very worried about you on the treacherous roads in B.C. We would love to read more about your adventures and see photos documenting your run across Canada. We are very proud of you.

It would be great if the media across Canada would run your story again to publicize the cause and to remind readers of what you endured on behalf of creatures who need our help. Perhaps you or a collaborator could write a press release to submit to the media electronically, including information regarding how to donate money to the cause. You and the animals deserve much more publicity than you have received so far.

Anonymous said. . .
Mich,
You are my hero. God bless you.
No.8

Anonymous said. . .
Michelle
YOUR FLYING HOME ON TUESDAY.
Tylar and I are here and sure wish we were there with you.
You have a great flight home and if you can, call us before you get to Vancouver or when you get to Vancouver.
Love you and well, words cannot say.
xoxoxoxoxoxoxoxoxoxoxoxo

Anonymous said. . .
Congratulations Michelle,
That was a truly amazing journey you embarked on and completed. By the sounds of this blog, you have touched many lives across Canada. You should be incredibly proud of yourself.
Take care,
Denise

October 30, 2007 – Ottawa

The night passed quietly. Dorit had an early flight and we would be in touch later in the week.

"Others will be inspired by this," Dorit tried to encourage me.

"I'm so glad you were here," I said as we exchanged a hug. "Thank you for coming. Thank you for everything." Then, she was gone.

I had some time to kill and people watching still fascinated me. One person's life and experience is never the same as another person's. We all have our own individual walk to take and everyone had a story to tell. This was mine.

Here I was again, sitting and waiting in the airport. Only this time, my great adventure was behind me. When I began this amazing journey, I couldn't have imagined the experience of it. It far exceeded my physical and emotional ability. However, my ability to stand tall in spite of the buffeting winds of my journey is directly related to the love and support I received from God and others.

Although it was often lonely and daunting, I was heartened by the help I received and awestruck by the kindness of strangers, family, and friends that helped get me here, and that God allowed an ordinary person like me to do something extraordinary.

In the beginning, I remember calculating my chances of success, or even survival, and the odds were stacked against me. There were just too many things that could go wrong. I never saw evidence that I made a difference, but my desire to make a difference made a difference to me. I have experienced what being relentless can do and it was one heck of a run. But, it was my struggles that made the accomplishment of it all the more worthwhile and my life has been enriched because of it. That is the reward for my efforts and energy.

As I sat there, I couldn't help but wonder why supporters and media were a no show yesterday. Although I was not pleased with the outcome, I was not discouraged either. Over the course of my journey, I had been heard and given consideration. I spoke my truth quietly and clearly and listened to others.

However small, I can build on the little successes from my journey. There's no such thing as failure as long as you keep on going and don't give up and you can never be disappointed if you keep the promises that you make.

Announcement after announcement, I watched as people boarded until my flight was called. Although I was excited about going home, my heart was filled with mixed emotions. I was relieved to be finished running, but missed the highway the way you would miss a loved one. Tears welled up in my eyes, but they no longer streamed down my face. My heart was already healing.

After the plane landed, it felt like a long walk to the baggage department. How much damage was done to my feet, only time would tell. For now, I was looking forward to putting my life back together and getting off this emotional roller coaster ride.

To my surprise, there was a group of about twenty or more friends waiting when I arrived. They started cheering at the sight of me and I was ecstatic to see their faces. It was one of those "wow" moments.

At the bottom of the escalator, I was happy to see my sister Angel and my niece Shannon standing there. I was caught up in the excitement and it felt like I was on top of the world.

One by one, I exchanged hugs and a word with everyone there. After we took some pictures, Sharron pushed me around on the luggage cart. "Hop on," she said. "You gotta get off those feet." It was so much fun that I couldn't stop laughing.

We left there and continued the celebration at a friend's house. Sharron presented me with a license plate that read "STOP FORREST STOP". It was too funny. There was other gifts of comfortable socks and foot cream.

My reception and homecoming party was heartwarming and sharing this moment with all of them heightened my happiness. It was good to be home and to be with friends.

Hey Mich,
I just wanted to say Welcome Home and way to go. You are one amazing person.
I've kept up with your blog through your whole journey. Thank you so much for sharing all your experiences.

I can't wait to read the book of your adventures. You're a true inspiration to everyone as to how to pursue something so huge and conquer it. You've accomplished such a feat and for a very good cause.

Take care - see you on the ice or at the rink - I'm really in total awe of what you have done.
Sharon

Michelle,
What an amazing woman you are. My heart is aching because of the lack of interest shown by the media.

Maybe you should have run the last mile in a bikini or topless. . . or naked for all that matter. Bet there would have been someone there besides your friend Dorit. Congratulations.
I am delighted that you are home safely. Take care my friend and keep in touch.
Bisous, Hugs
Cécile

Hi Michelle,
Sorry I was not able to greet you at the airport. I already had a commitment. I just want to let you know that I am so impressed with what you have done. I hope that this message has gotten to enough people to start making changes in this country. We need to try and get Vets to offer low cost spaying and neutering, especially for strays. I have some friends who trap strays and have them spayed and neutered. A lot of times they are paying from their pockets. I will continue supporting you in this cause and I will spread the news to as many people as possible. Thanks for speaking for our little furry friends. Take care and rest up. I'm sure you need to rest that body of yours.
Linda

Hi Mich.
Just want to say welcome home and congrats on a job well done. I surely admire your stamina, although I am sure it was tested many times out there all by yourself. Anyway just hope that you accomplished what you set out to do.(and please don't do it again) That was pretty scary for us back here wondering. Anyway we are all very proud of you and I am sure if the animals could talk they would send a great big Thank you to someone that cares.

Have a good rest in your own bed. I am sure it will feel wonderful.
Hope Sharron was able to meet up with you at the airport.
tc and rest well "Sharrons mom"
Gloria (not Flossie)

Anonymous said. . .
Way to go Mich. You should be so proud of your accomplishment, you did it on your own with all the prayers of your family and friends keeping watch over you.
Welcome back home.
Jackie and Elton

Congratulations Michelle. . . what a tremendous accomplishment. I'm sure you must be glad to be home but I can only imagine there must be a certain amount of adjustment even in that. I hope you are taking a much deserved break and are surrounded by lots of friends. Your journey was followed from afar. . . even Paris.
Congrats
Siobhan

My journey had come to an end but the run that had consumed me for the past six and a half months was difficult to turn off. Physically, my body wanted to kick in to running mode and emotionally my mind kept replaying one mile at a time.

This journey took all of me and the moment I was home alone, I felt lost – like walking into an empty room. Nothing about being home felt normal to me and I was no longer able to embrace a virtual world. You can't do something like this and be the same. Somehow, I had to take what I'd done and learned and make it part of my life.

That's when Sharron came up with a brilliant, but crazy, idea for a quick fix. "We'll setup a tent in the backyard and camp overnight so you feel more at home." She was dead serious. Up went the tent and that's what we did.

We bundled up and spent a cold November night in her backyard. It was hilarious and I was cured of my desire to sleep outdoors. It would take some time, but eventually I found a way for my life to find its routine again.

Nov 4
Hi Jody:
I wonder if I could ask you a favour? I'm certainly not savvy regarding the world of journalism and publications and exclusivity and all that, but I wonder if you could do a little bit of writing for us, other than for your magazine?.

When absolutely no one showed up for the completion ceremony in Ambleside Park in West Vancouver, Michelle and I were both a little bit shocked. We rode in silence for long stretches afterward, wondering what this means. We decided that if we were drinkers, we should go somewhere and get smashed - but neither of us drinks, so we had to deal with the profound disappointment with full consciousness (and no hangover).

We decided that we should try to engage the media in another way - write a one-page media release to be sent to all the national media outlets - one that would give the highlights of Michelle's journey and inspire them to seek to learn more and write about or report on her historic trip.

I asked Michelle to think about some key questions and what she sent us represents her response to some of those questions. Since I'm no writer, I wonder if you might be willing to condense it into a one-page article that would provoke media people to want more?

Please let me know if you can do this for us? I'm sure your experience and talents will produce something much more effective than what I could do.

Thanks in advance,
Dorit

In reality, we can't change society on a large scale but we can as individuals focus on changing hearts – starting with our own. When you want change, you have to target the heart. Change hearts and right behavior will follow. That's how powerful the heart is.

The story of my success is the victory of my heart. I can look back and see how the journey had been painful, but freeing. What started out as a willing commitment to make up for the mistake I made finished with the treasure of knowing peace and forgiveness.

My pursuit to raise awareness was for anyone entrusted with a life, including myself. I was guilty of the very thing I fought for. Along my path, there were lots of stories about animals that were saved, but I never got the name of one healthy cat or dog that was euthanized. I know of two dogs personally, Sheeba and Gizmo. They did nothing to deserve their fate and with God's help, I can live with that differently.

My life-changing journey taught me that receiving kindness is God's mercy and goodness and I've discovered what that means in my life. Surviving and enduring my trials has helped me see God's care and grace in everything. Experiencing God has left me better off spiritually than I was before.

Through the process of my life-changing journey, I found Jesus. My reward is with Jesus. He alone took down my Goliath and turned my time of sorrow into joy. Jesus brought my dead heart back to life. In the end, I was the one rescued.

When I began this marathon, I was sure it would be a spring-board for change in others; little did I know that I would be the one most changed.

I took kindly the counsel of my journey and gracefully surrendered the things I am not meant to carry. I do not regret my pursuit. I ran a road of faith believing the impossible and the unbelievable. The impossible happened.

Looking at the bigger picture, my attention shifted to what truly matters – life, God, and eternity. I choose life over death because there is no hope in death.

Chapter 8

A Deeper Battle

If you follow the political climate in Canada, you probably know as a nation, we are divided on how our country should handle the surplus of animals. No matter which side you agree with, or where your sympathies lie, it has to be troubling to you.

Whenever a healthy cat or dog is euthanized, it is our failure as people caring for the needs of our animals. Our government's lack of involvement and leadership means that all of us must share the responsibility. Pet owner or not, we are all impacted by the problem.

The tragedy of the overpopulation problem with cats and dogs is euthanasia is somehow the acceptable solution. The task of solving the problem is so overwhelming, it creates a danger and a trap that the problem cannot be solved any other way; consequently animal needs are not fully met.

It would be easy to launch accusations at our animal shelters and organizations, but finger pointing accomplishes little. Thank God for people in rescue who never give up trying to win for the abused and neglected in our society. Unless we have worked in a shelter, we cannot truly understand or appreciate the great pressure men and women face in their duties. They are, after all, human beings like you and me with strengths, dreams, and aspirations, but also human limitations.

The issues that divide shelters involve arguments and debates of which I am out of my depth of knowledge. If you want more information you will no doubt consult people who are more qualified than I am. The fact is, animal shelters are looking for relief from the problem and people are so far removed from the problem, they ignore it.

However, the problem is too big to ignore. The death rate is alarmingly high and not enough is done about the birth rate. From irresponsible pet owners to insufficient protection for animals, cats and dogs continue to be victimized by both the public and institutions. A fate they do not deserve.

> *"The consequence of setting up euthanizing as an absolute guide for controlling the population has become in the end a cruel injustice."*
>
> *–C.S. Lewis*

In this book, I am not trying to offend anyone or do a disservice to a cause, but to use it as a platform to keep raising awareness. My purpose is that others may be encouraged in heart and hope. From the beginning, I felt the best service I could do was to bring attention to the problem and inspire others to do what is right.

My strategy was to search out the facts to gain a better understanding of reality, listen to different sides of an issue, ask the experts for their insights and look for answers. What do animal shelters say? What does the public say? What does God say? How do they relate to each other? I took nothing for granted. What leaped out at me in the end was the silence about euthanasia.

There is no mystery about my position. It is my firm conviction and belief that it is morally wrong to euthanize a healthy cat or dog and that nonlethal methods are better. I'm aware that ending euthanasia is an unpopular subject by cultural standards. Concerns about "where do we put them all" runs deep in the shelters and this question cannot be dismissed.

However, euthanizing breeds more euthanizing. The results that come from euthanizing are anything but pleasurable. It causes sorrow of heart, loss, and regret. Once it's done, it cannot be undone. We must guard what is entrusted to our care and save life, not destroy it.

The battle between euthanasia and prevention is a deeper battle within people's hearts. It lies in our personal attitude of right and wrong and the problem is worsened by a lack of compassion. Ultimately, the problem is a moral one.

There may be no more important thing to say about the moral issue of euthanizing healthy cats and dogs, than the Word of God stands in direct opposition to this act. If anyone is unclear about what God says, I challenge you to read the Bible for yourself. God will tell you what is true. Then, you can judge for yourself if you should believe God or man.

Throughout my journey, I heard what people had to say. What convicted me is what God had to say. Our responsibility toward animals is to care for their needs. Euthanizing goes beyond our fundamental role of caring. In the pages of this book, several things stand out, but none more important than what Creator God says:

"A righteous man cares for the needs of his animals, but the kindest acts of the wicked are cruel."
–Proverbs 12:10 (NIV)

"Woe to those who call evil good, and good evil."
–Isaiah 5:20 (NIV)

"The Lord hates: hands that shed innocent blood."
–Proverbs 6:17 (NIV)

"But ask the animals, and they will teach you, or the birds of the air, and they will tell you; or speak to the earth, and it will teach you, or let the fish of the sea inform you. Which of all these does not know that the hand of the LORD has done this? In his hand is the life of every creature and the breath of all mankind."
–Job 12:7-10 (NIV)

"Everything under Heaven belongs to me."
–Job 41:11 (NIV)

We all need to question the acceptability of pet euthanasia. To remain silent is like giving consent and being ignorant about the truth does not exclude anyone from his or her personal responsibility.

As Canadians, we are right to object to euthanizing if it allows the problem to continue. The thought of a no-kill country is far-fetched unless a decision is made to replace euthanasia with prevention.

You can help make a difference. Even the smallest donation toward prevention methods helps. Let's not underestimate the impact we can have.

For more information and to hear what the experts have to say:

NO KILL ADVOCACY CENTER, www.nokilladvocacycenter.org

ALLEY CAT ALLIES, THE HUMANE SOLUTION, www.alleycat.org

MADDIES FUND, www.maddiesfund.org

JAZZPURR SOCIETY FOR ANIMAL PROTECTION, www.jazzpurr.org

DISPOSABLE ANIMALS: ENDING THE TRAGEDY OF THROW-AWAY PETS, by Bestrup, c. (Camino Bay Books, Leander, Texas 1997) Euthanasia is 'Unethical' for Dogs or Cats, as a Socialized Health Care Solution November 24, 2009 by Dean A. Ayers - Lead Investigative Reporter for NationalDogPress

COMPANION ANIMAL OVERPOPULATION: TRENDS AND RESULTS OF MAJOR EFFORTS TO REACH A "NO-KILL" NATION, by Joseph M. Frank and Pamela Carlisle-Frank. Foundation for Interdisciplinary Research and Education

ANIMAL WELFARE LEADERS, Nathan Winograd, Ed Boks, Michael Mountain

Appendix A

Public Response

Online Letter to bloggers:
Thursday, April 5, 2007

Dear Friend,

My name is Michelle Jameus and on April 15, 2007 I will begin running and carrying a flag across Canada to plead for our animals and to tell their tragic story. It needs to be told. Over a million abandoned and unwanted healthy and treatable pets are killed in Canada every year. Why do they have to die?

Homeless pets come from everywhere: your neighbor, a friend, your family, the street and the wild. We've failed to control the breeding of our animals and we have created a surplus of millions of animals that society has no homes for. What a heavy burden we have put on our animal shelters. For every animal that dies in a shelter someone is responsible.

The fact is, it's not necessary but the sad reality is some peoples' eyes and hearts see killing as the only solution to the overpopulation problem and have justified it in their own minds so that they are comfortable with it. Animals can't speak but they can suffer and we spare ourselves from the site of their suffering. They need us to be their voice. They need us to open our eyes and hearts.

There is good news! There is a better way that doesn't involve killing. There's a preventative program that solves the problem and it works. We just need all of Canada to step up and respond. We just have to make the decision that we will not destroy a healthy treatable animal just because society says there are too many. But the problem will continue as long as people only see killing as a solution and thousands and thousands and thousands will die in an animal shelter until we change their hearts.

The only solution that works is a preventative program that controls the overpopulation problem.

The solution rests on all our shoulders to be responsible owners and act now.

Please help us while they are still alive. Please have mercy on these helpless living creatures.

It's never too soon to do an act of kindness but for many of these animals it will soon be too late.

Any act of kindness will help because together everyone's gift will save lives and solve the problem without killing. Please help us solve the problem once and for all.

The animals thank you for your care and support.

A compassionate society takes care of the needs of their animals.

Response to article published from Cape Breton Post:

I agree pets are a responsibility and should be cared for humanely. Good for her, this is a big task.

My friend works in a shelter, she told me if nobody picks up the dog or cats, they have to kill it because they don't have funds, which is very sad. She said too many dogs and cats die because of lack of funds, this lady is raising a valid point.

Yes it is a valid point, but just exactly where does everyone suggest these animals go? Do we keep adding to already overburdened animal shelters so that we can keep all the "excess" animals alive? Do we enforce mandatory spay and neutering policies? I don't think either option is viable. There will always be irresponsible pet owners who allow their animals to wander around outside during "mating" season and they have puppies and kittens all over the place and then dump them off at the pound. Like most things, this is a people problem, not an animal one.

I am an animal lover and want to help Michelle. I live in Trois-Rivieres, which is located on highway 40 but is not far from highway 20 either. I am not sure which road she will be taking exactly but it will surely be in the vicinity. What I would like to offer is first to pay for one night in a hotel room so that she can rest, be quiet and comfortable and take a warm shower! I could pick her up at some convenient place for her and bring her to and back from the hotel. I will also make a donation.

Please let me know if this could be arranged.
Thank you for your work for the animals, I admire your dedication.

Patrick Labelle

Of course, irresponsible, uncaring people are at the root of the overpopulation problem. Cheap spay-neuter clinics would help enormously, but no way will the City agree to fund that. The few people such as you and Joanne (Jazzy-Jo) who truly feel compassion for the plight of the unwanted, abused animals have to work ten times as hard to make up for those who don't give a damn.

Mary Ann Dugal

Go Mich, love you and keeping you in my thoughts and prayers. It's a marvelous thing you are doing and I am proud of you.

Joyce Schwartz

We're all very proud of you for taking on such a challenge. Great stuff!

Lisa Langlois

Please make sure that Michelle knows that she is having an impact on the people around her—I was so inspired by her commitment, it is why I donated $500. It is important that she knows that I would not have donated if it wasn't for her, and her work at raising awareness. We need more people like her and she needs to know this.

Lady from Sudbury

Dear Michelle
A friend of a friend of yours has brought your cause and blog to my attention. I am greatly inspired by your commitment to help our four-footed friends by launching such a monumental effort in order to spread awareness to people across Canada.

However, the 'official' support you seem to be receiving in your endeavor is positively underwhelming. It is unbelievable that you are having to rely solely on your personal friends and family, however numerous they seem to be, and the chance 'angels' you encounter along the way.

To help remedy this situation, I would like to make a contribution (enclosed) to assist in covering any running / trip expenses you are personally out of pocket for to date. Please use it to help cover all and any of the expenses you have incurred along the way: whether it be accommodations, gear, food, physiotherapy, etc. If there is anything left over, please put it toward your future personal expenses, whatever you require to help make your monumental journey a little less daunting and safe.

This especially includes your safe passage home, when the time is come to pack it in. I think I speak for many of your friends, who are equally awe-struck at how far you have gone. We are all so proud of you. If you don't take one step further, you will remain our super-hero for life. Michelle, it is clear you are an extremely committed and disciplined individual, who still has much to offer to the safety and quality of life for our four-footed friends. Don't let them down - make sure you come home ***before*** *jeopardizing your health. That's what they would want.*

I hope this contribution will help in a small way to support your extraordinary efforts to raise awareness for our faithful canine and feline friends.

A Friend in your cause
(And the animals you are assisting, who can't speak for themselves)

PS: I had the map of Ontario laid out on the floor the other night as I was reading your blog. My dog, who had been playing in the mud in the back yard, trotted over it and left a partial paw print. The paw print fell right in the middle of your route, just past Thunder Bay – it looked just like the sign for a U turn.

Anonymous Angel
Ottawa, ON

It was good to see you in Calgary! I think what you are doing to bring awareness to the plight of our furry friends is just brilliant.

Good luck with the rest of your journey. Thanks for being a voice for our animals and Happy Thanksgiving!

Thought of the day ~
Humankind domesticated the cat; therefore, we have a greater responsibility to provide shelter, warmth, food and love to our feline creatures. Be a responsible pet owner; please spay and neuter your cat to put an end to cat overpopulation and the abandonment of thousands of cats and their unwanted offspring.

Patricia Gordon
Calgary

This is an incredible journey that you are undertaking and I am awed by your willpower and determination.

I wish you all the best and I do hope that the newspaper, radio and TV follow your journey so that the plight of animals can be rectified.

Thank you for this wonderful gift to the animals.
Monic Landry

So sorry I missed you in Montreal, I have just been informed of your wonderful journey. I wish you courage and loads of support which I am sure you will find in many along your way. Thank you so much!

Gloria Di Stefano
Montreal, Qc

WOW! Good luck. I am so extremely proud of you. Can I send you a donation?
Run with heart ~

Susie

Hi Michelle,

I just came across your blog and saw that you passed through Antigonish about 2 weeks ago. I am so sorry that I missed you! Besides being an animal lover, I also have a great backyard for camping and a guestroom. . . . I wish I had've known about this before you arrived. I am also the photographer for the A&G TransAction (a local community paper) and would have loved to get a photo of you. Care to run back here for a photo?? ;-)

Anyway, I saw your comments about not being able to reach the media and I wish that I had been aware of your journey as I would have loved to help you out and do a story on this. If you have time and would like to do something via email, you could perhaps write your thoughts or experiences in the Antigonish area and I could work it into a story about what you are doing. If you give me your mailing address I could also mail a copy of the paper to you if it is printed. If you happened to have had a photo of you taken in Antigonish that would be great- or any photo of you would work.

Here's the url for the paper I work for in case you want to check it out:
http://www.agtransaction.ca/

Lots of luck in your journey and if you ever pass through Antigonish again, please contact me.

Charlie

Hi Mich. Wow. What a courageous journey you're taking for a great cause. Our family has rescued 4 dogs. We wouldn't think of doing it any other way. If we can do anything to help-send a care package to 1 of your stops. . .let us know. You have our well-wishes.
Good luck, stay safe and healthy.
Lynne and Ron

I heard you on open line talking about your run to save the animals. I would like to wish you well and I hope you keep safe during your run. I was reading your blog and it seems that you have endured all kinds of weather since you started your journey. You are very brave to be on the road alone especially nighttime. Sounds like you have met a lot of nice and generous people, Newfoundlanders are known for their generosity and friendliness and I am glad that you have met so many that are eager to help you. Keep running, keep safe and God Bless You!

Donna Squires

I had no idea you were embarking on such a journey until Karen from the Octostars sent us your website with the details. I find it truly admirable that your are making this huge sacrifice for such a great cause.

Our family has had a beautiful chocolate Lab for 4 years now, and we had been contemplating getting another one. After looking over all the links on your site, I have come to the realization that there are a huge number of homeless dogs out there just waiting to be adopted. Even as a dog owner and lover, I had no idea of the magnitude of the problem until I was made aware of it by your campaign. I want you to know that as a result of your endeavor, I have completed an adoption application and am waiting for recommendations from a local shelter toward adopting a dog in need. So I will hopefully be doing my small part to help out. This has spurred me to act now to adopt a homeless dog, rather than going to a breeder. I will also be following up with a donation and possibly ongoing support for shelters.

I want to wish you all the best on your journey. I will check your site regularly to keep up on your progress. I hope you are very successful in raising awareness for the cause and I will forward your website to as many people as I can to spread the word about the need there is out there. Have a safe journey, and God bless you!

Rachelle

Hey there Michelle – you probably don't remember me. I am a friend of Marie's. We are keeping track of your progress here and I am creating a map on Google. I was wondering if I could publish you and your cause on a site called Google Maps? It would be able to be accessed by all. Right now – I have it started but have it unlisted as I thought I should check with you first. Sounds like you are having quite the trek – Keep up the challenge and see you when you get to Nipigon!

Brenda Dorosh

I've just learned about your journey. Wow. You've really picked a cause I share and believe in. And, WOW, again – you are really doing a brave thing in support of your belief. Stay strong. Keep the faith. It will see you through the toughest of times. I'll be thinking of you and cheering for you. I'll also be promoting what you're doing and thinking of ways to help your cause.

Hang in there Mich.
Love,
Barb

I am sure that as more and more people become aware of what you are doing you will have great support. What a worthy cause for the poor helpless creatures who need someone to act for them. I only wish you were coming to our city. I will be watching your journey and cheering you on. I have 2 little rescued puppymill dogs who were due to be euthanized. Here is a picture of one of them, Molly - a 9-month old bichon frise. They are priceless. We wouldn't give them up for any reason. They sleep with us, travel with us and they are insured to cover any unexpected expenses.

Wishing you success in your very unselfish endeavor. I am sure many otherwise forgotten animals will owe their very lives to your efforts. God bless you!

Carol Johnston,
Kitchener, Ontario

I just want to take a moment and let you know how proud I am of you. I really believe in what you are doing and I will try my best to get your word around. I have sent your blog to friends out in BC who work in the animal wellness industry. I have also passed your blog and donated some money to a local couple who feed, spay

and neuter the farel cats. They have over 30 cats living on their property in Gatineau. They have told me that they support you and will pass the word around. I thought that you were crazy to do this, but your compassion astounds me. I think you have to be a little crazy to be so compassionate about something. It's all good. I just want to say that you are amazing and keep going. You have a lot of supporters behind you and I'm sure you will have many more to come. Love you girl! Happy and safe running.
Linda Rinella

Good luck to her and Godspeed. My thoughts and prayers are with her every step of the way.

Jake says thank you for caring about the animals.
Gloria

I just wanted to say hi. I've been reading your blog and been keeping my folks updated on your progress. I just missed you when you were in Ottawa
(by about 15 minutes when you were at the Humane Society).

I hope all is well in the Sault, my old home. I have a few hills to warn you about. The first one you'll hit is downhill, called the Mile Hill. If you aren't careful, you may end up chasing Gidget, so hang on tight, or hop in and watch out for moose.
They congregate there.

The second hill is further along, past Batchewana Bay, in a place called Montreal River Harbour. This one is uphill. The transport trucks have a tough time with it. But on the bright side, you're getting into some really pretty scenery, since a lot of the highway is right on Superior.

You've got a lot of supporters back home.
Take care of yourself.
Jess

I've been following your blog with great interest,
best of luck with the rest of your run.

Murray Armstrong
London, ON.

Signatures and comments from iPetition;

Adele Bourque	
Adriana Gorrondona	
Allan R. Kirk	Power to you Girl; and God Bless You for doing what so many of us cannot. I crawl along with the aid of a cane and that's not much fun, but I still manage a regular monthly donation to Ontario ASPCA and Humane Society to help our sweetest creatures on the planet. Love to you and Good Luck on your "Goal" Thoughts and prayers are with you as you go/ Cecile Bertrand is a very close and Dear friend of mine for years; and this is how I found out about you. All the Best, Allan. Kirk
Alyssa	help save the cats
Anaëlle Lavoie	Cruelty toward animals is not acceptable at all. People that cause suffering to animals will have to pay for this. It is the law of cause and effect. Please stop doing this. How would you like to endure such pains?
Andrea Greening	This NEEDS to happen. Thank-you so much for initiating this petition and for all your other efforts to bring attention to the problem.

Andrea Hodgson	why kill helpless pets when they are not sick or on deaths door
Andrea Lewis	
Andreanne Emard	
Andy Watts/Nick Martin	Remus says thanks
Angel Heimerl	Who gets to decide that an animal should be destroyed for no reason. . .It is cruel and unnecessary to destroy a healthy life
Angela Barbera	
Angela Costelloe	let's not punish animals for human mistakes. . . .they have done nothing wrong, they have the right to live.
Ann M. West	
Ann Seymour	
Anna Del Monte	
Anne McWilliams	
Annick Lamoureux	I agree with the No-Kill Policy, let's spay/neuter our pets.
Ariane Cayer	No need to kill healthy animals for any reason whatsoever.
Arlene Bromaroff	
Arlene Rosochac	
Ashley Hunter	stop killing helpless animals
Ayse Akgun	I do volunteer in a NO KILL Cat sanctuary in Ottawa Ontario. We have currently more than 200 cats in our sanctuary and they will be cared for till their adoption or till the end of their natural life. It is done with no government support only by donations, fundraisers and out of pocket money. No paid employees any money goes directly to the felines care and comfort. No life should be taken on a whim, all God's creatures deserve better. If interested you can check our website and get more information www.countrycatrescue.com Thank you raising awareness for this issue and GOD BLESS YOU and Godspeed to you.
B, MacLean	
Barb Browczuk	

Barbara Price	
Barbara Silverman	Not only should Canada be no-kill, they also require stronger anti-abuse laws
Barbara Slater	
Barbara Ward	
Basil Kingstone	Congratulations to Michelle on drawing the attention of the whole of Canada to this. Our country has some catching-up to do
Becky Boyle	I hope this can finally come true, I have been telling people this forever, this can work here too.
Belynda Low	Hundreds of thousands of animals die each year thanks to neglectful people, we need tough laws to stop the killing. It baffles me how the press can cover bad wheat in pet food that kills a small number of pets, but totally ignores the daily abuse, suffering, and death, that takes place every day on the street, in the shelters and animal control buildings. We have NOT come a long way baby.
Bernie Villamil	
Bev Johnson	
Beverly Ryan	I have been a participant in the Jazzpurr TNR program since 2002, and to date they have spayed/neutered about 13 of my feral/strays. Without them I could not help the animals I love so much. God Bless
Bob McCoy	
Bren Belleperche	It is simply killing. There should be charges laid and consequences for anyone who kills an animal. There are other solutions. We need a task force to put together solutions and enforce them
Brenda Lucier	
Brenda Pilon	
Carla Cutway	It is our responsibility to solve the pet overpopulation problem, killing is not a solution
Carol Banks	Yes. . .let's get on board Canada
Carol Deckert	Hope you are successful. Please update me on how this petition goes and if any laws are changed.

Carol Johnston	One of the reasons we were put on this earth was to take care of the animals, NOT kill them
Carol Thorpe	
Carol Weale	
Catherine Elliott	
Catherine Godfrey	
Catherine Heinrichs	
Cathie Parsons	Great cause Michelle. May the universe guide you on your journey
Cecile Bertrand	Michelle and I met while she was running through Cobden, Pembroke (where I live), Petawawa, Chalk River, up to Deux Rivières. She is the most inspiring person I ever met. My prayers and thoughts are with you, my friend. Keep in touch. . . big HUGS
Charlene Hayes	Keep Going Michie, It is making a difference. Lots of love.Char
Cheryl	Way to go. 100% behind you on the spay/neuter programs. We have to get the community and organizations, and vets to help in this matter. I have been trying my best in promoting this across here in Sault Ste Marie, Ontario and people and vets don't want to listen. So I help by offering animal assistance to people on fixed incomes/or financial difficulties by taking their pets across the river (soo, michigan) and with aid and generous discount on the vets side, can offer these people to get their pets fixed, to stop the overpopulation of unwanted kittens and pups. If we could only get the vets to do the same thing here then maybe there wouldn't be so many animals put down unnecessarily.
Cheryl Simpson	It's time – way past time – that Canadians started to move beyond the "way we've always done things" We are so behind in our treatment of animals and the environment – and what about our ancient anti-cruelty laws in the criminal code – will they ever get updated? Those of us who care need to stand up and be counted.
Chris	sisters on earth and in heaven. My prayers are with you
Christine Audette	Good for Michelle can't wait to see you in Vancouver.

Christine Carle	You have my full support
Christine Hill	Killing should never be an option for pet overpopulation. We started the mess we must fix it in a kind and right manner.
Christine Reed	I support a no-kill shelter. It would be great to have more people caring for the voiceless. Thanks to all the supporters and lets become a country that dos NOT kill anymore
Christine Reed	Way to go
Cindy Hache	It's great to see someone so passionate about such an important issue. This will certainly arise awareness to this serious issue. Killing healthy, adoptable pets in our country is simply unacceptable and education as well as sterilization is most certainly the answer.
Cindy Lee	It's time all God's creatures are recognized and treated as such.
Claire Johnson	We must have laws against animal cruelty and abuse.
Claudia	I am proud of you thank you
Claudia Payment	
Claudia Settels	It is time to stop the cruelty and impose a system of control through spaying and neutering programs.
Corine Léger	STOP THE CRUELTY
Cynthia Scheible	
Dale Fraser	
Damian Follett	I agree that there are too many healthy dogs and cats euthanized every year in our country. I do think that some animals with aggression problems that threaten humans should be put down but not harmless animals who are healthy. Thank you. Damian Follett Paradise, Newfoundland
Daniel Mailloux	BRAVO
Danielle Tran	Michelle, you are truly an animal hero. I fully support a No-Kill Canada policy. Canada continually lags behind the rest of the world. Thank you for standing up for animal rights and for bringing attention to this most important matter. Animals do matter
Danika Smith	

Danny Mack	Proud of the job you are doing.
Darlene Quinsey	
Darlene Wennekes	
Dave Heffernan	
Dave Young	
David	
Dayle Lipson	no-kill is the way to go
Deanna	
Deanne Nurse	
Deb	spay or neuter is the best way an animal has a right to life too
Debbie	Michelle, as a fellow Canadian, I am so proud of you for your determination to protect our animals. You go girl. Bring this message to our country. Deb
Debbie Alleva	
Debbie Coles	
Debbie Patsack	
Debbie Tymura	
Deborah Ethier	
Denis Emard	I also think that the city laws should change. People with big houses, like me should be able to have more pet, since you are the room for it. Also, the Humane Society, should change their rules, adopting an animal from them is way too strict.
Denise Bogart	
Devan Jeffery	Please stop killing these poor little guys. They have so much love to share with us. Just give them a chance there are foster homes out there to help them all find new homes. Good homes. Spay and neuter is the way to go. A humane way for population control.
Dillon	I hate animal killing it needs to stop now and the ppl who do it i cant see how when u look in the animals eyes there a connection i guess they have no heart the messd you ill tell you that much
Dolly Digou	Thank you for your work in this area. It has been a long time in coming

Donata Seppala	Stop killing
Doris Dugas	Please convert Canada to a No-Kill Policy
Dorit	Michelle, your amazing courage and determination will inspire thousands of Canadians "make it happen"! There's no turning back now. We will have a No-Kill Country
Dorothy Bell	I currently have two 18 year old cats, a 14 year old dog, a 10 month old cat and two lovebirds all of which were waifs and strays. The 10 month old cat is one of three cats that I have been feeding over the past five months and was able to capture. He is now part of the household. I am providing food and an outside shelter for his two siblings and I'm still trying to capture them. I have set up a room in the basement for them but I will need assistance for vet bills for shots and spay/neutering of these two(my pension will only stretched so far). . . I fully support this action.
Dorothy Puddester	
Dr. Christine Storm	
E Allard	
Ellen Sturm	this is proof that angels walk among us.. thanks for thinking of the animals. . .they are our truest friends and companions. . .always there with unconditional love.
EllenFaith Atkinson	
Eva Mandri	
FOTA Rescue Society	our society has always advocated spay and neuter - it's the ONLY thing that works and it has been made MANDATORY by all municipalities including and in particular on Reserves. We have been around and active as a society for over 12 years - we know what we are talking about.
France Lapratte	
Francie O'Brien	
Gail	More education on spaying and neutering pets should also be a priority

Gail	Too many animals meet sad ends, mostly due to us humans. It's time we all take responsibility and do something to stop senseless deaths of animals.
Gail Gallant	WTG I totally support what you are doing. I wish you were coming to Halifax area, I know there would be a lot here to support you. Paws up to you.
Georgette	Let us become a No-Kill country
Gert Lawrence	
Gertie Dieleman	I am with you 110% I will pass the word to all my clients at Animal Care Centre Lobo.
GFredette	
Ghislaine Prince	Go Mich Go. . .You are a courageous girl. . .wish I had half your determination and courage. Will be thinking you. . Jessie
Ginette Manaigre	Animals should not be discarded like garbage. They enrich our lives more than our fellow human beings.
Ginger Hallett	Please support spay/neuter programs
Grace White	
Gwen Ireton	
Harry Alleva	
Heather and Craig	
Heather Christopher	
Heather Dryden	
Helen Hatton	Go Michele Go Canada must clean up her act, we're a 1st World Country for goodness sake, let's act it. Every dog and cat deserves to live his/her life, without fear, pain, suffering, abuse, hunger and being bred. STOP THIS MADNESS, THEY ARE GOD'S LOVING CREATURES God Bless you Michele. XXXXXXXXXXXXXXXXXXXX
Holly Power	
Ingulf Trettin	
Iris Carr	
Isabelle Grieves	Destroying unwanted animals (and babies too) is against all the laws of nature.

Jackie Dean	Michelle, know that you and the animals are in my prayers.
Jackie Gyorgy	
Jackie Sheridan	
Jacques Le Bourdais	
Janet Holburn	What a wonderful journey in support of a No-Kill Policy. I hope you have every Canadian sign your petition.
Janet Robertson	Good for you Michelle. . .wish you were coming to London, On. . .would really welcome all of you
Janice Campbell	
Janice Knight	
Janique Godin	
Jason Hatcher	
Jayde Evans	=(
Jazzy-Jo 's rescued felines	Michelle, you are our hero. My furry friends and I were honored to have met you and I pray for your success and safety every day of your brave journey. We will make a definite change this time not to save many but to save MILLIONS. This country must be awakened from its throwaway attitudes and comfy zone while thousands of our furry innocent friends suffer and die needlessly each day. WE WILL WIN THIS BATTLE AND GOD IS WITH US ALL THE WAY
Jean Warner	
Jennifer Gibson	
Jennifer Hayes	
Jennifer Lancaster	Accepting the continued routine murder of animals is no different than accepting mass extermination of humans. All are part of life on planet earth.
Jennifer Osborn	please stop. these animals can be loving pets. education is better that killing.
Jennifer Osborn	Killing healthy animals is no way to solve the problem of pet overpopulation. Catch and release spay/neuter and EDUCATION are solutions, not quick fixes. Killing is not a solution.

Jessica	No Kill is the only humane way to go.
Jessica Rivet	
Jill Dennis	
Jim Arkilander	I agree. We should be checking the population, instead of conveniently euthanizing animals.
Joanne Gontar	
Joanne Kennedy	
Jodi Balo	
Jodie Schafer	
Jody Crocker	
Joe Lingle	This is a really good cause. Way to go and keep it up
John Weir	
Jonathan Andress	
Josh	animals should be treated equal to humans and any other living thing. It's cruel to kill healthy animals.
Joyce	
Joyce Schwartz	I am so proud of you
Judith Irving	
Judy Horvath	There is so much senseless killing of animals we should be embarrassed of ourselves. Who decided that we - as humans - have the power of deciding an animal's fate? They have been created with love by God and placed on this earth with the gift of life, and yet with our superiority, we kill them at our discretion. All of those precious little lives - wasted. We need to stop the senseless slaughter of these beautiful creatures and devote more attention to programs where it can be more affordable for people to spay, neuter and vaccinate them.
Julia	
Julia White	
Julie	

Julie Witt	Support your local agencies that do spay/neuter programs by making a donation or volunteering. Talk to your city and town councilors. Write letters to your newspapers. Don't let your tax dollars go to 'Catch and Kill' programs that will NEVER solve the problem. It's always the complainers that get heard. It's time the animals and their supporters are heard. Together WE WILL make Canada a NO-KILL Nation
June Hodsdon	I fully support this type of program. . .good luck
Karen Hopkins, Saint John NB	
Karen Martin	Our domestic companions need our help here, we all know it is wrong to put down a healthy animal as a convenient means to deal with a preventable problem. Thank you Mich for bringing this to everyone's attention
Karen McDonald	
Karen Parker	What a great cause. Keep it going Mich.
Karen Ratushny	
Kari	I support you Michelle in all that you do.
Kathi Larson	
Kathleen Tolley	We have the means, the will to do so is long overdue. . . .
Katie Brogan	All living creatures have a desire to live just as much as we do. I support a loving environment for all animals in Canada, and for that matter, all over the world. No-kill Canada
Kayla McClay	
Kayla Paul	
Kelly Goodman	
Kelly Graham	Amazing Effort. Thanks for spreading the word.
Kelly Hayward	
Kelly Turco	
Kiara	I love animals
Kim Kerr	
Kim Petty	

Kim Thompson	
Kim Tousignant	
Kim Zebregts	
Kimberly MacDonald	I am with you 100% Michelle. Check out www.fixedfurlife.com to see what our little town is doing to end pet overpopulation.
Kirsteen Wrighte	I have just sent an e-mail to the Humane Society of Canada on this issue. Hopefully I will get a response.
Kirsty Mcconville	
Krassimir Vajarov	
Krista Black	GO MICH GO
Krista Zobolotny	
Kristen Caudle	
Kristina Blais	I have been involved with a no-kill animal rescue organization for years and know that it does work.
Kristine Chichkan	Let us all take care of our furry friends. Their love gives us all a reason to want to come home at night.
Kristine Cole	
Laura	we should love animals
Lauren Cheeseman	I look forward to signing your flag in support of your trek across Canada from your starting place in St. John's. Good luck, and I hope you achieve your goal with this important project. Lauren in St. John's, NL
Lauri Moffatt=Zawacki	
Lauri Pelletier	Way to go Michelle, I'm so proud of you and your accomplishments and the drive and determination to make a difference in the world. You are a hero. Keep up the great work and just know that our support is behind you 100%
Leigh Fettes	
Leisa Pieczonka	
Leslie Duh	I fully support a no kill policy nationwide. It truly is the only way to effectively prevent the unnecessary deaths of countless animals.

Leslie Hayward	Stop and think about it. . .There are solutions that don't involve killing. . .let's make the right choice. . .I am behind this. . .please support. We can make a difference. . .spread the word throughout Canada
Lillian Pyszniak	I am appalled and sickened by the needless murder of these poor, defenseless animals. It has to be stopped
Linda Bangay	Michelle's cross-Canada marathon is an amazing and selfless act. I admire her greatly for her tremendous compassion toward companion animals - they don't really have a voice except through people like Michelle.
Linda Graovac	These animals are of value to all beings, and it is only humane to allow them the right to live. People should spay their animals if they are allowing them to mix with other animals; and personally, I don't like it when people allow their indoor cats to roam at will during the day or night; it is one way they repopulate; as well, it is so easy for them to be hit by a car and killed, or poisoned by some malicious person.
Linda Horne	We must stop over breeding, overselling and disposing of far too many wonderful animals. We have made them into a throwaway item for our own selfish purposes. Put a limit on breeding and stop selling animals in pet stores.
Linda Rinella	Please stop the killing. People need to be responsible for their families. Pets are family and they have feelings too.
Linda Rinella	Canada needs to stop killing innocent animals and start spay and neuter programs to help control the population. There are other solutions. Animals have feelings too.
Linda Somers	We need to provide low-cost or free spay/neuter programs. We need bylaws that make the spaying/neutering of pets obligatory. We need to ban puppy mills.
Linda Toews	Excellent. I am so impressed that someone is taking on this much overdue cause. Bravo

Lindsay M. Bellaire	I think this is a brilliant idea. I could not agree more. I live in a neighborhood with many cats, and I witness cruelty from others in the neighborhood all the time. I try to stop it, but it's everywhere. We need to change the way people think. Animal's lives are just as important as ours. I don't know what makes people think they are not. You have my full and complete support.
Lindsay Simpson	
Lisa A. Taylor	
Lisa Mollagholamali	
Lisa Robinson	
Lisa Rowsell	
Lisanne Duku	
Lise Proulx	
Liz	Truly senseless acts. Humans don't kill humans because there are too many of them.
Liz Ringle	
Lois Jackson	We are very involved in rescuing dogs from death row. Walking the front line in pounds is so torturous. But we do it, and thank you for your efforts to effect change.
Lois Watt	I am glad to have this opportunity to sign. Canada must adopt a No-Kill Policy.
Lolita Roy	
Lorena Allen	
Lori Strike	
Lorne Cook	
Louise	Every animal has the right to live. Killing them is just wrong and heartless, it`s senseless. . .
Louise Frechette	
Louise Nettle	
Lucie Bechard	

Lucie Bisson	GO GO GO for it. Je suis entièrement avec vous. I am fed up of not sleeping at night because of animals being abused. Lucie I am 500% and more for this cause and my family and friends. LOVE and HUGS to all animals on this planet who have the right to live a normal life.
Lucie Bisson	STOP KILLING those poor souls. They deserve to live like you.
Lynda Gordon	
Lyne Cayer	
Lynn Anderson	
Lynn Hughes	Hi Michelle, you are amazing doing this and for such a needed and worthy cause. You may not recognize my name but I'm Sharon's friend, Lynn (the cop in Toronto) If you need anything on your way through just let me know. Be careful and know that lots of thoughts for you and the animals will help you through this. It's amazing. I will pass this on. Lynn
Lynne Perrault	Canadians need to put more emphasis on saving healthy pets. . .and enact legislation with teeth to deal with those who abuse or neglect their animals.
Madi Legere	Spay/neuter is the solution. Education is the way.
Marc Desjardins	
Marg Buckholtz	Effective low-cost spay neuter programs are the only way that the killing of healthy pets can be stopped.
Margaret Forrest	You are to be commended for your effort, Michelle – all the best.
Marie Myrick	Great Job you are doing. Thank you and God Bless you on your journey
Marie Parsons	In support of my sister's marathon across Canada for this cause, she has my full support.
Marina MacDougall	

Marj. Rapson	Hello: I have a mother cat and her three kittens, which I have been feeding every day all winter. They have a house on my patio where they sleep. One little female is missing now. Either she went into heat and wandered off or something happened to her. We haven't seen her in a few days. I want to help these cats by way of neutering and spaying them and I do not want any more cats running wild outside. The neighbors little boy has a sand box and I am afraid they will use it as a litter box. Also, I prefer they do not use my gardens. I took one in at the age of 5 weeks from some other litter and he makes a nice house cat but I had to bottle-feed him for a while. I am retired on a fixed income and can't afford all these cats and their meds and surgery etc. Who can help me? Also, My daughter and her husband are temporarily living with me and they have two pure bred cats, a British short hair and a Scottish fold. I can't expose them to wild cats. Marj. Rapson
Marjorie Coristine	
Mark Kekkonen	
Mark Kilborn	I AM TELLING ALL MY FRIENDS ABOUT U THEY ALL SAY GOOD LUCK AND HAVE A SAFE RUN LOVE YOU
Marnie Santarella	Best wishes, Michelle, I so admire you for doing this.
Mary Hostrup	
Mary Landry	Thanks to Michelle's courageous walk, more people are understanding the urgent need for action.
Maxine Penney	
Melanie Downey	
Melanie Schmidt	
Melissa	
Melissa Aubertin	
Melissa Cormier	
Melissa Mallette	
MF Ethier	To support a good cause and support Michelle Jameus's trek, for the cause.

Michel Trahan	J'aime tous les animaux, y compris les chats et les chiens, et je ne serais jamais du genre à placer une tête de cerf ou d'orignal sur mon véhicule.
Michele	For doing something - Thank you
Michele Parent	Michelle, thank you for doing this—today I am donating $500 to your cause—don't hesitate to contact me if I can help you in any way.
Michelle	
Michelle Gibson	
Michelle Hashem	
Michelle Power	People helped to create this problem and everyone should help to fix it. It's our fault, not theirs. Please encourage everyone you know to adopt an animal and have their pets spade or neutered. You can save a life today.
Michelle Seaman	
Mike Finnegan	
Mike Halman	This is a no brainer let's just adopt laws to this cruelty
Monica Reynolds	This petition is an absolute MUST for EVERYONE to sign, I will be forwarding it on, we desperately need a spay and neuter program. If you have a pet then you should be responsible it is NOT "JUST AN ANIMAL".
Monique Mullin	Please stop killing healthy animals) 0:Killing is so wrong.
Mrs G Carrigan	
Mrs. Mary ("Mare") Moore	
Nancy Ball	I agree and support this important issue.
Nancy Dunphy	Hey Mich. . .YOU GO GIRL Have a blast in my homeland. Hope to see you soon and sign your flag. THANK YOU for doing this for the cats and dogs whom All deserve a chance to Live. GOD BLESS you Mich.Nancyxo
Nancy Nuessler	
Natasha Danschinko	Best of Luck to Mich Jameus. The Rebels are all rooting for you. You Go Girl. Tash
Nathalie Henderson	

Nathalie Petrin	What you're doing for all of our furry friends is truly amazing Michelle. Keep up the great work.
Nicole Joncas	We should all sign this very important petition. We should also ask our governments to BAN puppy mills, and ban pet stores from selling living creatures kept in tiny cages. There wouldn't be so many abandoned pets,
Nicole Messier	NO KILL is a must. We must be the change we want to see in our world (Gandhi) The Militia for @nimals in Quebec supports this petition.
Nicole White	Good Cause
Ninette Maga	
Nora Livingstone	Over population can be stopped, killing isn't the answer.
Norma	Please People who ever you are help save pets don't Kill them. It's a Life TOO. Thank You Norma Picken
Olivia Cheng	
Pam Knowles	
Pam Rockel	I support the no Kill policy 100%. There is no need to put down perfectly healthy animals because 'we' don't want them. We are responsible for the plight they are in, the least we can do is to take care of them.
Pamela Keetch	
Pat. Smith	
Patricia Murray	I am signing the petition in honor of Michelle Jameus and her cross-Canada run to raise awareness and support for Let Live Canada.
Paul Belanger	Stop killing healthy pets. No one deserves to die.
Paula M.A. Campkin	
Paula Wannamaker	May God bless the humans who speak up for these animals. My hope is that Canada will support a No-Kill Policy which I thought we already had. We are way too slow in this endeavor to help companions that give us nothing but love and devotion. Please make this policy happen as we wouldn't want to be the last nation to do so. It will happen, it's just a matter of when. The sooner the better. Thank You.

Peggy Hickey	
Peggy Zulauf	Good Luck, Michelle.
PeggySue	life isnt fair if u have no voice
Philip Rose	
Priscilla Brown	
R Allard	
Rachelle Belcourt	
Randi Gallant	You are doing a fabulous thing. Best of luck, we support you 100% Randi
Ranette Thorpe	
Rebecca Fahringer	
Rebekah Allen	
Rejeanne Landry	I LOVE CATS AND WISH THAT I COULD HAVE A BIG PLACE TO TAKE CARE OF THOSE IN NEEDS AS I LIVE IN THE COUNTRY AND SEE SO MANY GETTING KILLED ON THE ROADS AND I DESPISE PEOPLE WHO HAVE ANIMALS AND DO NOT TAKE CARE OF THEM BETTER THAN THAT. MINE IS TREATED LIKE HE WAS MY OWN KID AND I WOULD NOT LET MY KID GO OUT AT NIGHT ON THE STREETS AND GET KILLED BY CARS OR PEOPLE WHO HATE ANIMALS.THANK YOU
Rosa-Maria Edmonds	
Rose-Marie Trowell	I can hardly wait for NO KILL to become a reality. I have worked with others for many years to have low cost spay/neuter clinics all over. But the vested interested interest groups have more money and know all the people in high places Thanks Rose-marie
Rosemary Mack	Way to go Michelle
Roxy Atwill	Mich, you have great heart and great courage to take this journey for our little furry friends, keep up your efforts
Ruth Sachsalber	
S Sargent	
S. Potter	

S.Malott	
Sandra Barro	
Sandra Halliday	I feel that no dog or cat should be put to death like any other human being should be put to death. I feel those people who put animals down should be punished fully and all people who abused there pets should be punished.
Sandra Tarrant	
Sandy Bolton	
Sara Sutton	
Sarah Little	
Sarah Steptoe	I really love animals. Animals have a right at life
Serge Gagnon	
Shannon Aubut	
Sharon Donnelly	The world needs more people with hearts like yours.
Sharon Macklin	
Sharron Malott	
Shawn	Canada needs to promote spay/neuter programs for those who cannot afford regular vet services and eliminate the senseless killing of healthy animals.
Shelby Feigen	STOP KILLING ANIMALS THAT DONT DESERVE TO BE KILLED
Shelley Callaghan	
Sinem	good job. . . I support you with all my heart. . .
Stacey Browning	
Stephanie Bata	
Stephanie Bigras	
StephanieBrunetteD'Souza	
Stephanie Caron	
Stephanie Heaton	We need to all work together to stop the killing of animals. They deserve to live long, healthy and happy lives. God bless to all animals and congrats on the marathon.
Stephanie MacNeill	Thank you for being the voice for Canadian shelter animals.

Stephanie Olsen	If the veterinarians across Canada would donate 10% of their annual practice time performing pro bono spays and neuters, we could have the over-population problem licked in a year.
Stephanie Rivers	
Stephanie Shepley	As an animal lover and owner I can't wait till the day I can stop reading about all the poor helpless animals who are put down every year.
Sue Beaulieu	
Sue Lemieux	Wonderful thing you are doing for all animals, they need much more protection under the laws than they presently have.
Susan Blissett	On behalf of the voiceless and the innocent.
Susan Longmuir	Every living creature has a right to be here, or why were they put here in the first place?
SusanLR	I believe in NO Kill of healthy animals, BUT I expect every person who signs this petition to realize they now have a moral/ethical obligation now to step up and either foster/adopt or help us pay for vet bills for these animals. I currently have a 13yr old 95lb dog from a NO Kill pound in Quebec who has lived 12 yrs of her life there. She is currently afraid of the world (too big) but lucked out with now having a forever home. Some didn't fare so well. Signing this is a step BUT tkng actn is by HELPING us take care of these animals. Once you are AWARE of a situation you now OWN it morally/ethically.
SusanLR	I believe in NO KILL, but what do we do with the lack of fostering/adoption? Every person who signs this petition is morally/ethically obligated to either foster/adopt r help us ay these animals!!!! There are not enough of us doing this. I currently have an animal who came from a NO KILL pound in Quebec. This 13 yr old, 95lbs of sweetness has lived 12 of her yrs in a kennel. What kind of life was that? Currently she is lucky enough to now have a FOREVER HOME, who loves her and indulges her neurotic behaviors because we feel she deserves it. She is afraid of the world.
Susannah Wash	

Suzanne Desilets	I can't believe we still have this happening in this day and age. Shameful.
Suzanne Friemann	
Sylvia Suchonski	I am strong for a No-Kill Policy I strongly believe all animals should have their chance of living a happy and full life. It's great that there are people out there like you, which make a difference for our friends.
T. Tellier	
Tanya Brazeau	
Tanya Harry	No more killing
Tanya Proulx	
Tara Grinage	
Tasha Hodsdon	
Theresa Hatcher	
Theresa McKinley	There is no reason in this day and age to kill animals. A low cost spay and neuter clinic will eradicate most of the unwanted animals. Stringent laws for puppy and kitten mills will also help solve the problem. These people should be jailed, not just given a slap on the wrist.
Theresa McKinley	God bless you Michelle and God speed as you run for the lives of the animals who may never feel the wind on their faces and the open fields beneath their feet. Our prayers are with you on this journey of hope. Terry
Therese Audette	
Tom and Maryann Rutledge	
Tom Webb	You are a true inspiration to many and we are very proud of what you are doing to raise awareness. Thank you for your efforts and high concern level. Truly outstanding. God be with you. Tom, Kamloops
Tracey Grodzicky	
Traci Moor	A job very well done. Congrats Michelle

Tracy Jacobson	It is time that Canada got with the program and initiated the No-Kill Policy. These animals have a right to live. As a pet owner you have responsibilities. It is all about education, and this needs to be pushed and supported.
Tracy Luck	
Tracy Pansier	
Tremellat Eric	
Tricia Selwood	
Tylar Parsons	I am Michelle Jameus's nephew. I joined her on her journey for a short time. I understand how hard she is fighting for these animals and she needs your support. Donate, sign a petition or help raise awareness and together we can save our innocent animals.
U. Lee	All animal lovers should participate in this petition. This is a worthy cause that I am proud to be a participant.
Valerie St-Louis	
Vanessa Cassalman	
Victor Cronin	you will be successful, because you decided to *do* something rather than just complain. congrats to you
Viki Johnson	I run a cat rescue organization in S-W Ontario and see the results of unaffordable spay/neutering every day. As a No-Kill organization, I know it can be done
W Robertson	
Wendy McIndoo	I believe this is a very important petition to have - animals mean so much in our lives and become so much a part of "people" lives. Good luck.
William Bryant	
William Taylor	
Ximena Apestegui	
Yvette Labatte	Turtle Gardens has been no-kill since its inception – 1989 Implemented Low Cost Spay Neuter Voucher Program in 2006 The solution is spay/neuter.

Appendix B

Shelter Response

Online Letter to animal shelters:

— Original Message —

From: Michelle Jameus
To: *shelters*
Sent: Friday, February 16, 2007 12:28 PM
Subject: Imagine! No more killing healthy pets.

Some people don't think that saving the lives of healthy cats and dogs is important.

Imagine living in a society where killing a healthy living creature is acceptable.

If we don't change that, what kind of message are we sending?

Hello,

My name is Michelle. Starting in the spring, and throughout the summer, I will be traveling across Canada along the TransCanada Highway to raise awareness about this very important issue.

Please visit the following link for more information about the 'No Kill Canada Marathon'; www.jazzpurr.org

I believe if more people knew what the issues are and why this issue is so important we can bring an end to a very old practice and convert Canada to a no kill country. At the end of the day, I believe we all want to save the life of every living creature.

I would welcome the opportunity to visit your animal shelter for a tour and meet the animals and the people who care for them. If possible, I would like to participate in any event you may have scheduled at the same time as I pass through your area. It is with regret that it will not be possible to visit every shelter but those closest to the TransCanada Highway.

I believe there is some room in the hearts of Canadians to be a life savor for our companion friends and together we can make a difference.

I look forward to hearing from you.
Michelle Jameus
Ottawa, ON

I am greatly encouraged by your ambition to run across Canada on behalf of the homeless pets.
What a great mission!
I wish to encourage you. My prayers and support are with you all the way.
I have built my own shelter and have rescued thousands of animals over the years. It is also my mission and will as long as God gives me the health and strength to carry on.
The thought struck me, when will someone pick up the torch and do the same for all the aborted babies that have no voice?
May God give you the strength and health to reach your goal! It will be done!
Gertie Dieleman
Animal Care Centre Lobo

You are certainly welcome to visit our shelter in St. John's, Newfoundland when you begin your trip. Please be advised that we do not operate a no kill shelter but we will be glad to give you a tour.

We ask that you call out shelter in advance of your arrival and we may be reached at (709) 576-8598 between 9:00AM and 4:30PM.

Thank you,
Michael Lewis
Shelter staff
SPCA Shelter, St. John's, NL

Thanks for your email. We don't actually have a shelter yet (are still fundraising) and are quite a distance from the Trans Canada, but good luck to you in your journey. I hope it's a grand success.

Sincerely,

Evie Gagne
Charlotte County SPCA
St. Stephen, New Brunswick

I feel it would be more productive to educate the public on the indiscriminate and commercial breeding practices currently allowed by Canada's weak legislation, the need for low-cost spay/neuter clinics in all municipalities, more commitment to training, behaviour and education, and what really goes on at some H.S. shelters that trumpet that they are "no kill" (selective admission through temperament testing, with the rejects referred to the local animal control where they are likely euthanized, unadopted dogs living in the shelter environment for years, and the mental health issues this contributes to).

Many of the so-called "no kill" shelters pass the buck on animals with behavioural issues, and call rescue. Two dogs with broken bones lay in separate Ontario shelters over last Christmas, the shelters did not seek medical treatment for their injuries. The young Border Collie that got shipped to me (400 kilometers away) died in surgery. He was young and strong, but infection had set in over the week he lay untreated, his heart stopped, he could not be revived. Thankfully, the other survived, but required extensive orthopedic surgery, a cost borne by the rescue that saved him from euthanasia when his hold period as a stray was up. A young sweet Jack Russell pup lived with a shattered hind leg for a month, the muscles and tendons literally torn off the bone, while the owner (who bought him from P.J.s Pets) tried to give him away rather than pay for his care after one of her kids "fell on" the dog. Jack Russell Rescue has paid out thousands to repair what could be fixed, which is far less fixable than if he had been treated promptly.

Awareness and access to spay/neuter clinics, tighter controls on pets stores who sell puppies and kittens (and other pets) and strict regulations on breeding practices for everyone. If those were implemented the number of healthy animals killed every year would drop drastically!

Right now there is a whole culture in Ontario dog rescue pulling dogs for little or no cost from kill shelters in Ohio and other U.S. states (and Quebec) and shipping them up to Ontario for "adoption". Some of these rescue groups do not vet, nor do they spay/neuter these animals prior to adoption. Yet they charge $250 - $450 "adoption fees". If the adoption fails, they are not available to take the animal back, even if they have undertaken to do so. It is always the adopter's fault. Someone should expose these practices.

I will euthanize, if an animal is physically healthy but mentally unsafe. A dog that bites repeatedly or unpredictably should be humanely put down. I have had to do this twice in ten years. Generally, I will not accept biters into rescue, I try to rehome those who need it, and retrain some behaviours, but rescue is not there to fix someone's poor training, poor breeding or poor choices if doing so puts others at risk.

Some people are idiots, and should not be allowed to possess animals. If you can do something to prevent them from becoming pet owners or caregivers, from breeding for greed, selfish reasons or carelessness, by all means do so.

Luan Egan
Border Collie Rescue
Toronto

Thank you for caring
Give A Dog A Chance

I admire your zeal and positive outlook! You are very welcome to visit or stay (if you require overnight accommodation you are welcome to stay for as long as needed).

Love For Life Pet Rescue isn't a shelter. . .The animals listed on the website are only a few of the many that live here in my home with my sons (10 & years) and I. It's a long story but these and numerous other cats were abandoned by another rescue for whom I was giving foster care. . .I am a former Vet Tech and have been home from work for medical problems and offered to foster. Most of the cats were scheduled to be euthanized at the Hamilton Animal Shelter within 12twelve hours of coming to live with me. . .Many are feral and terrified of humans and will never be adopted. . .They have full run of the house .. the exception being a few that are restricted because of picking on or bullying. . .There are also frequently a variety of dogs and cats that I foster for other rescues and a number of parrots and rodents. . .

I am located in Burlington which might be too far south of the route you are following if you should happen to make it to the GTA, (Greater Toronto Area), it would be terrific to have you visit. . .perhaps a tour of the Hamilton High Volume (which translates to high kill), Shelter can be arranged by my rescue friend who is quite active there.

Best of luck!

Merya
Love For Life Pet Rescue

I will post this for you on my webpage. Feel free to stop in, would love to have you, although we are no where near the Trans Canada highway. . .let us know if you are coming this way.
Renee
osas@bmts.com

You do realize that unfortunately euthanasia for many is a form of population control and in many circumstances is necessary. Puppy mills pet shops have a big responsibility in regards to the issue on pet overpopulation. I find it sad that municipalities, provincial and federal governments do not invest in low cost spay and neuter clinic be mobile or a location dedicated to speutering. It would end so much suffering.

Merci
Johanne Tasse

It's wonderful to hear that you'll be doing this important marathon. I hope you won't be traveling alone. Our group helps stray and feral cats in this area (Clare municipality, Nova Scotia). Some people don't think it's important, but fortunately there are more people who are interested in helping. We've taken in 80 cats in our 1st 7 months, 37 were feral kittens we found homes for, 15 were ill and had to be euthanized and the rest were spayed/neutered. We've also built winter shelters for the feral colonies and feed them every day. We have no shelter and not much money, but we do our best.

Good luck on your marathon. Hope you'll be visiting Nova Scotia.

Adele Bourque
Clare Feral Friends Society, NS

Hello, my name is Tracey and I am a volunteer with the Lethbridge and District Humane Society. I just want to start by saying that I think what you are doing is absolutely wonderful, and I know that I can speak for all of the volunteers at the Humane Society when I say that we support you one hundred percent. We are a no kill society and try our best to help spread the word about how precious each and every animal's life is. I understand that you will be traveling along the Trans Canada highway and since we are off the highway we would like the opportunity to come to you and show our support. We are fairly close to Calgary and hope that we may be able to meet you at one of your stops and have the opportunity to tell you a bit about our Humane Society and also learn more about the society that you are involved with, and most importantly help support you and spread the word about "The No Kill Canada Marathon"

Tracey Grodzicky
Lethbridge Humane Society, AB

Yes, we would love it if you would stop at our shelter. We are very close to the Trans Canada.

Kirsteen Thomson
L.A. Animal Shelter
Amherst, NS

I've just received a message of your effort this spring. Truly, it is commendable. I, too, am a huge animal supporter.

I would agree that to save all healthy animals would be ideal – but where do you put them? . . .all 1,000,000 of them? That's the estimated number in Canada that are destroyed annually. There needs to be work done on the front-end of this issue. i.e. animal laws and regulations.

I'm concerned for the noble efforts of community shelters that try to manage this major over population issue – may feel negativity toward their efforts of a 'No Kill Canada' campaign. Will this message of 'No Kill' at shelter levels somehow push back on the pet owners looking to surrender their animals? A better campaign message may be 'spay / neuter your pet' and 'Pets are for life'.

I wish you great success with your quest for change in support of our domestic animal friends. :)

If you need a place to stay in Halifax area. . .
Good luck and all the best.
Cheers!
Joyce Nifort
SPCA, NS

This is great to see. I can just hear you say the words as I read them. I know that you will inspire thousands and make a real difference in the policy of our society toward the unnecessary killing of cats. Perhaps people will one day think differently about our relationship to animals in the same way that many are now realizing that our environment has been treated cruelly.

Peter d'Entremont
C-A-R-MA

Oh Michelle. That is so wonderful. . .this really speaks to my heart. I wish more than anything that rescues would stand united and support one another, there is so much conflict and it is so self-defeating. I hope that things are going very well for you and I will follow your progress. . .you must let me know if you'll be heading this way. . .or anywhere in the Greater Toronto Area. . . the offer remains open if you or your entourage need ANYTHING . . .if you get stranded, become ill or run into problems, need someone to come and pick you up. . .whatever you need, please don't hesitate to call me at anytime and I will do whatever I can to help. . . I am worried about you.

Love For Life Pet Rescue
Burlington

These animals and we humans who care too much SHOULD NEVER have to live through this. Again with education and with more conscientious efforts we will be able to have some control and hopefully regulate HOW, WHO, WHEN animals are adopted. This has to go hand in hand with what you are doing.

I, myself have had some ideas for some years now regarding laws, not by-laws, implemented to have a national registry of all the people who breed who MUST FIRST obtain a license to do so, and I believe that with the numbers that are strays, we will never be able to catch up UNLESS there is a BAN ON ALL BREEDING, COMMERCIAL AND PERSONAL, for 5 YEARS. The fine for breeding without a license for individuals should be triple the cost of a low-cost spay/neuter clinic cost. Professional breeders SHOULD have their own legislation act to insure they are qualified for breeding and must pay a yearly breeding fee. This fee could be used for education and support of rescue groups who are going to still be out there trapping/spaying/releasing of ferals etc.

Also anyone who rents MUST register their NEUTERED PET ON THE LEASE. This would be a good preventative to stop pets abandoned in apartments and a hefty fine of $1500 and a criminal record would be enforced.

For rural areas, vets should be able to neuter farm cats free of charge to the farmer and there should be a limited number of cats aloud in ratio to the size of the operation. Of course dogs must also be neutered and fines for letting their dogs run amuck, as many do.

When an individual finds a cat, they can have free spay/neuter, only if the cat has a home afterward, and, after they have applied 3 times they must then be visited by an association that has implemented these regulations. After their 4th free neuter of a rescued cat they will have to pay a pro-rated fee and after the 8th cat be required to register as a sanctuary and follow guidelines to insure health and behaviour of the animals and prove no destruction of property or infringement on the rights of neighbors or the community. They must also submit a vet report once per year (a discounted visit) which would reinsure the animals are properly cared for.

Anyhow that's just the tip of the iceberg and we are at least beginning to take these steps in the right direction.

Jo
JazztJo Havenly Felines

Appendix C

Media Response

Thank you to the following:

Canadian Pets and Animals Magazine, by Jody Cowan, 3-part feature

Best Friends Network, Jill Dennis

Rogers Talk Ottawa Show, Ottawa, ON, by host James Hendricks, Monday June 25, 2007

CTV, Lethbridge, AB, by cameraman Moses, Monday October 1, 2007, feature, drove all the way to Medicine Hat with Barb, Tracey, Laney

VOCM Openline Radio, St. John's, NL, April 13, 2007

"Woman Crossing Country To Keep Animals Alive", *Cape Breton Post*, North Sydney, NS, by Julie Collins, Wednesday, May 9, 2007

"Going the distance for Pets", New Glasgow, by New Glasgow, NS, May 16, 2007

"Animal activist to visit L.A. Animal Shelter", *The Amherst Daily News*, Amherst, NS, by Terri McCormick, May 18, 2007

"Let Live Canada Marathon Runner Makes Stop In Tantramar", *The Sackville Tribune Post*, Sackville, NS, by Joan LeBlanc, May 23, 2007

Photo, June 1, 2007, *The Bugle-Observer*, Woodstock, NS, by Angela Ferguson "Pet of the Week", *The Bugle-Observer*, Woodstock, NS, by Angela Ferguson, November 16, 2007

Vision, Rockland, ON, by Gregg Chamberlain

"On The Run To Save Pets", *The Ottawa Sun*, Ottawa, ON, by Laura Czekaj, Tuesday June 26, 2007

"Cross-Country Runner Brings No-Kill Message To Arnprior", *The Arnprior Chronicle-Guide*, Arnprior, ON, by Peter DeWolf, July 10, 2007

Biz, web media, Pembroke, ON, by Cecile Bertrand

"Marathoner Runs To Keep Healthy Dogs And Cats Alive", *The Daily Observer*, Pembroke, ON, by Anthony Dixon, Saturday June 30, 2007

"Saving Pets One Step At A Time", *The North Bay Nugget*, North Bay, ON, by Bryn Weese, Thursday July 5, 2007

CTV News Sudbury

CBC Northern Ontario Radio, Sudbury, ON, by Dan Lasard

"Fast Feet", *The Sault Star*, Sault St Marie, ON, by Micheal Purvis, Friday July 20, 2007

"Cross-Canada Marathon Hopes To Raise Awareness", *The Mirror*, reporter unknown, Scarborough, ON, August 1, 2007

CFNO Radio North, Marathon, ON, by Al Crezwall

"Spade/Neutering: Running to Raise Awareness", *Nipigon-Red Rock Gazette*, Nipigon, ON, by Paulette Lalonde Forsyth, Tuesday August 14, 2007

"Marathon Runner Pushes Pet Control", *Thunder Bay News Source*, Thunder Bay, ON, Kristi St. Cyr, August 9, 2007

The Dryden Observer, Dryden, ON, by Josh Johnson

"Journey Of Awareness", *Winnipeg Free Press*, Winnipeg, MB, by Michelle Melanson, Wednesday August 29, 2007

"Petsmart Hosting Pet Adoption Weekend", *Leader-Post*, Regina, MB, by Ciaran Dickson, Saturday September 15, 2007

"Protecting Animals", Times Herald, Moose Jaw, Sask, by Shelby Parker, Tuesday September 18, 2007

Medicine Hat News, by Ian at SPCA

"Pet Run", Shaw TV, Calgary, AB, Oct 9, 2007

Global TV, Calgary, AB

Acknowledgments

First and foremost, I thank my God through Jesus Christ for allowing me to take such an amazing journey. I'm especially grateful to Him for putting so many kind people in my path. I also thank Him for giving me the desire to publish this book. While I was writing it, the experience was emotional for me. I often wondered what was more difficult: running solitary across Canada, or writing about it.

I also want to express my appreciation to Taylor Graham at Xulon Press for his help in the editing of this book.

Secondly, I'm grateful to family and friends and everyone who took this journey with me. Especially the shelters I visited and for the privilege of meeting them. Without your support and words of encouragement, I would not have been able to face all my challenges or complete this run.

Lastly, I'm thankful for the media that took an interest and helped inform people about this tragedy. This should be a testimony that change is needed.

I could not have done something like this without a lot of support and there are so many people to thank that I've had to categorize: special mention, family & relatives, shelters, receptions, food and accommodations, supporters, running buddies, medical care, equipment, road warriors, photographs, and media. These are the incredible people I remembered as I wrote *To Companion Friends, With Love*.

Thank you everyone for taking this incredible journey with me.
I couldn't have done it without you!

Special Mention:

Dorit Girash, Windsor, ON, Let Live Canada and Jazzpurr Society for Animal Protection

Julia White, Windsor, ON, Jazzpurr Society for Animal Protection, Let Live Canada

Family & Relatives:

Mom and Dad, Terrebonne, QC
Chris (sister), Thunder Bay, ON
Marie (sister), Nipigon, ON
Angel (sister), Blainville, QC
Marcel (brother), Terrebonne, QC
Shannon (niece), Ottawa, ON
Tylar (nephew), Nipigon, ON
Melissa (niece), Blainville, QC
Andre (cousin) and Cathy, Chapeau, QC
Blanche-Helene (cousin), Bonfield, ON
Francine (cousin), North Bay, ON
Auntie May, North Bay, ON
Kim (cousin) and Lorenzo, Caprial, ON
Auntie Jeanie, Caprial, ON
John and Susan (in-laws), Worthington, ON
Rose and Mike (in-laws), Worthington, ON
Jim and Helen (in-laws), Thunder Bay, ON
Uncle Bert and Auntie Darling, Kamloops, BC

Shelters:

Jessica, Heavenly Creatures, St. John's, NL
Tammy and staff, Animal Care and Adoption Centre, St. John's, NL
Annie and Alison, SPCA, St. John's, NL
Kelly, Beagle Paws, St. John's, NL

Ann Marie and staff, SPCA, Clarenville, NL
Carol, Exploits Valley SPCA, Grand Falls, NL
Betty, Antigonish Animal Shelter, Antigonish, NS
Kirsteen, L.A. Shelter, Amherst, NS
Kelly and staff, Humane Society, Charlottetown, P.E.I.
Peter and Corinna, C-A-R-MA, Shemogue, NB
Jo, Jazzy-Jo Heavenly Felines, St. Eugene, ON
Stephanie and Jill, Humane Society, Arnprior, ON
Staff, Humane Society, North Bay, ON
Valerie and volunteers, New Hope Rescue, Thunder Bay, ON
Aileen, Bill and staff, Humane Society, Winnipeg, MB
Volunteers, D'Arcy's A.R.C., Winnipeg, MB
Winnipeg Pet Rescue Shelter, Winnipeg, MB
Gail and staff, Humane Society, Regina, Sask.
Ray and staff, Humane Society, Moose Jaw, Sask.
Rhonda and Audrey, SPCA, Medicine Hat, AB
Tracey, Barb, Laney, Heather and staff, Humane Society, Lethbridge, AB
Kelly, Jake, Deb and volunteers, Meow Foundation, Calgary, AB
Cheryl and staff, Humane Society, Calgary, AB
Jennifer and Sonya, Carla Cumming Adoption Centre, Canmore, AB

Receptions:

Kelly and staff, Humane Society, Charlottetown, P.E.I.
Sharron, R.A. Center, Ottawa, ON
Valerie and volunteers, New Hope Rescue, Terry Fox Monument, Thunder Bay, ON
Aileen, Bill and staff, Humane Society, Winnipeg, MB
Gail and staff, Humane Society, Regina, Sask.
Tracey, Barb, Laney, Heather and staff, Humane Society, Lethbridge, AB
Kelly (MEOW), Cheryl (HS), Joanne (The Cat House), Calgary, AB
Sharron, Ottawa Airport, Ottawa, ON – Homecoming

Food and Accommodations:

Family and relatives
Bev and Rob, Sheila's Restaurant, Gambo, NL
Gerard and Paula, Gambo, NL
Laura Blackwood Pike, Gander, NL
Ruby and Laura, Hampden, NL, Junction 421
Diana Peddle, Comfort Inn, Corner Brook, NL
Susan and Mark, East Bay, NS
Ivan, East Bay, NS
Frank and Ruthie, East Bay, NS
Mary and Alain, Monastery, NS
Mary, Darryl, Matthew and Megan, Thorburn, NS
Ruth, Thorburn, NS
The Rhynold family, Oasis Campground, Antigonish, NS
Trevor and Judy, ShipWright Inn, Charlottetown, P.E.I.
Earl, McCready's Motel, Young's Cove, NB
Joy, Days Inn, Oromocto, NB
Peter and Corinna, C-A-R-MA, Shemogue, NB
Madi and Dave, Moncton, NB
Flo and Stan, Fredericton, NB
Pastor Charles and Shirley, Meductic, NB
SMHV, Woodstock, NB
River Country Campground, NB
Guildo, Comfort Inn, Edmunston, NB
J.P., Pierreville, QC
Rolland and Therese, Campground, St. Gregoire, QC
Comfort Inn, Levi, QC
Claude, Motels de la Rive, Deschaillons, QC
Camping au Plateau, Terrebonne, QC
Jo, Jazzy-Jo Heavenly Felines, St. Eugene, ON
Sandy and Doug, Antler Campground, Deux Rivieres, ON
Linda and Jen, Renfrew, ON
Michelle and David, Elliot Lake, ON
Kay and Lorne, Bruce Mines Campground
Ray and Beth, Bruce Mines Campground
Marian and Peggy, Del Mar Campground, Iron Bridge, ON

Pancake Bay Provincial Park, ON
Neys Provincial Park, ON
Travelodge Inn, Marathon, ON
Penny, Ojibway Park, Echo Bay, ON
Betty, Sault Ste Marie, ON
Ady, McAuleys Motel, SSM, ON
Vicki and Laura, McAuleys Restaurant, SSM, ON
Dennis, Rabbit Blanket Lake Campground, ON
Jesse and Josette, Information Centre, White River, ON
Carol, Kenora, ON
Jim and Karen, Prawda, ON
Tanner, Hostel, Winnipeg, MB
Linda and Jean, L'Auberge Clemence B&B, Elie, MB
Robin, Virden Motel, Virden, MB
Perry, Sweet Dream Motel, Broadview, Sask,
Perry, Wolsely Motel, Wolsely, Sask.
Ray and Karen, Moose Jaw, Sask,
Laney, Barb, Lethbridge, AB
Jen and Allen, Calgary, AB
Magi, Canmore, AB
Waitress at Esso, Sorrento, BC

Bike/Running Buddies:

Andree, Ottawa, ON
Tylar, Nipigon, ON
New Hope Rescue, Thunder Bay, ON
Tracey, LHS, Lethbridge, AB
Kelly, MEOW Foundation, Calgary, AB
Jennifer, Calgary, AB
Barb, Roadrunner Group, Calgary, AB

Medical Care:

Andree, Massage Express, Ottawa, ON
Laura, PT Works, North Bay, ON
Nipigon Hospital, Nipigon, ON
Mark, BIO Pad, Thunder Bay, ON

Equipment:

Matthew and Tim, SkiWolf, Fredericton, NB, running stroller #1
Shaf, Canadian Tire, Espanola, ON, tire repair
Steve and Nick, The Hardware Company, Kenora, ON, running stroller #2
Candice and Stu, Chariot head office, Calgary, AB, warranty repairs

Road Warriors:

Bob Lewis, Walk for Family Peace, Vancouver to New York City
Richard Ralph, rollerblading across Canada for cancer
Gordon Robb, cycling across Canada for lymphoma research
Francis Graf, cycling across Canada for cancer
Christie, cycling across Canada

Supporters:

Mile One, St. John's, NL
Florence, Ruff Spots, Mount Pearl, NL
Bill and Jeannie, Downtown Hostel, St. John's, NL
Driver who rescued me from the rain before Bellevue Cove, NL
Leone, Junction 421, NL
Driver who brought me through the Wreckhouse in Newfoundland
Captain and crew of the Caribou Ferry to North Sydney
Lester, Charlie, Bruno, Indian Reservation of Poklotek, NS
Herald, Port Hastings, NS

Amy and Marilyn, Veterinarian Clinic, New Glasgow, NS
Driver who dropped me off at Tim Horton's in Charlottetown, P.E.I.
Joy, SpayAid, Charlottetown, P.E.I.
Dave, Fredericton, NB
Tom Gibson, MRDC, Kings Landing, NB
Richard, Big Stop Irving, Saint-Andre, NB
A special "angel" who requested to remain anonymous, Ottawa, ON
Staff, Cumberland Veterinarian Hospital, Orleans, ON
Nicole, Teja's Animal Rescue, Alexandria, ON
Gertie D, Animal Care Center Lobo, London, ON
Ashley Adam, K-911 Rescue, Ottawa, ON
Beth and Heather, ReformtheOHS, Ottawa, ON
Sharron, Ottawa, ON
Sharron's Dad, ON
Sharron's Mom, ON
Andree, Ottawa, ON
Karen M, Ottawa ON
Karen S, Ottawa, ON
Nathalie and her two sons, Ottawa, ON
Peggy-Sue, Ottawa, ON
Michele, Orleans, ON
K.P., Ottawa, ON
Traci Moor, ON
Supporters attending Ottawa Media Conference
Friends who came to Ottawa Airport
Leslie H, Ottawa, ON
Isabelle A, Ottawa, ON
Kim and parents, Ottawa, ON
Carol and France, Ottawa, ON
Jodie and Grade 5 students, Ottawa, ON
Cecile, Pembroke, ON
Colette, Pembroke, ON
Diane, Marathon, ON
Rose and John and MNR staff, Nipigon, ON
Nipigon Baptist Church, ON
Lawrence, Kenora, ON
OPP

Jim, Roadrunner group, Calgary, AB
Tracey, her daughter Brooke, and grandmother, Vancouver, B.C.
Siobhan Mlacak, Paris Europe
Bloggers and email
Online petitioners
Donators

Photographs:

Peter d'Entremont (cover) – permission granted
Supporters, family and friends (inserts) – permission granted

Media:

Please see 'Appendix C, Media Response'.

Notes

Chapter 2: Cape Breton, Nova Scotia, P.E.I.

p.67 "Euthanasia" defined in *Webster's Seventh New Collegiate Dictionary, 1967*

p.67 "Compassion" defined in *Funk & Wagnalls Standard College Dictionary, 1978*